ETHIOPIA AND
THE BIBLE

ETHIOPIA AND THE BIBLE

EDWARD ULLENDORFF

M.A. (Jerusalem), D.Phil. (Oxford)

Fellow of the Academy

THE SCHWEICH LECTURES
OF THE BRITISH ACADEMY
1967

PUBLISHED FOR THE BRITISH ACADEMY
BY THE OXFORD UNIVERSITY PRESS

Oxford University Press, Great Clarendon Street, Oxford OX2 6DP

Oxford New York

Auckland Cape Town Dar es Salaam Hong Kong Karachi
Kuala Lumpur Madrid Melbourne Mexico City Nairobi
New Delhi Shanghai Taipei Toronto

With offices in
Argentina Austria Brazil Chile Czech Republic France Greece
Guatemala Hungary Italy Japan Poland Portugal Singapore
South Korea Switzerland Thailand Turkey Ukraine Vietnam

Published in the United States
by Oxford University Press Inc., New York

First published 1968
Reprinted 1983
Paperback edition 1988
Reprinted 1989, 1992, 1997, 2006

British Library Cataloguing in Publication Data
Data available

Library of Congress Cataloging in Publication Data
Data available

Printed in Great Britain
on acid-free paper by
Antony Rowe Limited
Chippenham, Wiltshire

ISBN 0–19–726076–4   978–0–19–726076–0

TO

EDWARD AND PATRICIA

KORRY

...and the gain of Ethiopia and of Sabaeans,
men of stature, shall come unto you and
shall be yours

ISAIAH 45: 14

PREFACE

THE present volume is a survey rather than a study in depth. This limitation arises, partly, from the purpose and character of the Schweich Lectures and, partly, from a lack of prolegomena of serious dimensions in the field of the Ethiopic Bible translations. On a few of the other subjects here treated I have touched in some earlier studies. I have considered carefully what has been written, especially by M. Rodinson, since I first discussed—in the mid 1950s—the Hebraic ingredients in Abyssinian Christianity. I have, however, not hesitated to plagiarize those previous writings of mine in cases where I felt unable to progress beyond those earlier positions. In any event, I expect this to be my final contribution to the study of Hebraic-Jewish elements in Ethiopian monophysite Christianity or to the ramifications of the Sheba legend. In foreseeable circumstances I would not wish to return to these subjects, as I feel that I have now said everything in this sphere that I am capable of saying.

I should like to express my sincere gratitude to the members of the Schweich Committee for the great honour they have done me in inviting me to deliver this series of lectures. There are so many illustrious names among my predecessors, including those of some of my own teachers, that I have at all times contemplated this task with awe and reverence as well as with a genuine sense of inadequacy on my part.

I wish to thank Sir Mortimer Wheeler, C.H., and his most helpful staff for their unfailing kindness during the period of the lectures and the printing of this volume.

My colleague, Dr. A. K. Irvine, has been good enough to read the typescript and to offer some valuable criticisms.

My wife has subjected my manuscript to critical scrutiny and has, as usual, made herself responsible for all the physical aspects of preparing the typescript for the printers.

CONTENTS

LIST OF ABBREVIATIONS

ANET	*Ancient Near Eastern Texts* (ed. Pritchard).
B. & F.B.S.	British & Foreign Bible Society.
Bi Or	*Bibliotheca Orientalis.*
B.M.	British Museum.
B.N.	Bibliothèque Nationale, Paris.
BSOAS	*Bulletin of the School of Oriental & African Studies.*
C.I.H.	*Corpus Inscriptionum Himyariticarum.*
C.S.C.O.	*Corpus Scriptorum Christianorum Orientalium.*
E. of I.	*Encyclopaedia of Islam.*
E.O.T.	Ethiopic Old Testament.
ESA	Epigraphic South Arabian.
GGA	*Göttingische Gelehrte Anzeigen.*
GLECS	*Groupe Linguistique d'Études Chamito-Sémitiques.*
I.C.C.	*International Critical Commentary.*
JA	*Journal Asiatique.*
JES	*Journal of Ethiopian Studies.*
JQR	*Jewish Quarterly Review.*
JRAS	*Journal of the Royal Asiatic Society.*
JSS	*Journal of Semitic Studies.*
JTS	*Journal of Theological Studies.*
MO	*Monde Oriental.*
MRAL	*Memorie, Regia Accademia dei Lincei.*
OLZ	*Orientalistische Literaturzeitung.*
OM	*Oriente Moderno.*
RRAL	*Rendiconti, Regia Accademia dei Lincei.*
RSE	*Rassegna di Studi Etiopici.*
RSO	*Rivista degli Studi Orientali.*
Tňa	*təgrəňňa.*
ZA	*Zeitschrift für Assyriologie.*
ZAW	*Zeitschrift für Alttestamentliche Wissenschaft.*
ZDMG	*Zeitschrift der Deutschen Morgenländischen Gesellschaft.*

INTRODUCTION

The Ethiopian scene: the Biblical setting

W H I L E recent political events and decisions have placed Ethiopia firmly within her geographical setting, the continent of Africa, her traditional historical role—extending over two millennia or more—had made her a bridge between the civilizations of Africa and Asia. Many of her inhabitants were migrants from South Arabia who had introduced their language, their writing system (which underwent, however, material alterations on the western side of the Red Sea), and other vital facets of their cultural inheritance. With her ancestry across two continents and her commanding position in the horn of Africa, Ethiopia has always occupied a favoured place at a crossroad of civilizations and a meeting point of many races and influences. Jerusalem became as vital as Aksum in Ethiopian national consciousness, and the religion that had sprung from Mecca has exerted a more than intermittent pressure on the creed of Alexandria which is so deeply rooted in the realm of Prester John.[1]

Ethiopia—more than four times the size of Great Britain—is a country of great natural beauty, marked by a vast mountain massif with a mean height of some 8,000 feet.[2] These highlands rise from the torrid plains, abruptly and almost perpendicularly, and the steep escarpment has had a profound influence on the course of Ethiopian history: it has attracted Semitic immigrants from South Arabia, deterred the would-be conqueror, and preserved a civilization of Biblical hue in a cocoon of archaic and antique style. It has also for many centuries enabled the people to live in isolation from the outside world and to stem the onslaught of advancing Islam. The abruptness of the physical contours is reflected in astonishing contrasts of climate within a distance of a few miles and in linguistic barriers of uncompromising incisiveness.

This great massif is cleft, in a direction from north-east to south-west, by the rift valley—that enormous geological depression which extends northwards from the fault zone of the Red Sea towards the Dead Sea and the Jordan valley and is marked, in Ethiopia, by the Dankali depression and the deep trench

---

[1] For a masterly study of the ramifications of this mythical concept cf. C. F. Beckingham's Inaugural Lecture *The Achievements of Prester John*, S.O.A.S., 1966.

[2] Cf. my *The Ethiopians*, 2nd ed., O.U.P., 1965.

　　　　　　　B

which cuts the plateau along the course of the Awash river and the group of large lakes in south-west Ethiopia.[1] To the west of these mountain ranges lies the immense valley of the Nile and its tributaries which is fed, in part, by the romantic Abbay (or Blue Nile), winding its tortuous course to and from Lake Tana, and by the torrential rains which, from June to September, gush down the mountains as mighty rivers.

The Abbay or Blue Nile plays a profoundly important part in Ethiopian life and history. To Ethiopians it is the Gihon of Genesis 2: 13 ('and the name of the second river is Gihon: the one that compasseth the whole land of Ethiopia [Cush]'); and to this day the Nile springs are called Giyon,[2] i.e. Ethiopic for Gihon. There is no valid reason to doubt the essential accuracy of this identification:[3] in Jeremiah 2: 18 Shiḥor, the river of Egypt, is rendered as Γηων by the Septuagint; in Ben Sira 24, 27 Gihon appears in parallelism to the Nile;[4] cf. also Jubilees 8: 15 and 23,[5] as well as Josephus, *Antiquities*, i. 1, 3.[6] The secret of the Nile's source had roused the passionate curiosity of men, from Alexander the Great and Julius Caesar to James Bruce and, in our own day, R. E. Cheesman[7] who has made a most able survey of the area.

A recent student of Ethiopia[8] has told us how he has been seduced by the charm of traditional Ethiopian life: 'Played out by an extraordinarily handsome people in a setting of great natural beauty and a climate often called "idyllic", it offers a gate through time to a state of being that is richly medieval'— or, one may add, full of the flavour of Old Testament times. For outside the bustling modern towns Ethiopia remains a haven of peace where priests are dancing before the ark and the courtesies of the ancient Orient continue to live.[9] The scene of David and

---

[1] Cf. Reale Società Geogr. Ital., *L'Africa Orientale*, p. 116; W. B. Fisher, *The Middle East*, pp. 14 ff.; U.S. Army, *Area Handbook for Ethiopia*, p. 46.

[2] Cf. Cheesman, *Lake Tana and the Blue Nile*, London, 1936, pp. 71 and 75.

[3] Cf. Skinner, *Genesis*, ad locum (I.C.C., 2nd ed.).

[4] המשפיעה כיאור מוסר וכגיחון בימי בציר (M. Z. Segal, *Ben Sira* [in Hebrew], Jerusalem, 1953, p. 146).

[5] Charles, *The Ethiopic Version of the Hebrew Book of Jubilees*, Oxford, 1895, pp. 32–33: አሰሕ፡ ተፈርሐብ፡ ጎብ፡ ማየ፡ ደዮጎ፡ ፈለገ፡; See also the note to *Gihon* in Charles's translation of *Jubilees* (1902), p. 71.

[6] 'and Geon runs through Egypt, and denotes what arises from the east, which the Greeks call Nile' (in W. Whiston's translation, London, 1841, p. 33).

[7] Op. cit.

[8] D. N. Levine, *Wax and Gold*, University of Chicago Press, 1965, p. vii.

[9] 'It will always be the Emperor Haile Sellassie's greatest glory that he has been able to bring these two worlds into harmony: gently to restrain the impatient and quietly to urge on the tardy, to preserve and also to discard without loss of Ethiopia's ancient and historic identity' (Ullendorff, *The Ethiopians*[2], p. 208). As time goes on, it will become increasingly

all the house of Israel playing before the Lord on harps and lyres, drums and sistra, dancing with all their might, and bringing up the ark with shouting and the sound of the trumpet[1] is a spectacle that is eminently alive in Ethiopia and can be seen each year at Timqat[2] and on many other occasions.

The Biblical atmosphere manifests itself in Ethiopia not only in attitudes, beliefs, and a general quality of life that is forcefully reminiscent of the Old Testament world, but it is also expressed in numerous more tangible ways: the council of elders resolving a dispute, sitting by the gate or under a tree in the field, reminds one of the scene in Deuteronomy 25: 7–9 or Ruth 4: 2 ('then the elders of the city shall call him and speak unto him' or 'he took ten men of the elders of the city and said, Sit ye down here [by the gate]'). An Ethiopian notable's stately progress, in the cold mist of dawn, on ass or mule, accompanied by his retainers, is precisely as described in Genesis 22: 3 ('and Abraham rose up early in the morning and saddled his ass and took two of his young men with him, and Isaac his son . . .'). And David with his harp or lyre differs little from the Ethiopian minstrel playing on instruments that have scarcely changed since the days when Saul's spirit needed to be soothed.[3] Who can fail to think, when watching an Ethiopian child washing the feet of his father's guest, of the similar scene when Abraham received the three men,[4] or the woman washing Jesus' feet,[5] or he himself those of his disciples?[6] The dignity of the bow, so vividly described in Genesis 33: 6–7 when Jacob's wives and handmaidens and children bowed to Esau,[7] is a daily occurrence of touching spontaneity in contemporary Ethiopia.

The people who inhabit this beautiful land and who consider themselves the lawful successors of Israel[8] have been established in the horn of Africa for several millennia and constitute an amalgam of Hamites, Semites, and Nilotic groups. Whether the Cushitic (i.e. Hamitic Ethiopian) peoples originally came from southern Arabia, whence the Hamito-Semites may have sprung,[9] or whether the cradle of the once united Hamito-Semitic race

difficult to maintain this judgement (first expressed in 1958) as the strains and pressures of modern life and social upheaval begin to impinge even on the traditional framework of Ethiopian society.

[1] See 2 Sam. 6: 5, 14–16.
[2] i.e. Epiphany; cf. H. M. Hyatt, *The Church of Abyssinia*, pp. 169 ff.
[3] Cf. 1 Sam. 16: 16, 23; 2 Kings 3: 15.   [4] Cf. Gen. 18: 4.
[5] Cf. Luke 7: 38.   [6] Cf. John 13: 5.
[7] Or Ruth to Boaz: 'she fell on her face and bowed herself to the ground' (Ruth 2: 10).
[8] *Kebra Nagast*, chaps. 45, 50, 55, 60, *et passim*. Conti Rossini, *Liber Axumae*, C.S.C.O., 1909, p. 72. See also below, p. 31 (Gəʿəz passage).
[9] Cf. Hitti, *History of the Arabs*[4] (1949), pp. 10 ff.

was—as some scholars have conjectured—in that part of Africa[1] which is now called Ethiopia, need not concern us at present. In any event, the prolonged influx of Semitic elements from south-west Arabia, in pre-Christian centuries and later, has once again brought about a union of Hamites and Semites. The stage is the Abyssinian plateau where the result of this renewed fusion has been the emergence of the Hamites as the predominant ethnic factor and of the Semites as the principal linguistic and cultural element.

Physically, the Hamito-Semitic union has produced a handsome race, elegant, subtle, and nervous. Most travellers and observers have gained the impression that Ethiopians are exceptionally intelligent, mentally agile, and quick to absorb knowledge. They are proud, yet courteous, and good manners are highly esteemed; they are also accomplished diplomats, perhaps somewhat suspicious, but generous and uncalculating. Ethiopians are given to litigiousness, but their sense of honour and justice is satisfied once the matter has been argued out at length; they will present a case with great dexterity and a distinct flair for oratory. Their hospitality retains something of a Biblical and patriarchal flavour; and few of those who have savoured it have been able to resist their exquisite sense of humour and their compelling charm.

Nobody quite knows how many people there are within the boundaries of the Ethiopian empire. Since no properly controlled census has ever been undertaken, all population figures are bound to be estimates. In 1936, L'Africa Orientale[2] thought that 6–7 millions was a realistic guess, while the figure in the Guida dell'Africa Orientale (p. 82) is $7\frac{1}{2}$ million. The 1954 Ethiopian Guide Book[3] contains an estimate of just under 17 millions, and the U.S. Army Area Handbook considers a total of 21 millions 'far beyond all competent estimates' (p. 53). The Ethiopian geographer, Ato Mesfin Walda Maryam, in a carefully documented study,[4] has convinced me that previous guesses[5] ranging between 10 and 15 millions were too low and failed to take account of the modern growth-rate which Ato Mesfin assumes to be at least 2 per cent. I am not competent to judge whether his own estimate of close on 25 millions (in 1961) is not slightly excessive. At any rate, Ethiopia ranks after Nigeria and Egypt as the most populous state in Africa.

[1] Cf. Nöldeke, Semitic Languages in Encycl. Brit.[13], xxiv. 620; Skinner, Genesis, pp. 201 and 207.   [2] R. Soc. Geogr. Ital., pp. 195–7.
[3] Issued by the Ethiopian Chamber of Commerce.
[4] Ethiopia Observer, v. 2, pp. 135–42.   [5] Including my own (The Ethiopians, p. 32).

Biblical references to Ethiopia

In assessing the significance of Biblical references to Ethiopia one has to bear in mind that the Hebrew 'Cush', which has been rendered by the Septuagint as Αἰθιοπία,[1] lacks any precise connotation. Moreover, many of the scriptural references are of difficult interpretation. The same is very largely true of classical writers as well: thus Homer speaks (*Odyssey*, i. 22 ff.) of 'the distant Ethiopians, the farthest outposts of mankind, half of whom live where the Sun goes down, and half where he rises'. This division into eastern and western Ethiopians probably indicates that the name Αἰθίοπες[2] referred to all peoples of dark skin, from the country south of Egypt, Nubia, to India.[3] Herodotus is at times a good deal more precise, for he clearly identifies Ethiopia with the kingdom of Meroe, Nubia: 'Ethiopians inhabit the country immediately above Elephantine, and one half of the island; the other half is inhabited by Egyptians; . . . finally, you will arrive at a large city called Meroe: this city is said to be the capital of all Ethiopia.'[4]

It is clear, therefore, that the Biblical 'Cush' is a vague term connoting the entire Nile Valley, south of Egypt, including Nubia and Abyssinia.[5] מהדו ועד כוש (Esther 1: 1) describes the utmost limits of the world. We have already discussed[6] the river Gihon which 'compasseth the whole land of Ethiopia' (Gen. 2: 13), an apt description of the Nile's course in Meroe and Abyssinia. The genealogical table (Gen. 10: 6–8) is of the utmost importance, but the confusion it induces and the problems it poses seem wellnigh incapable of solution: the sons of Ham are Cush[7] and Mizraim, Phut and Canaan; and the sons of Cush are Seba, Havilah, Sabtah, Raamah, and Sabtecha; and the sons of Raamah are Sheba and Dedan. And Cush also begat Nimrod.[8]

---

[1] On two occasions (Ps. 72: 9 and 74: 14) Αἰθίοπες appears as a translation of צײם.

[2] This word is usually explained as αἴθω and ὄψ (Liddell and Scott or W. Max Müller, *Äthiopien*, Leipzig, 1904, p. 4) 'burnt face', but it might also be derived from αἴθοψ which means 'sparkling, brilliant'; and Conti Rossini (*Storia d'Etiopia*, p. 56) renders this as 'dal viso ardente, rilucente'. αἴθοψ is also 'red, fiery' and might be compared to Amharic *qay* 'red' where 'questo, nel linguaggio corrente, è il colore degli Abissini, opposto a *ṭaqur* colore dei negri, Sciangalla, ecc.' (Suppl. to Guidi's *Vocabolario Amarico*, col. 75).

[3] Cf. Herodotus vii. 70.   [4] Herodotus ii. 29.

[5] For the distinction between 'Ethiopia' and 'Abyssinia', see my *Semitic Languages of Ethiopia*, p. 4. Cf. also Glaser, *Abessinier in Arabien und Afrika*, pp. 6 ff.

[6] p. 2, above.

[7] Instead of the usual Αἰθίοπες, the Septuagint here renders 'Cush' as Χους.

[8] In the 'Testament of Naphtali' the Lord commanded Michael and the seventy angels to teach the seventy languages to mankind. Then spoke Nimrod the wicked: 'In my eyes there is none greater than he who taught me the language of Cush' (cf. *Zawaat Naphtali* in Ginzberg, *Legends of the Jews*, ii. 215; Charles, *Pseudepigrapha*, p. 363).

For Nimrod as the offspring of Cush, cf. Skinner, *Genesis*, pp. 207 ff.

Of the two sets of names mentioned as Ham's progeny, each reads from south to north (Cush and Egypt; Phut and Canaan). Phut = Punt is probably the Somali coast,[1] and Canaan is the only non-African location cited. The sons of Cush all appear to be situated in Asia; no doubt the compiler of the table believed these Arabian peoples either to be of African descent (or migration) or to be under African dominion—by no means an extravagantly eccentric suggestion. By far the best known of these names are Sheba and Dedan;[2] the literature on Sheba and the Sabaeans is too extensive to be quoted here,[3] while Dedan has been generally associated with el-'Ulā in the northern Ḥedjāz.[4]

There are several places in the Old Testament where Cush is mentioned as the border region south of Egypt: 'from Migdol to Aswan up to the border of Ethiopia' (Ezek. 29: 10); 'Ethiopia was strong and Egypt without end . . .' (Nahum 3: 9). The messengers who were sent to frighten Ethiopia travel in ships (Ezek. 30: 9), an obvious allusion to navigation on the upper Nile. The rivers of Ethiopia are also referred to in Isaiah 18: 1: 'a land . . . which is beyond the rivers of Ethiopia.'[5] No doubt we have to think here of the White and Blue Niles and the Atbara. The papyrus boats, mentioned in Isaiah 18: 2, can be seen in Ethiopia to this day, especially on Lake Tana.[6]

The prophet Isaiah refers to 'Cush' on a number of other occasions as well: the Lord promises to recover the remnant of his people from various countries of the diaspora, among them Egypt, Upper Egypt (Pathros), and Cush (Isaiah 11: 11);[7] the placing of Cush within the setting of this verse fixes its geographical position south of Upper Egypt. The same is true of Isaiah 43: 3, where God is ready to offer the richest and furthest countries (among them Ethiopia, Egypt, and Seba) as ransom for Israel, or of Isaiah 45: 14 where the labour of Egypt and the trade of Ethiopians and of Sabaeans appear in juxtaposition. In Isaiah 20: 3-5, in the prophecy on Egypt and Ethiopia, we hear

[1] See *The Ethiopians*[2], p. 47; F. Hommel, *Ethnologie und Geographie des Alten Orients*, pp. 634-650; Breasted, *History of Egypt*[2], pp. 127, 142.

[2] For the other names, see the detailed discussion in Skinner, *Genesis*, pp. 200 ff.; also Hommel, op. cit., index; and H. v. Wissmann, *Zur Geschichte und Landeskunde von Alt-Südarabien*, index.

[3] See H. v. Wissmann and M. Höfner, *Zur hist. Geogr. d. vorislam. Südarabien*, p. 109 *et passim*.

[4] See especially Albright's article 'Dedan' in the *Albrecht Alt Festschrift* (*Geschichte und Altes Testament*), Tübingen, 1953.

[5] The same expression also occurs in Zeph. 3: 10.—The other reference to Ethiopia in Zephaniah (2: 12) yields nothing of any particular interest ('Ethiopians slain by my sword').

[6] Cf. Cheesman, op. cit., pp. 90 ff. For the *tankwa* 'papyrus boat' see p. 111 in Ursin's *Äthiopien*.

[7] Ethiopia as a seat of a Jewish diaspora may also be the background to Ps. 87: 4 (see below).

of the Egyptians being led away as prisoners and the Ethiopians as captives;[1] and Isaiah 37: 9 (= 2 Kings 19: 9) gives Tirhaqa as the name of מלך כוש (LXX: θαράκα βασιλεὺς Αἰθιόπων). He is Taharqa of the 25th (Ethiopian) dynasty who was defeated by Sennacherib during the latter's campaign against Judaea.[2]

Jeremiah 46: 9 speaks of 'the mighty men, Ethiopia and Pu[n]t who handle the shield'. That the Ethiopians were dark-skinned was well known to Jeremiah: 'Can the Ethiopian change his skin?' (13: 23). And Ebed-Melech, the Ethiopian[3] eunuch, was the man at whose intercession Jeremiah was released from the pit (38: 7, 10, 12) and who was promised deliverance from the fate that was to befall the city (39: 16–18). Dark-skinned Ethiopians are thus shown to have been in the service of King Zedekiah; Ebed-Melech himself must have attained a fairly senior position at court, for otherwise he would have been unlikely to have had such ready access to the person of the king (38: 8–10).

Ezekiel warns of 'the sword that shall come upon Egypt and the anguish that will be in Ethiopia' (30: 4); and in the following verse he enumerates Egypt's provinces and allies, in order to picture the approaching disaster in all its magnitude: 'Ethiopia and Pu[n]t and Lydia and all the mingled people.'[4] From most of these references there emerges a fairly stable idea of Cush as a country commonly bracketed with Egypt (and situated to the south of it) or the north-east African littoral. In Psalm 87: 4 we would appear to have a hint[5] to a number of centres with sizeable Jewish colonies: Rahab (an emblematic name of Egypt), Babylon, Philistia, Tyre, and Ethiopia.[6]

Egypt, with Libya in the west and Ethiopia in the south, is also mentioned in Daniel 11: 43, 2 Chronicles 12: 3 and 16: 8.

---

[1] Cf. Breasted, op. cit., p. 551.

[2] Cf. TIRHAKAH in Hastings's *Dictionary of the Bible*, and Breasted, op. cit., pp. 552 ff.

[3] Cf. the discussion in Talmud *Mo'ed Ḳaṭan* 16b dealing with Ethiopians and dark-skinned people.

Ebed-Melech is called Ethiopian, i.e. black, antiphrastically, because he was the only white, i.e. pious, man at the court of King Zedekiah (Ginzberg, *Legends of the Jews*, vi. 412).

[4] While the Septuagint has Αἰθιοπία in Ezek. 30: 4 and 9, in v. 5 כוש ופוט ולוד appear, oddly enough, as Πέρσαι καὶ Κρῆτες καὶ Λυδοί. This may well be an echo of the similar text in Ezek. 27: 10. It is, however, interesting to note that the Ethiopic version—in contrast to the LXX—follows the text of the Hebrew original in this particular detail (as is also the case with the Peshitta). This is an aspect deserving of consideration when we come to discuss the *Vorlage* of the Ethiopic Bible text (Chapter I).

In Ezek. 38: 5 we have 'Persia, Ethiopia, and Pu[n]t'; there appears to be some confusion, therefore, in the geographical distribution of these peoples as between Ezek. 27: 10, 30: 5, and 38: 5.

[5] According to Duhm (Marti's *Hand-Kommentar*), ad loc.

[6] The Hebrew עָם כוש was understood by the LXX (and E.O.T.) as עָם כוש.

Although the reference in 2 Chronicles 21: 16[1] to a (South) Arabian military campaign against Judah presents historical and geographical difficulties, the very mention of הערבים אשר על יד כושים is of the greatest interest, for it shows the close proximity between the South Arabians and Ethiopians and might well be an early pointer to South Arabian migrations to Ethiopia.

The 'topaz of Ethiopia' (Job 28: 19) is the yellow topaz found on the islands of the Red Sea; this has to be read in conjunction with naval expeditions to Ophir, the gold-producing country,[2] which has probably to be sought either somewhere in South Arabia or along the Somali coast (1 Kings 9: 27–28). In 2 Samuel 18: 21 ff. we are told about an Ethiopian servant employed by King David; he was clearly in a much less senior position than Ebed-Melech under Zedekiah (see above), for he is simply referred to as הכושי.[3] This appellation would suggest that he was the only one thus employed at that particular time.

One of the most famous Ethiopian references in the Old Testament is, of course, in Numbers 12: 1 where Miriam and Aaron speak against Moses because of האשה הכשית[4] whom he had taken. Jewish commentators, since the days of the Targum, have been embarrassed by the obvious interpretation that Moses had married an Ethiopian slave-girl. Some have argued (and so have some modern exegetes) that 'Ethiopian, Cushite' is a blanket term that might well have been applied to Zipporah, the Midianite (i.e. North Arabian), but it seems very unlikely that this explanation would satisfactorily account for the indignation expressed by Miriam and Aaron. The Targum renders the 'offending' words as אתתא שפירתא 'a beautiful woman' which is based on an ancient Gematria[5] of כושית and יפת מראה (each producing 736 in numerical value).[6]

The prophet Amos explains in chapter 9: 7 that God did not only bring up Israel out of Egypt but was equally concerned in

[1] Cf. also 2 Chron. 14: 8, 11, 12.

I cannot agree with M. Rodinson (*Bi Or*, 1964, p. 239, 1st col.) that 'il n'y a rien à tirer du texte . . . fort tardif'. The inferences seem to me patent and clear, and the lateness of the text is neither proved nor relevant, for even if this were a late gloss it would still be a very early allusion to the geographical and historical situation.

[2] 'Commercial relations on a large scale between Palestine and Arabia certainly go back to the days of Solomon; and many books of the Old Testament, particularly Job and Proverbs, which are strongly marked by the presence of Arabic words, show that the connexion was steadily maintained' (A. Guillaume in *Legacy of Israel*, p. 132).

[3] It is obvious that in v. 21*b* we should read הכושי in conformity with the other occurrences of the word in this chapter. The Septuagint misunderstood this as a proper name: Χουσεί.

[4] LXX: Αἰθιόπισσα; E.O.T.: ኢትዮጵያዊት ፨   [5] Cf. Rashi, ad loc.

[6] For further Midrashic elaborations on this theme see below, pp. 13 ff.

other historical migrations. In fact, what reason was there to assume that Israel held any special position: 'Are ye not as the Ethiopians unto me?'[1] The climactic inference of these words can only be fully appreciated if the Ethiopians serve, in the present context, as the epitome of a far-distant, uncivilized, and despised black race.[2]

To conclude this survey of Old Testament references we must turn to Psalm 68: 32[3] which contains the much-quoted כוש תריץ ידיו לאלהים: ኢትዮጵያ፡ ታበጽሕ፡ እደዊ፡ ኀበ፡ እግዚአብሔር።[4] This is undoubtedly Ethiopia's favourite Bible quotation; it occurs twice in the *Kebra Nagast*[5] and is frequently used as a motto[6] or in heraldic devices in present-day Ethiopia. The Ethiopic and Greek texts are clear, but the Hebrew original is not without its textual problems.[7] 'Ethiopia stretching out her hands unto God' has become a proof-text and a symbol of the country's passionate adherence to the orthodox faith.

The principal New Testament reference occurs in Acts 8: 27, where we hear of 'a man of Ethiopia, an eunuch of great authority under Candace queen of the Ethiopians'. While there can scarcely be any doubt that the eunuch who was baptized by St. Philip must have been a servant of one of the Meroitic queens who bore the name Candace,[8] Ethiopians have, from a very early period, applied this episode to themselves and have identified Candace with the Queen of Sheba. In the New Testament there is, of course, no connexion between Candace and the 'Queen of the South'[9] (Matt. 12: 42; Luke 11: 31), but the *Kebra Nagast*[10] ('Glory of the Kings'—the Ethiopian national

---

[1] בני כשיים; υἱοὶ Αἰθιόπων; ደቂ፡ ኢትዮጵያ።
[2] Cf. Harper, *Amos and Hosea* (I.C.C.), p. 192.
[3] LXX and E.O.T. 67: 32.   [4] Αἰθιοπία προφθάσει χεῖρα αὐτῆς τῷ θεῷ.
[5] Chapter 50 (end):

ኢትዮጵያ፡ ትሜጥፕ፡ እደዊ፡ በእግዚአብሔር፡
ወውእቱ፡ ይትሜጠፕ፡ በክብር፡

'Ethiopia will extend her hands to God and He will turn to her with honour.' The last part is, of course, an addition designed to underline the appositeness of the Biblical quotation. The text of the substantive part differs from the Ethiopic Old Testament and, indeed, from *Kebra Nagast*, chapter 113 (end); the text of the latter tallies with E.O.T. Cf. Hubbard, *Kebra Nagast* (thesis), pp. 21–22.
[6] e.g. in leaflets dropped by the British and Ethiopian governments during the Ethiopian campaign in 1940/1.
[7] Cf. Duhm, *Psalmen*, pp. 262–3; Cassuto–Hartom, *Psalms* (in Hebrew), p. 151.
[8] Cf. Ullendorff, *New Testament Studies*, ii (1955), 53.
[9] βασίλισσα νότου appears to go back to a Semitic idiom (cf. M. Black, *Aramaic Approach*[2], p. 68) such as מלכת שבא.
[10] Cf. Bodleian MS. Bruce 93 (= Dillmann, *Catalogus Cod. MSS. Bibl. Bodl. Oxon.*, Oxford, 1848, no. xxvi); C. Bezold, *Kebra Nagast*, Munich, 1905; E. A. W. Budge, *The Queen of Sheba*

saga) fuses the two queens, belonging to such different periods, into one person.

The *loci classici* of the blending of the two traditions about the 'Queen of the South' and 'Candace Queen of the Ethiopians' are in the 21st and 33rd chapters of the *Kebra Nagast*. Here the great Sheba cycle is introduced by references to Matthew 12: 42 and Luke 11: 31; and we are then informed that 'the Queen of the South is the Queen of Ethiopia'.[1] At this point Bodleian MS. Bruce 93 adds: 'the patrimony and country of birth of this Queen of the South is Aksum [the ancient capital of Abyssinia], for she originates from there.'[2] In chapter 33 the conflation goes so far as to assert: Gaza is 'the city which King Solomon had given to the Queen of Ethiopia; for in the Acts of the Apostles Luke the Evangelist wrote, saying: "He is the governor of the whole country of Gaza, a eunuch of Queen Candace" . . .'. We observe here not only the identification of the Queen of Sheba with Queen Candace as an essential step in the christianization of Ethiopia's traditional past,[3] but also the misinterpretation, possibly unintentional,[4] of ἐπὶ πάσης τῆς γάζης αὐτῆς as administrator of 'Gaza' instead of 'her treasure'—probably conduced to by the mention of Gaza in the preceding verse (8: 26).

It has, incidentally, been suggested[5] that the text which the Ethiopian eunuch was heard to read was the Septuagint version of Isaiah 53: 7–8. This does appear to be the case, especially in view of the beginning of v. 8 where the LXX diverges from the Masoretic text. It is, however, worthy of note that the Ethiopic New Testament (Acts 8: 33) here follows a text that differs both from the LXX and the Greek New Testament but is close to the Masoretic text and the Syriac New Testament (though quite distinct from da Bassano's Ethiopic Old Testament).

Details of the Queen of Sheba cycle of legends will be discussed in Chapter III, below, but it ought to be mentioned here that some versions of the Old Testament narrative (1 Kings 10) are likely to have reached Ethiopia already in pre-Christian

and her Only Son Menyelek, Oxford, 1932; Hubbard, *Literary Sources of the Kebra Nagast*, St. Andrews Ph.D. thesis, 1956; Ullendorff, *The Ethiopians*², pp. 143–4.

1 ንግሥት፡ አዜብ፡ ንግሥት፡ ኢትዮጵያ፡ ይእቲ፡ (chapter 21).

2 ዘቲሰ፡ ንግሥት፡ አዜብ፡ ርስታ፡ ወምድረ፡ ሙላዳ፡ አክሱም፡ እስመ፡ እምኔሃ፡ ተወልደት። (*Kebra Nagast*, ibidem; cf. also Bezold, op. cit., p. 12 [Ethiopic text]).

3 The anachronistic treatment of pre-Christian events is, perhaps, best known from the versions of the Alexander legends which have all been given a Christian character, and Alexander himself is depicted as a devout Christian.

4 Yet the Ethiopic New Testament has the correct ላዕለ፡ ኵሉ፡ መዛግብቲሃ። (Acts 8: 27).

5 e.g. by D. S. Margoliouth in Hastings's *Dictionary of the Bible*, i. 790.

times. They were no doubt brought into the country by some of the South Arabian immigrants and were subsequently adapted in such a manner as to contribute in the most effective way to the ennoblement of the Ethiopian nation. With the introduction of Christianity into Ethiopia, in the fourth century, a Christian layer was superimposed on the Hebraic-Semitic traditions prevalent at the time. It was thus natural, and even essential, that the national ancestress of the Abyssinian nation, the Queen of Sheba, should come to be identified with 'Candace queen of the Ethiopians', the only express mention of Ethiopia in the New Testament. Parallels are not lacking for the blending of diverse elements and the acquisition of an ennobled national ancestry: one need only think of the Quraysh genealogies which have been adopted by many converts to Islam who could have had no possible connexion with that Meccan family.[1]

Another New Testament verse that has attained great prominence in Ethiopia is Revelation 5: 5. 'No man in heaven nor in earth' had been found worthy to open the book 'sealed with seven seals.' Finally, one of the elders comforted St. John saying: 'Weep not: behold, the Lion of the tribe of Judah,[2] the Root of David, hath prevailed to open the book and to loose the seven seals thereof.' The idea of the lion of Judah is, of course, as old as Genesis 49: 9,[3] but its application to the royal house of Ethiopia, as part of the Imperial styles, is of no great antiquity.[4] The phrase does not occur in the *Kebra Nagast*, although in chapter 107 the relevant passage from Genesis 49: 8–10 is quoted *in extenso* together with suitable embellishments.

On one of his maps[5] Ludolf prints the *Insignia Regis Regum Aethiopiae* consisting of a lion holding a cross accompanied by the text (see footnote 2, below) in Latin and Gəʿəz. This is further explained:[6] 'Insigne Regis, quo etiam in consignandis literis utitur, est Leo crucem tenens cum symbolo: ምእ: እንበለ: ዘእምነገደ: ይሁዳ:: Vicit leo de tribu Iuda.' And again:[7] 'Habessinos etiamnum Regum suorum posteros Israelitas vocare, neque alios praeter Menileheci generis masculos regio solio dignos putare: atque eam ob causam insignia regia Leonem habere cum symbolo:

---

[1] Cf. Nöldeke, *Geschichte des Qorans*, ii. 159; Goldziher, *Muhammedanische Studien*, i. 81, 85, 97, 180–1, 188–9.

[2] ἐνίκησεν ὁ λέων ὁ ἐκ τῆς φυλῆς Ἰούδα

ምእ: እንበለ: ዘእምነገደ: ይሁዳ::

[3] גור אריה יהודה.

[4] See now S. Rubenson's interesting article in the *Journal of Ethiopian Studies*, iii. 2, July 1965 (but published 1966). [5] *Historia Aethiopica*, book i, beginning of chap. 4.

[6] Ibid., book ii, chap. 1: 41. [7] Ibid., book ii, chap. 3: 27–28.

Vicit Leo de Tribu Juda; ut demonstrent, quod ex tribu Judae & stemmate Davidis oriundi sint. . . .'[1]

Rubenson argues,[2] rightly I believe, that the lion rampant, the Latin cross, and the Latin text in the blazon point to a European origin of this heraldic device. In any event, the use of the scriptural 'The Lion of the tribe of Judah hath prevailed' as a constituent part of the royal styles is of comparatively recent date.

References to Ethiopia in the Apocrypha and Pseudepigrapha of the Old Testament are of rather limited significance. They are generally of the same type as may be encountered in the Old Testament itself, i.e. allusions to the borders of Ethiopia south of Egypt, from India to Ethiopia, etc.[3] There are, however, one or two partial—and fairly interesting—exceptions: in the Sibylline Books we are told that the land of Gog and Magog is 'in the midst of the rivers of Ethiopia'.[4] This is, I believe, the only occurrence where Gog and Magog are located in Nubia-Abyssinia; as these adversaries of God and his Messiah are consigned to perdition, the 'rivers of Ethiopia' must represent a particularly remote and nasty location. The same thought is repeated, in a somewhat expanded form, in Sib. iii: 512–19 where Gog and Magog are cursed, together with many tribes who will fall and upon whom the Most High will send a grievous scourge. Among these peoples are 'Moors and Ethiopians and nations of barbarous speech'.[5] In Sib. v: 194 Syene (Aswan) shall be destroyed by 'an Ethiopian hero', yet in v: 206–13 the 'stout-hearted' Ethiopians and the 'whole land of the Ethiopians shall perish with fire and moanings'.

Turning to the Apocrypha of the New Testament, we find that additional colour is lent to the claim of Abyssinia as the first Christian nation by the narrative in the seventh book of the Apocryphal Acts of the Apostles, according to which Matthew baptized the king of Ethiopia. Matthew had arrived at Naddaver, the capital of Ethiopia, where King Aeglippus reigned and where magicians and charmed serpents held sway over the people. Matthew was welcomed by a eunuch named Candacis (*sic*), whom Philip had baptized, and succeeded in breaking the spell of the magicians and serpents. He baptized king, court,

---

[1] Cf. also Ludolf, *Commentarius*, pp. 531, 547.   [2] Op. cit., p. 80.

[3] e.g. Judith 1: 10; *Add.* Esther B: 1, etc. Cf. Charles, *Apocrypha and Pseudepigrapha* (index under 'Ethiopia').

[4] Charles, *Pseudepigrapha*, The Sibylline Books, iii. 319–20.

[5] For a discussion of the speech of Ethiopia as the epitome of a barbarous language, see my paper 'C'est de l'hébreu pour moi!' in the Winton Thomas issue of *JSS* 1968.

and country, and the people built a large church in thirty days. Aeglippus was succeeded as king by his brother Hyrtacus who killed Matthew because he had refused to sanction Hyrtacus' marriage to Ephigenia, the daughter of Aeglippus.

The ascription by the Ethiopians of this apocryphal story to themselves is no doubt due to the ambiguity of the term 'Ethiopia', and is thus on a par with their appropriation of Candace queen of the Ethiopians. In fact, in this narrative of the Apocryphal Acts the names alone make it plain that the document cannot have referred to Abyssinia.[1]

Another apocryphal account, which relates to Matthew 2: 13 ff. and some of the Infancy Gospels, has gained some currency in Ethiopia. It is contained in the British Museum Ethiopic MS. Add. 16 193 (= Dillmann, B.M. *Catalogus*, xlii) and deals with the Flight of the Holy Family to Ethiopia. The sojourn in Ethiopia lasted for 3½ years, and during the return to Palestine the Virgin Mary wrought a large number of miracles. The compilation is of a complex character with a conflation of many disparate strands.[2]

Ethiopia also plays some part in the Midrashic elaborations of Rabbinical literature which continues and embroiders themes more or less tenuously touched upon in the Old Testament. The most detailed of these embellishments concerns the alleged sojourn in Ethiopia of Moses and his reign as king of that country.[3] The Biblical elements that were woven into this tale are derived from Moses' flight from Egypt (after he had slain the Egyptian overseer), the uncertainty about the location of Midian, and Moses' marriage to an Ethiopian woman. The Midrash relates that, when Moses escaped from the Egyptians, a war was raging between Ethiopia and the nations of the East. Moses appeared in the Ethiopian king's camp and found great favour with the king (named Ḳiḳanos) and his people. When the king died, the nobles made Moses king over them and gave him Adoniah, Ḳiḳanos' widow, as his wife and queen. Moses was victorious in all his campaigns, lifted the siege of the capital, and made the country prosper. He ruled over Ethiopia for

[1] This had already been pointed out by C. Conti Rossini, *Storia d'Etiopia*, p. 145. See also Dillmann, *Zur Gesch. d. Axum. Reichs*, pp. 4 ff.
[2] R. H. Emery has edited and annotated this manuscript, under my supervision, in a doctoral thesis accepted by St. Andrews University in 1959. A fresh study of this manuscript, based on the collation of manuscripts hitherto not considered, will shortly appear in a *C.S.C.O.* volume on the Flight of the Holy Family, edited by Ullendorff and Emery.
[3] Cf. *Yashar Shemot*, an eleventh-century compilation of *midrashim* to the Pentateuch; Ginzberg, *Legends of the Jews*, ii. 283–9, and v. 407–10. See also, in a more general context: M. Abraham, *Légendes juives apocryphes sur la vie de Moïse*.

forty years, and in the 67th year of his life the time came to leave Ethiopia and to release Israel from Egypt.

Josephus[1] has a rather different account, though many details and stratagems used by Moses are identical in both versions. Here Moses is appointed commander of the Egyptian army when the country is invaded by the Ethiopians. His campaign against Ethiopia is successful—except that the capture of Saba ('which was a royal city of Ethiopia, which Cambyses afterwards named Meroe after the name of his own sister')[1] eludes him. However, Tharbis, the daughter of the Ethiopian king, falls passionately in love with Moses; he promises to marry her—provided she procures the surrender of the city. It is clear that the object of all these Midrashic embroideries is to explain Moses' union with an Ethiopian woman (Num. 12: 1).

A rather different subject is touched upon in the Talmudic discussion on the nations of the earth offering gifts to the Messiah.[2] Egypt's gifts will at first be rejected by the Messiah, but Ethiopia's offering will no doubt be accepted, for she was never Israel's taskmaster; and in her favour is also adduced the psalmist's כוש תריץ ידיו לאלהים (Ps. 68: 32).—Eldad had-Dani reports that the Danites, prompted to leave Palestine, passed through Egypt and settled in Ethiopia where they slew many of the inhabitants and exacted tribute from the survivors.[3]

According to the *Targum Sheni* on Esther, Ahasuerus—who reigned 'from India unto Ethiopia'—had received coronation gifts from countries as far afield as Ethiopia[4] and Africa (ממדינת אפריקי). Elsewhere Ethiopia is described as 'the pearl of all countries'.[5] And because of the Ethiopians' fondness of Moses they accepted from him the custom of circumcision[6] which they have maintained to this day.

These quotations will suffice to demonstrate that Ethiopia-Cush makes a relatively modest appearance in Biblical literature (and in some of its immediate offshoots) and that the picture which emerges from this material is, even in its cumulative effect, rather blurred. It is not always clear what Biblical

---

[1] *Antiquities*, ii. 10 and 11.
[2] *Pesaḥim*, 118b. Cf. also Ginzberg, op. cit. iii. 166–7.
[3] *Eldad had-Dani*, ed. Epstein, Pressburg, 1891, pp. 25–26; cf. also Ginzberg, op. cit. iv. 182.
[4] *Targum Sheni* in מקראות גדולות, Warsaw, 1874, part vi (חמש מגילות), p. 138a, col. b (top):

וסב מתמן ספסירא ושרייאנא דילי דאייתין לי יתיה מן כוש מדינתא (ביומא קדמאה דקמית במלכותא)

'and fetch from there the sword and my coat of mail which they brought me from Ethiopia (on the day I ascended the throne).'
[5] See Ginzberg, op. cit. vi. 365.   [6] Ginzberg, op. cit. v. 407.

writers have in mind when they refer to Ethiopia; her location remains imprecise, and her people's characteristics vary from utter remoteness and awareness of their black skin to an innocent piety reaching out for God's mercy. Yet we cannot afford to neglect the historical crumbs and the legendary embellishments which this literature throws out. And furthermore: even if the Bible is not too generous in the space it allocates to Ethiopia, the latter's consciousness of the former is overwhelming and occupies a prominent part in the Ethiopian national scene and atmosphere.

Historical background

Old Testament influences and reflections had probably reached Ethiopia even before the introduction of Christianity in the fourth century and before the translation of the Bible.[1] Monophysite Christianity, once it had taken root, became not only the official religion of the Ethiopian empire but also the most profound expression of the national existence of the Ethiopians. In its peculiar indigenized form, impregnated with strong Hebraic and archaic Semitic elements as well as pagan residua, Abyssinian Christianity constitutes a store-house of the cultural, political, and social life of the people. In speaking of this distinctive conglomerate one has to bear in mind three major religious manifestations in Ethiopia—Judaism, paganism, and Islam—which are either genetic ingredients of Abyssinian Christianity or at least elements of a long historical symbiosis.

For a possible infiltration into pre-Christian Abyssinia of Jewish migrants from the north, from the direction of Egypt, we possess very scanty material only. Jeremiah (44: 1) speaks of Jews who had settled in Egypt, in the north (Migdol and

---

[1] M. Rodinson has recently subjected my views (expressed in 'Hebraic-Jewish elements in Abyssinian (monophysite) Christianity', *JSS* 1956, pp. 216–56, and in *The Ethiopians*) to a searching examination carried out with exceptional erudition and characteristic courtesy. It will not be possible, in the present context, to deal with these matters at length, but they will be briefly considered in Chapter II. If I understand M. Rodinson's position aright, it hinges on his doubts that Hebraic and Old Testament influences penetrated into Ethiopia *before* the introduction of Christianity. Such influences as he concedes are, instead, due to an 'imitation de l'Ancien Testament, parfois poussée jusqu'à l'identification avec Israël' (*JSS* 1964, p. 18; also: *Bi Or*, xxi (1964), 238–45). I can find no reason to dissent from many of M. Rodinson's views; I may well have underestimated the force and importance of the *imitatio Iudaeorum et Veteris Testamenti*, but I have made it plain that I was *not* thinking of an *émigration massive* (*JSS* 1964, p. 16) but of small groups not constituting a complete tribal *golah* (*JSS* 1956, p. 223). I have also given repeated warnings of the extreme caution needed in the analysis of this problem (ibid., pp. 216 and 253).

I should like to take this opportunity of thanking M. Rodinson for his extremely important and valuable criticisms which will have to be taken into consideration in any future discussion of this matter.

Tahpanhes) as well as in the south (Upper Egypt = Pathros).
The prophet Zephaniah (seventh century B.C.) refers to a diaspora in Cush: 'From beyond the rivers of Cush my suppliants,
my dispersed community, shall bring my offering' (Zeph. 3: 10).
Verses 1 and 2 in chapter 18 of Isaiah seem to be based on the
information of eye-witnesses, but the value of these scattered
Old Testament verses is, nonetheless, limited—even though it
seems reasonable to suppose that Jews had penetrated as far as
Upper Egypt, Nubia, and possibly beyond. Herodotus (ii. 30)
relates how certain Egyptian garrisons, after having been on
duty at Elephantine for three years without being relieved,
revolted against Psammetichus and went to Ethiopia. Even if
this referred to the time of Psammetichus II (593–588 B.C.), it
would clearly be too early to have any connexion with the
Jewish military garrison at Elephantine of whom we hear in
the Aramaic papyri of the fifth century B.C. It is, of course,
conceivable that similar revolts and desertions occurred also
under the Persian Government later on. Yet, neither do we
possess any historical information about this nor is a desertion
to Ethiopia (= Nubia) tantamount to the settlement of Jews in
Abyssinia (= Ethiopia in its present connotation).

It must thus be realized that the frequently canvassed origin
of the Falashas[1] from the Jewish garrison at Elephantine or the
conjecture that Jewish influences in Abyssinia had penetrated
by way of Egypt are devoid of any reliable historical basis.[2] It is
mainly thanks to the deservedly great authority of Ignazio
Guidi[3] that these views have received any serious consideration. Not only do they remain entirely within the realm of
pure conjecture, but there are a number of facts which militate
against their acceptance. Conti Rossini[4] has suggested that the
Judaism professed by the military garrison diverges considerably
from such Jewish forms as have been preserved in Ethiopia.
There is no mention of the Sabbath in the Elephantine papyri,[5]
and the only feast specifically referred to is the festival of Un-
leavened Bread. Members of the Jewish military garrison at
Elephantine intermarried with their neighbours (document no.
14) and appear to have lived on equal terms with them. Such
aspects of Elephantine religious life as emerge from the papyri

[1] See excursus on the Falashas—appended to Chapter II.
[2] My views on this subject are shared by M. Rodinson, *JSS* 1964, p. 16.
[3] [Breve] *Storia della letteratura etiopica*, p. 95, note 2.
[4] *Storia d'Etiopia*, p. 144.
[5] Cf. A. Cowley, *Aramaic Papyri of the Fifth Century B.C.*, pp. xvii ff.; R. Yaron, *The Law of the Elephantine Documents* (in Hebrew), Jerusalem, 1961.

are in sharp contrast to the entire cast of religious expression among the Falashas in particular and the Judaizing trends of the Abyssinian Church in general. This estimate remains true even when the fullest allowances are made for the inevitable deficiencies in our knowledge of the Elephantine community.

The position is different with regard to Jewish and Old Testament influences that may have entered Abyssinia via South Arabia:[1] the source material here is a good deal ampler, and the evidence for migratory movements across the Red Sea is indisputable.[2] The Hebrew Bible abounds, of course, in direct or indirect references to ישמעאלים, ערביים, ערב, etc.; and the desert origin of the Hebrews points in the same direction. Solomon and his successors had an outlet to the Red Sea at Elath (= 'Aqabah, 2 Kings 14: 22; 16: 6), and we have already alluded to naval expeditions to Ophir (p. 8, above). While none of the Biblical references reveals any intimate and detailed knowledge of Arabia, and South Arabia in particular, they nevertheless give an indication of Jewish contacts with that country. Three of the South Arabian kingdoms occur in the Old Testament: Saba (Gen. 10: 7 and other places), Ma'in[3] (1 Chron. 4: 41), Ḥaḍramawt (Gen. 10: 26).

In Rabbinical literature there are a few references to Jewish connexions with Arabia. In Midrash *Bemidbar Rabba* ix we hear that ... שאל מלך ערביים את רבי עקיבא אני כושי ואשתי כושית. The date (about A.D. 130) is given by the mention of R. 'Aqiba. The fact that this 'King of the Arabs' was black (an Ethiopian) clearly shows that R. 'Aqiba must have travelled as far as South Arabia.[4] The passage also reveals, incidentally, that an Ethiopian prince or kinglet ruled at that time over at least a province of South Arabia. In the days of R. 'Aqiba a sizeable Jewish community must already have existed in Arabia,[5] for otherwise it would scarcely have been worthwhile for R. 'Aqiba to undertake so arduous a journey, whose purpose presumably was to incite the Jews of Arabia to fight against Rome.[6] This is likely to be one of the first pieces of direct evidence for the

[1] See C. Rathjens, *Die Juden in Abessinien*, esp. chap. 2; H. Z. Hirschberg, ישראל בערב, Tel Aviv, 1946, esp. chap. 4; Glaser, *Abessinier*, pp. 174 ff.

[2] Cf. M. Höfner, 'Über sprachl. u. kult. Bez. zw. Südarab. u. Äth. im Altertum' in *Atti del Convegno*, pp. 435 ff.

[3] M. Rodinson (*Bi Or*, 1964, p. 239) seems a trifle too categorical in rejecting this identification. Not only is there the evidence of the Septuagint and of the *kaṯib* of the Masoretic text, but the mention of similar South Arabian locations in the Old Testament affords this identification reasonable support. Cf. also Hirschberg, op. cit., p. 34.

[4] See also Hirschberg, op. cit., pp. 40, 280.   [5] Cf. Hirschberg, op. cit., pp. 50 ff.

[6] A reference to R. 'Aqiba's journey occurs also in Talmud Bab. *Rosh Hashanah* 26a: אמר רבי עקיבא כשהלכתי לערביא. See also S. Krauss, *ZDMG* 1916, p. 331.

existence of Jewish colonies in Arabia.[1] So early and far-flung
a settlement of Jews in the Arabian peninsula makes it probable
that some Jewish elements at least were included in the South
Arabian waves of migration across the Red Sea into Abyssinia.

This latter point is accepted also by M. Rodinson,[2] but he
argues that 'la chronologie s'oppose à ce qu'une influence im-
portante du judaïsme se soit exercée en Éthiopie avant les
débuts de l'évangélisation de ce dernier pays'.[3] This view is
based on the assumption that monotheism ('plus ou moins
judaïsant') did not become dominant in South Arabia until
about A.D. 375, i.e. later even than the introduction of Christianity into Ethiopia. The justification of this opinion will
depend primarily on the interpretation of what precisely a
'dominant' position entails, but the existence of Jewish nuclei
in many parts of the Arabian peninsula, ever since the destruction of the Second Temple in A.D. 70, is not in doubt.[4]

Details of the location and activities of these Jewish colonies
in pre-Islamic Arabia need not be reiterated here; we know of
the Jewish population of Yathrib (Medina),[5] of Jewish tribes,[6]
and of the Khaibar oasis.[7] While the Jews of Arabia cherish the
tradition that some Jewish refugees came to Arabia as early as
the time of the destruction of the First Temple,[8] there is no
doubt that the bulk entered the peninsula only after the events

[1] Strabo (*Geogr.* xvi. 23) mentions that Aelius Gallus collected for his expedition to South
Arabia some 10,000 men '. . . ὧν ἦσαν 'Ιουδαῖοι μὲν πεντακόσιοι'. And Josephus (*Ant. Iud.* xv.
9, 3) explains: . . . 'sub illo tempore [Herodes] misit et Caesari subsidio quingentos lectos
homines de suis satellitibus, quos Aelius Gallus ad Mare Rubrum duxit et qui ei magno usui
fuerunt.' Here we have a definite reference to Jewish contact with South Arabia shortly
before the Christian era, and it is not impossible that some of Aelius Gallus' Jewish warriors
may have remained in South Arabia to settle there. The extent of Aelius Gallus' penetration
into Arabia has been discussed in Wissmann–Höfner's *Histor. Geographie des vorislamischen
Südarabien*, pp. 31 ff.

[2] *JSS* 1964, p. 16: 'il est inconcevable certes qu'il ne se soit produit aucun développement
de cette influence au delà de la Mer Rouge, et même qu'aucun Juif d'Arabie du Sud ne soit
venu s'installer en Éthiopie.'   [3] Ibid.

[4] Apart from the sources cited above, cf. especially E. Glaser, *Abessinier*, p. 174: 'Das
Vorschieben des Judenthums aus politischen Motiven scheint aber etwas älteren Datums zu
sein als die Christianisirung Axums'; Rathjens, *Juden in Abessinien*, p. 10; Conti Rossini,
Storia, p. 144: 'È verisimile che realmente in Etiopia sieno esistiti nuclei giudaici prima che il
paese passasse al cristianesimo.' And ibid.: 'Che, in ogni caso, il giudaismo sia antico in
Etiopia, è dimostrato in modo positivo. . . .' While M. Rodinson quotes with approval (*JSS*
1964, p. 14) Conti Rossini's view (ibid.) that 'altri apparenti influssi giudaici spiegansi con
l'adozione del Vecchio Testamento; altri, effettivi, sono d'età più tarda' (and who could fail
to assent to these propositions with alacrity?), he makes no mention of the equally positive
opinions expressed by C. C. R. on the same page (quoted above in this note).

[5] W. Montgomery Watt, *Muhammad at Medina*, pp. 192 ff.

[6] Ibid., and Guillaume in *Legacy of Israel*, p. 133: 'Whole tribes seem to have gone over to
Judaism and accepted monotheism before the rise of Muhammad.'

[7] Hirschberg, op. cit., pp. 132–3 *et passim*.

[8] Cf. H. Graetz, *Geschichte der Juden*², v, 68; and especially Hirschberg's comprehensive
Yisra'el ba'Arab.

of A.D. 70. Al-Jumaḥi mentions in his biographies several Jewish poets of Medina,[1] and the story of the last Himyarite king, Ḏu Nuwās, who was converted to Judaism, is too well known to warrant repetition:[2] his defeat ushered in the period of Abyssinian rule in South-West Arabia. Much of the traditional Jewish Aggadic material[3] became part of the general Semitic heritage and found its literary reflexion, often in a very changed and distorted form, in the Qur'an[4] or the *Kebra Nagast*.[5] The Qur'an in its foreign vocabulary underlines this Semitic medley in its numerous loan-words from Hebrew, Aramaic-Syriac, and Ethiopic,[6] several in strangely hybrid disguises. The religious syncretism of pre-Islamic Arabia has yet to be disentangled in detail—despite such valuable existing studies as D. Nielsen's chapter in the *Handbuch der altarabischen Altertumskunde* and G. Ryckmans's *Les Religions arabes préislamiques*, 3rd ed.[7] The impact of Jewish settlements in Arabia may be felt in the gradual displacement of pagan deities in favour of such names as *Ḏu-Samawi* and even *Raḥmanan*[8] which are clearly derived from (at least originally) Judaic conceptions. A direct link with these settlements has, perhaps, existed until recently in the long history of the Yemenite Jews.[9]

With the defeat of Ḏu Nuwās at the hands of the Abyssinian conquerors (about A.D. 525) Judaism in South Arabia was severely checked.[10] But the Christian predominance,[11] in its turn,

[1] *Ṭabaqāt aš-šuʿarāʾ*, ed. Hell (1916), pp. 70 ff.

[2] See *Dhū Nuwās* in *Encyclopaedia of Islam*[2];. M. Guidi, *Storia e cultura degli Arabi*, pp. 143 ff.; Ryckmans, *Le Muséon*, lxvi (1953), 284 ff., where, in Ry. 507 and 508, we hear of Ḏu Nuwās' real name YSF and his epithet *ʾsʾr*. See also S. D. Goitein's article in *Haʾarets* (25 Mar. 1955): גלויים חדשים על בית המלוכה היהודי בתימן. Cf. Jamme 1028: *ywsf ʾsʾr yẓʾr*.

[3] See Ginzberg, *Legends*, vol. vii under 'Arabs', 'Arabia', 'Arabic', and 'Ishmaelites'.

[4] Cf. A. Geiger, *Was hat Mohammed aus dem Judenthum aufgenommen*, Bonn, 1833; M. Grünbaum, *Neue Beiträge zur semitischen Sagenkunde*, passim.

[5] Hubbard, op. cit., pp. 140–83.

[6] See excursus to Chapter II, below; Nöldeke, *Neue Beiträge*, pp. 46–64; Fraenkel, *Aram. Fremdw. im Arab.*

[7] In *L'Histoire Générale des Religions* (1960). See also J. Ryckmans, 'Le christianisme en Arabie du Sud préislamique' in *L'Oriente cristiano nella storia della civiltà*, Rome, 1964 (Accademia dei Lincei).

[8] Cf. G. Ryckmans, op. cit., pp. 223, 227; see also note 612. *C.I.H.* 543 begins: *brk wtbrk sm rḥmnn ḏbsmyn wyšrʾl wʾlhhmw rbyhd. . . .* 'Praised and blessed be the name of RḤMNn, who is in heaven, and YŠRʾL and their God, the lord of the Jews. . . .' A similar passage occurs in Ry. 515 (*Le Muséon*, lxvi (1953), 314–15) where we find *rbhwd brhmnn* 'par le Miséricordieux, Seigneur des Juifs'.

[9] 'It is generally accepted that the Yemenite Jewish communities known to us in the twentieth century were descendants of the pre-Islamic Jews and Jewish proselytes' (R. B. Serjeant in *JRAS* 1953, p. 117).

[10] A valuable document for the history of Christianity and Judaism in the Yemen may be found in the Ethiopic Acts of Azqir (ኣኅፁC: ፁቢቢ: Hፁ7ፁ7:—B.M. MS. Orient. 689 = Wright, *Catalogue*, ccliii. 20). Cf. also Conti Rossini's 'Un documento sul Cristianesimo nello Iemen' in *Rend. R. Acc. Linc.*, 1910.

[11] Cf. I. Guidi, *L'Arabie antéislamique*, p. 73: 'Le judaïsme et le christianisme étaient alors

was short-lived and came to an end with the Persian occupation
of South Arabia at the end of the sixth century. The Roman–
Persian antagonism found its reflection in the political-religious
events in the Red Sea area: the Persians were anti-Christian
because Christianity had become identified with Roman rule,
and they encouraged all religious manifestations which might
be instrumental in dislodging Roman influence. In this way the
Jews as well as Christian sects hostile to Rome were favoured,
but the Persian hegemony in Arabia soon disintegrated under
the dynamic onslaught of nascent Islam.

The Jews, Jewish proselytes,[1] and Judaism were thus strongly
entrenched in pre-Islamic Arabia and had come to play an
increasingly important part in the religious and cultural life of
the peninsula ever since the first century A.D. While it is undoubtedly true—as M. Rodinson has argued—that, after the
adoption of Christianity, the Bible exerted a strongly imitative
impact in Ethiopia, it is equally clear that many cultic, literary,
and cultural facets cannot be ascribed to that *imitatio Veteris
Testamenti* for the simple reason that they go back to extra-
Biblical sources. Here we have to envisage aspects of Jewish lore
which were assimilated in Ethiopia in much the same way as
Hebraic and post-Biblical elements entered into Qur'an and
Ḥadith, i.e. by living contact and direct communication. The
meeting of both strands—the relatively early presence of small
Jewish groups[2] (or even only individuals) in the Aksumite king-
dom together with the later imitation of Israel and the Old
Testament—eventually produced the complex and highly syn-
cretistic Ethiopian civilization.

The penetration of Hebraic-Jewish elements from Arabia into
Abyssinia will have to be visualized in a twofold manner:

(*a*) It has already been suggested that among the South

également répandus dans le Yémen; le premier grâce aux Israélites, très nombreux en
Arabie, et le second grâce probablement aux missionnaires syriens monophysites, qui fuyaient
la persécution des empereurs grecs; à Negran surtout, les chrétiens étaient nombreux.'

[1] An epigraphic hint to Jewish missionary zeal in pre-Islamic South Arabia may well be
detected in Ry. 520 (*Le Muséon*, 1954, pp. 100–1) where, in an inscription dedicated to
RḤMNn, we find the words: *wlḫmrhw rḫmnn wldm ṣlḫm sb'm lsmrḫmnn* 'et que lui accorde le
Miséricordieux des enfants bien constitués, *combattant pour le nom du Miséricordieux*'. This is also
Goitein's understanding of this passage (*Ha'arets*, loc. cit.).

The penetration of Judaism and Judaizing tendencies into Arabia reached at times
astonishing proportions and was accompanied by forceful proselytizing activities (cf. Sidney
Smith in *BSOAS* 1954, p. 462).

[2] So also Rodinson (*JSS* 1964, pp. 16–17): '. . . le mode d'explication par une influence
idéologique juive paraît solidement étayé. Elle ne semble pas dispenser de supposer la présence réelle d'un certain nombre de Juifs. C'est cette présence seule, semble-t-il, qui peut
expliquer que des mots venus évidemment de l'hébreu ou du judéo-araméen aient été adoptés
par le guèze dans les traductions de la Bible. . . .'

Arabian immigrants into the Aksumite empire there must have been some Jews.[1] This seems obvious when one considers the comparatively large number of Jews in Arabia and their distribution. It is not likely that they entered Abyssinia as a compact community, a complete tribal *golah*, but they probably came in small groups together with their non-Jewish fellow merchants and settlers. The diffusion of Judaizing practices and influences would suggest that they did not establish separate Jewish colonies on Abyssinian soil but mixed with other immigrants. I hope to be able to show below (excursus to Chapter II) that the Falashas, in their geographically circumscribed habitat, are unlikely to have any bearing on a solution of this question.

(*b*) There were, it appears, several military interventions by Ḥabashat[2] in Arabia. They all occurred at a time when the Jewish impact on South Arabia was considerable. The last Abyssinian expedition in Arabia, which defeated Ḏu Nuwās, took over the country from a Judaized king and a Judaized culture. It may be doubted that the process of Judaization had gone very deep, but it seems certain that Hebraic sediments, traditions, practices, and customs were subtly absorbed and, in due course, brought back—often in a much changed and adulterated form—across the Red Sea into Abyssinia.

South Arabia must thus be considered the principal avenue by which Jewish and early Biblical elements reached the kingdom of Aksum and gained admission in a variety of forms to be discussed in Chapter II. At the same time, it must be clearly understood that those elements bore a general Hebraic cast reflecting an early form of Judaism still fairly free from Talmudic accretions. That is, of course, to be expected when one recalls the early date of some Jewish migrations into Arabia, although we should not exclude either customs or literary

[1] Cf. Wellhausen, *Reste arabischen Heidentums*[3], p. 230: 'Im Südwesten der arabischen Halbinsel und im gegenüber liegenden Ostafrika hat das Judentum längere Zeit mit dem Christentum um die Herrschaft gekämpft. Zeitweilig hat es im Jaman den Sieg davon getragen; in Habesch hat es wenigstens starke Spuren an dem dort durchgedrungenen Christentume hinterlassen.'

[2] Conti Rossini 'Expéditions et possessions des Ḥabašat en Arabie', *JA* 1921, pp. 35–36. See also A. F. L. Beeston's article *Abraha* in *Encyclopaedia of Islam*[2].

The views expressed by Conti Rossini (and, in his footsteps, by the present writer) have recently been subjected to severely critical scrutiny by A. J. Drewes, *Inscriptions de l'Éthiopie antique*, esp. chaps. i and vi. Drewes argues with great knowledge and acumen, but he is, perhaps, at times inclined to throw out the baby with the bathwater. His great achievement is that everyone has been compelled to re-examine the linguistic and historical material *ab initio*. A. K. Irvine has ably done so with regard to the identity of Ḥabashat (*JSS* 1965 and *E. of I.*[2] under *Ḥabashat*) and has arrived at the conclusion that this name refers to a region (and not a people) and that there is insufficient evidence to connect it with a South Arabian tribe ('the equation of *ḥbšt* with Abyssinia is the most natural one').

allusions which later on appear in the literature of the Talmud. The period of Talmudic 'gestation' extends over several centuries, and we must therefore expect to find some of its ingredients among Jewish communities which were severed from the main stream of tradition before its committal to writing.[1]

It must not, of course, be supposed that Judaism was either the only or even the principal monotheistic religion in pre-Islamic Arabia. The great expansion of the monophysite (and, to a lesser extent, the Nestorian) church beyond the fringes of the desert brought Christianity right into the heart of Arabia.[2] The Syriac story of the Jacobite bishop Akhudemmeh[3] shows the intense missionary endeavour of this monophysite zealot among many Arabian tribes. No less important were the religious activities of the monophysite kingdom of Ghassan (or of the Nestorians at Ḥirah) who, by their numerous contacts with the large tribes of the interior of Arabia, contributed so notably to the diffusion of that type of Christianity over wide areas of the Arabian peninsula. The same form of Christianity was, of course, brought into Arabia not only by the Abyssinian conquerors, but also by the vigorous trade in Abyssinian slaves and by commercial relations in general. The importance of these commercial activities between the Quraysh and Abyssinia is attested in Ibn Hishām's recension of Ibn Isḥaq's life of the Prophet.[4]

It must be appreciated that those forms of Judaism and Christianity which were found in south-west Arabia at that time were not only imbued with a markedly oriental ceremonial, but their general Semitic character, the circumstances of their development as well as their entire religious, historical, and emotional atmosphere, rendered them much closer and more akin to each other than is the case with their westernized counterparts. Monophysite Christianity had a distinctly Hebraic mould, while Judaism in Arabia, at that period, could not but reflect some of the imprint of the missionary zeal and vigour of

---

[1] 'The abundance of Jewish thought and ideas contained in the Koran and in its early authoritative commentaries testifies to the profound knowledge of Judaism possessed by Arabian Jews. They may even help us to restore some Aggadic concepts lost in the course of time and unknown to Jewish scholarship today, as well as to gain much-sought data about the life and practices of the Jews in Arabia. . . . The unusual number of Aggadic stories quoted in the writings of Zamakhshari, Baiḍawi, Bukhāri and Ṭabari testify to the fact that the Arabian Jews took an active part in Jewish spiritual life' (A. I. Katsh, *Judaism in Islam*, 1954, p. xxv).

[2] Cf. J. Ryckmans, *Le Christianisme, passim*; Wellhausen, *Reste*[3], pp. 230–4, and esp. p. 232.

[3] Cf. F. Nau's edition of the *Histoire de Akhoudemmeh* (*Patrologia Orientalis*, iii, 1909).

[4] Cf. M. Guidi, *Storia e cultura*, p. 153; S. Smith, *BSOAS* 1954, pp. 462–3.

early Christianity.[1] The pertinency of these considerations seems evident.

The cultural and historical affinity between the two shores of the Red Sea, brought about by intense commercial activities, had long been known in antiquity. It is implicit in the picture which emerges from the *Periplus Maris Erythraei*,[2] an anonymous second-century account of travel and trade in the Red Sea area. Here we hear of the famous harbour of Adulis, 'a fair-sized village', and here we also encounter what is probably the first reference to 'the city of the people called Auxumites'.[3] A far more detailed story is told by Cosmas Indicopleustes in his *Christian Topography*;[4] when he visited the kingdom of Aksum about the year A.D. 525, he found Adulis a flourishing port and in close commercial relations with Arabia and beyond: '. . . Ethiopia, though separated from Sheba by the Arabian gulf, lay in its vicinity. . . . For the Homerites are not far distant from Barbaria, as the sea which lies between them can be crossed in a couple of days. . . .'[5] In the Semitic culture which the immigrants from South Arabia had transplanted across the Red Sea into the Aksumite kingdom the Jewish ingredient must have been fairly prominent. That was due not only to the un-doubted presence of some Jews and Jewish proselytes among the immigrant traders[6] and settlers, but also to the notable Hebraic-Jewish admixture in South Arabian civilization at that period.

For the history of the carriers of those influences we lack nearly all genuine and trustworthy source material. Generalizations of all sorts abound, but there is an almost complete absence of historical detail:

> . . . il est incontestable qu'un fond de judaïsme est venu s'implanter dans le pays à une époque assez largement antérieure à l'introduction du christianisme, et que ce substratum hébraïque a laissé des traces profondes.[7]

[1] M. Rodinson (*Bi Or*, 1964, p. 239, col. *b*) has described the similar characterization, which I offered in *JSS* 1956, as generalizations and as such inadequate. It would be difficult to dissent from this verdict; yet it is, perhaps, a little harsh, for I still think that this paragraph describes the atmosphere in which these religious forms flourished in a manner that is recognizable and essentially true to reality—even though it is couched, inevitably, in im-pressionistic terms.

[2] Translated from the Greek and annotated by W. H. Schoff, 1912.

[3] Op. cit., § 4.

[4] Translated from the Greek by J. W. McCrindle, Hakluyt Society, 1897.

[5] Op. cit., p. 52.

[6] 'Sembra anche assai probabile che il giudaismo sia stato portato in Etiopia (forse anche prima che vi si diffondesse il cristianesimo) da Ebrei mercatanti d'Arabia . . .' (Conti Rossini in *OM* 1921, p. 53; review of Rathjens's *Die Juden in Abessinien*).

[7] Kammerer, *Essai sur l'histoire antique d'Abyssinie*, p. 25.

Littmann believes to have found[1] the title 'King of Zion' on Aksumite coins, and Kammerer thinks that this

impliquerait que, sous ce souverain déjà, la tradition de la reine de Saba et des très anciennes relations qui ont pu exister avec la capitale des Juifs, avait plus ou moins servi de base à l'introduction d'une religion nouvelle qu'on considérait comme apparentée à la religion juive. . . .[2]

The absence of relevant and reliable historical sources is, however, compensated for, at least in part, by fairly numerous threads of indirect evidence which, in their cumulative effect, present an impressive array. The important linguistic factors will be reviewed in an excursus to Chapter II, while the main part of that chapter will be concerned with the cultural and religious elements. On the linguistic side it need only be observed here that some words and concepts must have been introduced by Judaized emigrants from Arabia at an early date, for they show Hebrew or Jewish-Aramaic forms and a specifically Jewish connotation.[3] Nöldeke has stated[4] that *maṣwat* 'würde allein genügen, jüdischen religiösen Einfluß bei den alten Abessiniern zu konstatieren'. Dillmann had already found:[5]

Ab Aramaeis et Judaeis Aramaice loquentibus ut Arabes ita Aethiopes multa nomina et verba, maxime quae ad res sacras et literarias pertinent (plurima sine dubio jam eo tempore quo Arabiae meridionali imperabant et cum Judaeis Arabiae commercium habebant) adoptarunt.

And H. J. Polotsky has averred, apropos of this quotation, that 'nothing more sensible has ever been written on this subject'.[6] He has also endeavoured to dispose of the 'theory attempting to connect the Aramaic words and other Aramaic features with the Christianization of Ethiopia and with the translation of the Bible into Ethiopic'.[7] The linguistic and semantic evidence[8] thus clearly demonstrates that an *imitatio Veteris Testamenti* alone, without the presence of early Judaized nuclei, could not account for the historical and religious situation as it presents itself in subsequent centuries.

We shall later on (Chapter II) refer in some detail to Old Testament elements in Abyssinian life. The story of the Queen of Sheba (Chapter III), in all its manifold ramifications, has given rise to, or possibly provided the *ex post facto* rationale of such deeply rooted traditions as the Aaronite origin of the Aksumite clergy, the reference to Ethiopians as *däqiqä 'əsra'el*,

---

[1] *Askum Expedition*, i. 50.　　　　[2] Kammerer, op. cit., p. 86.
[3] Cf. Conti Rossini, *Storia d'Etiopia*, p. 143; and Nöldeke, *Neue Beiträge*, pp. 32–46.
[4] Op. cit., p. 36.　　[5] *Lexicon*, col. xxii.　　[6] *JSS* 1964, p. 4.　　[7] Ibid.
[8] For details see excursus to Chapter II, below.

and the consciousness of having inherited from Israel the legiti-
mate claim to being regarded as the chosen people of God. It
stands to reason that these and other traditions, in particular
that of the Ark of the Covenant at Aksum, would have been an
integral part of the Abyssinian national heritage before the
introduction of Christianity in the fourth century. For it seems
difficult to imagine that a people recently converted to Christianity (not by a Christian Jew, but by the Syrian missionary
Frumentius) should *thereafter* have begun to boast of Jewish
descent and to insist on Hebraic customs and institutions.

Rathjens has expressed the view[1] that after the introduction
of Christianity into the Aksumite kingdom the Jews were probably subjected to severe persecutions. There exist, of course, no
records to substantiate this opinion, but in view of the cherished
descent from Israel and at least a measure of Judaization in pre-
Christian Abyssinia one may well question the cogency of this
conjecture. Moreover, it seems likely that many of the immigrant Judaic elements, spiritually isolated as they must have
been, became voluntary adherents of Christianity. To what
extent Abyssinian Christianity reacted, by way of local retalia-
tion, against the anti-Christian excesses perpetrated by the
Judaized Ḍu Nuwās in South Arabia, it is impossible to determine. In any event, it appears probable that those Abyssinian
Jews who had been converted to Christianity became the effective carriers of Hebraic elements, rites, and forms current in the
Christian Church of Ethiopia.

We possess little direct information on Jews and Judaism in
Abyssinia during the Middle Ages. The legend of the foundation of a Jewish dynasty by Judith, a 'Jewish' queen, was given
currency by James Bruce,[2] and has been echoed by Rathjens[3]
and others, but it has been shown by Conti Rossini to possess
no basis in historical fact.[4] The narrative of the ninth-century
Jewish traveller, Eldad had-Dani,[5] is more in the nature of
a fanciful geographical tale, though it has exerted an enduring
influence throughout the Middle Ages. His story of the Jewish
kingdom 'beyond the rivers of Cush' is unlikely to relate to
Ethiopia. His language reveals no traces of Ethiopic, nor does
his narrative betray a first-hand knowledge of Abyssinia. He
shows, however, more than a casual acquaintance with Arabia,

[1] *Juden in Abessinien*, p. 17.   [2] *Travels*[3], ii. 441–2.   [3] Op. cit., pp. 18 ff.
[4] *OM* 1921, p. 53.
[5] Cf. my article in the latest edition of the *Encyclopaedia Britannica*.
For a detailed study see Conti Rossini's 'Leggende geografiche giudaiche del IX secolo
(*Il Sefer Eldad*)', in *Boll. d. R. Soc. Geogr. Ital.* 1925, pp. 160–90.

and his Hebrew offers some evidence of an Arabic substratum. It is, therefore, likely that he was a Jew from South Arabia and one of its Jewish settlements.[1]

Abu Ṣāliḥ, the Armenian (very early thirteenth century), testifies to the Judaic leaven in Abyssinian Christianity:[2]

والحبشة مملكة سابا ومنها حضرت ملكة اليمن الى اورشليم لتسمع من سليمان كلام الحكمة

Abyssinia is the kingdom of Sheba; from it the Queen of the Yemen came to Jerusalem to hear words of wisdom from Solomon.

وعندهم تابوت[3] العهد الذى فيه اللوحى[4] الحجارة المكتوبة باصبع الله بالوصايا التى امر الله بها بنى اسرائيل ... وحمله بجماعة كبيرة من بنى اسرائيل منسويين الى نسل داوود النبى وهم بيض حمر شقر ... وذكر ان النجاشى كان ابيض احمر اشقر وجميع نسله الى اليوم وذكر انه من نسل هارون موسى عند وصوله الى بلاد الحبشة وتزوج موسى ابنة الملك

The Abyssinians possess the Ark of the Covenant, in which are the two tables of stone, inscribed by the finger of God with the commandments which he ordained for the children of Israel. . . . And the Ark is carried by a large number of Israelites descended from the family of the prophet David,[5] who are white and red (in complexion), with blond hair. . . . It is said that the Negus was white and red of complexion, with blond hair, and so are all his family to the present day; and it is said that he was of the family of Moses and Aaron, on account of the coming of Moses into Abyssinia. And Moses married the King's daughter.[6]

Abu Ṣāliḥ also reports[7] that at the consecration of churches the Abyssinians were directed to slay twelve beasts. A. J. Butler notes[8] that this custom of animal sacrifices was

quite unexampled in Coptic Church history and quite against the Coptic canons. It can only mean . . . that the patriarch sanctioned the

---

[1] Other Jewish travellers with information on Ethiopia in general and the Falashas in particular were Benjamin of Tudela (twelfth century) whose account has been discussed by Conti Rossini (*ZA* xxvii (1911–12), 358 ff.); Elia of Ferrara (Cerulli, *Etiopi in Palestina*, i. 234–6); and Obadiah of Bertinoro (op. cit., pp. 320–4), both in the fifteenth century. Cf. also Aescoly, ספר הפלשים, esp. pp. 146–78.

[2] *Churches and Monasteries of Egypt*, ff. 105a to 107a.

[3] On the linguistic aspects of this word see excursus to Chapter II.

[4] For oddities of language see op. cit., pp. xxiv–xxv.

[5] i.e. the father of Solomon who is the father of Menelik I (*Kebra Nagast*).

[6] According to the Midrash and Josephus (pp. 13–14, above). It is interesting that Abu Ṣāliḥ was familiar with this Jewish story which, together with many similar aspects, bears witness to the currency of this material in early Abyssinia—unaffected by the introduction of Christianity and the translation of the Scriptures.

[7] Ff. 106b–107a.

[8] Op. cit., p. 291.

maintenance of a purely Abyssinian practice. From the earliest times there were large Jewish settlements in Abyssinia, and it is probable that the custom of religious sacrifice derived from the Jews remained after the conversion of the people to Christianity. . . .

Abu Ṣāliḥ wrote well over two centuries before the religious reforms of Zar'a Ya'qob (mid fifteenth century), and his testimony alone would appear to invalidate the theory that it was Zar'a Ya'qob who was responsible for the introduction of Judaizing trends into the life of the Ethiopian nation and church. As this judgement was expressed by no less an authority than Dillmann,[1] it naturally deserves the greatest respect. But the operative passage does not take sufficient account[2] of the considerable body of earlier evidence which points to the prevalence of a Judaic sediment prior to Zar'a Ya'qob:[3]

. . . und vieles von dem, was wir von unserem Standpunkt aus reine Misbräuche nennen müssen, erst durch ihn [i.e. Zar'a Ya'qob] zu allgemeiner Herrschaft gelangt ist. Namentlich zeigt sich jetzt klar, daß die eigenthümliche Verquickung des Christenthums mit mosaischen Satzungen und Gebräuchen, in welcher die abessinische Kirche fast einzig dasteht, nicht *aus dem früheren jüdischen Bekenntnißstand des ganzen Volks oder großer Theile desselben* [my italics] zu erklären ist, sondern auf bewußter Zurückdrängung einer schon stark ausgebreiteten reineren christlichen Sitte[4] und rücksichtsloser Erneuerung altkirchlicher, in den Canones fixirter Übungen beruht.

Dillmann accepts, of course, that Judaic customs existed before Zar'a Ya'qob, but avers that it was he who accorded them general acceptance ('allgemeine Herrschaft'). In one respect Dillmann goes much further than most by suggesting (in the italicized sentence) that at an early period either the entire people or at least large parts were adherents of the Jewish faith. So widespread a diffusion of Judaism goes, I believe, beyond the evidence at our disposal. Dillmann proceeds to state that 'ohne Frage waren ja Juden im Reich',[5] but he rejects the surmise,

[1] And echoed by so eminent a scholar as M. Rodinson: '[Dillmann] montrait que ces réformes étaient en bonne partie responsables de ces coutumes qui avaient semblé si nettement judaïques par la suite' (*JSS* 1964, p. 13).

[2] This is also the gravamen of Nöldeke's criticism (*GGA* 1884, pp. 580–1): 'Wir möchten seinen [i.e. of Judaism] direkten Einfluß auf die abessinische Kirche für weit größer halten, als es Dillmann zu thun scheint. Man bedenke nur, daß es blos Juden gewesen sein können, welche die zahlreichen Korrekturen der Geezbibel nach dem Hebräischen vorgenommen haben.' This last point will be discussed in Chapter I.

[3] Dillmann, *Über die Regierung* . . ., p. 68.

[4] Rodinson (loc. cit.) misunderstands this phrase by rendering *eine reinere christliche Sitte* as 'coutumes purement chrétiennes', i.e. 'purely Christian customs' instead of 'higher Christian ethics' or 'more refined Christian morals'.

[5] Op. cit., p. 69. I am not certain that there were, in fact, large Jewish segments in the Ethiopian population during the fifteenth century.

rightly I think, that Zar'a Ya'qob encouraged the introduction of Jewish practices to curry favour with these heterogeneous elements. A glance at the *Mashafa Bərhan*[1] shows with what distaste Zar'a Ya'qob looked upon the Jews and how improbable it is that he would have adjusted his policies to suit their prejudices and requirements. In fact, his 'reforms' represent an amalgam of deeply rooted and ancient Judaic practices with a renewed emphasis on the lore and customs of the Old Testament.

Earlier, in the fourteenth century, 'Amda Şəyon had sent troops to the province of Begamedr to fight against 'renegades, who had once been Christians but who now denied Christ like the Jews'.[2] These are vague references to Jewish proselytizing activities (or, more likely, physical coercion) in the north-west of Ethiopia, and it would be unsafe to describe these elements either as Jews or as Falashas[3] *simpliciter*. Much more specific is the information contained in Shihāb ad-Dīn's sixteenth-century *Futūḥ al-Ḥabaša*:

وكانت بلاد سمين يملكها يهود الحبشة واسمهم بلغتهم فلاشة انهم يقرون بالله واحدا ولا يعرفون غير ذلك من الايمان ولا نبى ولا صديق، وكان اهل بحر عنبا قد استعبدوهم اربعين سنة يستخدمونهم ويحرثون لهم . . .[4]

The Semien province was ruled by the Jews of Abyssinia who are called Falashas in their own language; they recognize one God only and nothing else in the way of faith: neither prophet nor saint. The people of Baḥr Amba have subjugated them for the past forty years and employed them to work the land for them. . . .

Beginning with the fifteenth century we find, in occidental sources, several references to Jewish influences on the Abyssinian type of Christianity. These indications have usually been transmitted by travellers to the Holy Land who came into contact with members of the Ethiopian Church. Most of this information has been assembled, with characteristic learning, in Cerulli's masterly *Etiopi in Palestina*.[5] In the 1480s, on a pilgrimage to Jerusalem, Felix Faber made the acquaintance of the Abyssinian community of whom he remarks, *inter alia*:

. . . et quamquam ista faciant et observent, tamen perniciosis erroribus

---

[1] Edited and translated by C. Conti Rossini and L. Ricci, *C.S.C.O.*, Aeth. 47, 48, 51, 52, Louvain, 1964–5; see esp. vol. 52, pp. 51 ff. and index under *Giudei*.
[2] Cf. Perruchon, 'Histoire des guerres d'Amda Syon', *JA* 1889, p. 293; Dillmann, *Kriegsthaten des Königs 'Amda-Ṣion*, p. 1017.
[3] As was done by Huntingford, *Glorious Victories*, pp. 61–62; cf. *BSOAS* 1966, p. 610.
[4] Ed. R. Basset, p. 342 (Arabic part); see also note (4) on pp. 456–8.
[5] Two vols., Rome, 1943–7.

infecti sunt, et haeretici abhorribiles ecclesiae sanctae. Accipiunt enim cum Judaeis, Sarracenis et Jacobitis inutilem, immo damnabilem circumcisionem. . . .[1]

Close on a hundred years later Leonard Rauwolff (or Rauchwolff), a physician from Augsburg, wrote a more detailed account which also included a sketch of the Solomon–Sheba legend:

. . . haltens noch in vielen andern Stücken die alte Weise der Jüden. Als da sie den Sabbath-tag heyligen, und für jren gewöhnlichen Feiertag halten. Item, daß sie nicht von allerley Speisen essen, die im alten Testament als unreyne verbothen. Wenden zu jrer entschüldigung für, der heylige Apostel Philippus habe, da er mit dem Kämmerer der Königin Candaces in Mohrenlandt, hinab nach Gaza reyset, und jn bekehret, diß und anders mehr, als gebornen Jüden, zugelassen. . . .[2]

At about the same time (late sixteenth century) Pêro Pais apparently accepted the Ethiopian view of the Jewish origin of Abyssinian culture and institutions:

Antes q̃ a Rainha Sabba fosse a Ierusalem a ouuir a sabedoria de Salomão, todos os da Ethiopia erão gentios e adorauão differentes Idolos; mas quando ella tornou de Ierusalem lhes trouxe a historia dos Genesis, e estiuerão na ley dos Iudeos até a vinda de Christo, sojeitandose a seus ritos e çeremonias e guardando os mandamentos de Deos. . . .[3]

Jerome Lobo (early seventeenth century) is more specific:

. . . their [i.e. the 'Abyssins'] present Religion is nothing but a kind of confused Miscellany of Jewish and Mahometan Superstitions, with which they have corrupted those Remnants of Christianity which they still retain.[4]

The great Ludolf has a remarkably balanced chapter *De prisca Habessinorum religione et ritibus eorum Iudaicis* in his *Historia Aethiopica* (1681; book iii, chap. 1) which is supplemented by precious observations in the *Commentarius*. Ludolf discusses the origin of these Judaic rites and dwells on such practices as circumcision (pointing to its prevalence among other peoples), dietary observances, Sabbath legislation, levirate marriage, etc. He also published, in his *Commentarius*, the important *Confessio Claudii* in which the sixteenth-century King Galawdewos defends the monophysite faith against Roman Catholic polemics,

---

[1] Cerulli, op. cit. i. 312–13. [2] Cited after Cerulli, op. cit. ii. 27.
[3] Pais, *História da Etiópia*, Porto edition, ii. 9.
[4] Lobo, *A Voyage to Abyssinia*, translated into English (from the Abbé Le Grand's version) by Samuel Johnson, 1735, p. 59.
See now C. F. Beckingham's account of the long lost manuscript of Lobo's original version in *JSS* 1965, pp. 262 ff.

especially the accusation of Jewish rites and practices. The *Confessio* will have to be considered in greater detail in Chapter II.

A century later, James Bruce of Kinnaird makes frequent references to the Judaic customs of the Ethiopians and censures the first Christian missionaries [who], finding these and other Jewish traditions confirmed in the country, chose to respect them rather than refute them. Circumcision, the doctrine of clean and unclean meats, and many other Jewish rites and ceremonies are therefore part of the religion of the Abyssinians at this day.[1]

It would, of course, be impossible to quote here all the numerous expressions of opinion by modern writers who speak of the Abyssinian 'Christians, both in their religious and social customs' as bearing 'signs of the influence of Judaism';[2] or who describe, generally without detail, 'the whole cast of religious expression in Ethiopia as antique and ceremonial and imbued with an undercurrent of Judaic practice'.[3] The 'caractère judaïsant de l'Église éthiopienne' has been stressed by a Hebrew and rabbinic scholar,[4] and the Nestor of modern *éthiopisants*, Carlo Conti Rossini, has affirmed the antiquity of Judaism in Ethiopia and the existence, since the early third century, of 'nuclei giudaici qua e là sparsi . . .'.[5]

Early Judaic influences and deep-rooted Old Testament practices and customs have thus combined to produce this complex pattern which we shall have to probe in some detail in subsequent chapters.

---

[1] Bruce, *Travels*[3], iii. 13.
[2] R. S. Whiteway in his introduction to *The Portuguese Expedition to Abyssinia*, p. xxi.
[3] This opinion was expressed by no less an authority than Archbishop David Mathew, *Ethiopia*, p 12.
[4] A. Z. Aešcoly, *Recueil de textes falachas*, p. 4.
[5] *Storia d'Etiopia*, pp. 144–5.

I

BIBLE TRANSLATIONS

General considerations

THIS series of lectures might have been devoted entirely to the question of Bible translations into Ethiopic, but unhappily the absence of adequate preliminary work would have rendered such an undertaking premature and, indeed, impossible. No critical edition of the entire Bible (despite excellent work on some of its books) is yet available, and it is still a matter of controversy when the Scriptures were translated into Gəʿəz, by whom, from what language or languages, and which versions at what period sponsored a series of revisions and corrections.

There is no unanimity in Ethiopian tradition as to the translation of the Bible, but there has survived an interesting traditional account about the rendering into Gəʿəz of the Old and New Testaments:[1]

. . . ወመኅብበ፡ መጻሕፍቲሃስ፡ ዘብሉይ፡ ተዐልፀ፡ እምዕብራይስጢ፡ ኁበ፡ ገዐዝ፡ በመዋዕሊሃ፡ ለንጉሥተ፡ አዜብ፡ እንተ፡ ሐወጸት፡ ለሰሎሞን፡፡ ወበእንተዝ፡ ኩነ፡ ጽሩየ፡ ፍካሬሆሙ፡ ለመጻሕፍት፡ ነቢያት፡ ዘውስተ፡ ብሔር፡ አግዓዚ፡ እስመ፡ በሀገ፡ እይሁድ፡ ነበሩ፡ እምቅድም፡ ልደተ፡ ክርስቶስ፡፡ ወእሙኬ፡ አዕለውዎ፡ እምድኅሪ፡ ልደተ፡ ክርስቶስ፡ ግጮ፡ ሰቃልያን፡ ቃለ፡ ጽዱቀ፡ ውስተ፡ ስምዐ፡ ሐስት፡፡ ወኮመ፡ ተዐልፀ፡ መጻሕፍት፡ ነቢያት፡ እምዕብራይስጢ፡ ኁበ፡ ገዐዝ፡ ትረከብ፡ ትእምርተ፡ በውስተ፡ መጽሐፈ፡ ነገሥት፡ ዘይብል፡ ትርጓሜ፡ ነገረ፡ ዐብራይስጢ፡ ኁበ፡ ገዐዝ። ሔሎ፡ ብዜል፡ አምላክ፡ አይናይ፡ ብዜል፡ እግዚእ፡፡ ጸባኦት፡ ብዜል፡ ዘኖይሳት፡፡ ወመኅብበ፡ መጻሕፍቲሃስ፡ ዘሐዲስ፡ ለምድርኔ፡ ኢትዮጵያ፡ ተዐልፀ፡ እምሮማይስጢ፡ ኁበ፡ ገዐዝ፡ እምቅድም፡ ያስተርኤ፡ ሃይማኖት፡ ኦስጥሮስ፡ ወእምቅድም፡ ይትፈጠር፡ ሃይማኖት፡ ልዮን፡፡ ወእምቅድም፡ ይትጋብኡ፡ ማኅበር፡ ከሰባት፡ ዘውእቶሙ፡ ኤጲስ፡ ቆጾሳት፡ ዘከልቄዶን፡፡ ወበእንተዝ፡ ኮነ፡ ፍካሬ፡ መጻሕፍቲሃ፡ ለብሔረ፡ አግዓዚ፡ ዘብሉዪ፡ ወዘሐዲስኒ፡ ንጹሔ፡ ከመ፡ ወርቅ፡ ወፍቱነ፡ ከመ፡ ብሩር፡ . . .

. . . and as to the books of the O.T., they were translated from Hebrew into Gəʿəz in the days of the Queen of the South who visited

[1] Bibliothèque Nationale, Paris, MS. Éth. 113, ff. 63 seqq. (= Zotenberg, *Catalogue*, pp. 127–8).

Solomon. Hence the interpretation (rendering) of the prophetic books extant in Ethiopia was faithful, as the population were of the Jewish religion before the birth of Christ. However, in the translation after the birth of Christ the crucifiers distorted the true word into a testimony of falsehood. As to the manner in which the books of the prophets have been translated from Hebrew into Gǝ'ǝz, one will find an indication in the Book of Kings which gives a translation of Hebrew words into Gǝ'ǝz, i.e. ኤሎኂ: meaning 'God', አዶናይ: meaning 'Lord', ጸባኦት: meaning 'of hosts' (cf. Zotenberg, op. cit., p. 8, 2nd col., lines 10–13). As to the books of the N.T. of our country Ethiopia, they were translated from ርግይስጡ: (Latin?) into Gǝ'ǝz' before the appearance of the Nestorian Faith and before the creation of the doctrine of Leo and before the assembly of the Council of Dogs, i.e. the bishops of Chalcedon. Hence the Ethiopian rendering of the Old and New Testaments was pure as gold and proven as silver. . . .[1]

Another traditional ascription will be found in the Synaxarium for the 21st of Nahase[2] (20 Nahase in Zotenberg, *Catalogue*, p. 194, no. 20):

በዝቲ: ዕለት: አዕረፈ: አባ: ሰላማ: መተርጕም: . . .

ሰላም: ለከ: ለእሞ: ሃይማኖት: ስርዋ::

ትእዛዛት: ኦሪት: ወወንጌል: እንተ: ደቤክ: ትኩዐዋ::

ሰላማ: ዝክርከ: ከሞ: በነቢነ: ነዋ::

በከናፍሪከ: ምዑዛት: እመዓዝ: ክርቤ: ወዐልዋ::

እምነ: ዓረቢ: ለጌዐዝ: መጻሕፍት: ተግልዋ::

On this day died Abba Sälama, the translator [of the Scriptures]. . . .
Greetings to you, root of the tree of faith,
Upon whom the commandments of the Law and the Gospels have been poured;
Sälama, how your memory has abided with us!
By your lips sweeter than the scent of myrrh and aloe
Have the Scriptures been translated from Arabic into Gǝ'ǝz.

We shall discuss later on whether the reference to Arabic relates to translation or revision. A lot has been written[3] about

---

[1] Cf. the observations on this passage by A. Rahlfs in a posthumously published essay 'Die äthiopische Bibelübersetzung' (written about 1916) in the 2nd ed. of his *Septuaginta-Studien*, Göttingen, 1965, pp. 667–8 (I am indebted to Professor Polotsky for drawing my attention to this article); also Conti Rossini, *ZA* x (1895), 236–41.

[2] Guidi, *Le Synaxaire éthiopien (Patrologia Orientalis*, ix. 4, Paris—no date), p. 359 [563]; Ludolf, *Commentarius*, p. 295.

[3] Ludolf, op. cit., p. 296; Dillmann, *Zur Geschichte . . .*, p. 20; Conti Rossini, *ZA* 1895 and 1912; Praetorius in Herzog's *Realencyclopaedie*[3] iii (1897), 87; Zotenberg, *Catalogue*, p. 263, col. I, O, 14: 'Abba Salama, le traducteur de l'Écriture Sainte, qui est enterré à Ḥaqalet';

the identity of Abba Salama, but Ethiopian tradition seems clear, for Frumentius is referred to as አባ፡ ሰላማ፡ ከሣቴ፡ ብርሃን፡ and his commemoration day is 26 Hamle, whereas the present prelate is described as መተርጕም፡ and his day is 20 (or 21) Nahase.

Although Ethiopic studies proper may be said to have begun with scholarly attention to Bible translations and editions, such interest has sadly abated of late; and the oldest and most extensive non-epigraphic monument of Ethiopic literature[1] still remains without a proper critical edition. In a masterly paper, submitted to the Third International Conference of Ethiopian Studies at Addis Ababa in 1966 (still unpublished at the time of writing),[2] O. Löfgren has deplored this present-day lack of interest, particularly among young scholars, in the text of the Gə'əz Old Testament and has proposed the establishment of an international body to organize a critical edition of the Ethiopic Bible:[3] 'The first task of such an institute would be the preparation of a list of all Bible MSS. in Gə'əz known to exist in Europe as well as in Ethiopia' to be followed by the assignment of text editions to individual scholars.[4]

It is just over 450 years ago that Johannes Potken printed the first Ethiopic text, the 1513 Psalter published at Rome,[5] but naturally this was not a work of critical scholarship. For that we had to await the advent of the polymathic talents of Job Ludolf who gave us the first critical edition of *Psalterium Davidis aethiopice et latine*.[6] August Dillmann, in the nineteenth century, carried a great deal further what had been begun by Ludolf 150 years earlier: he published, between 1853 and 1894, the Octateuch, Samuel and Kings as well as the Old Testament Apocrypha.[7] Among those who followed in Dillmann's footsteps

---

Lantschoot, 'Abba Salama, métropolite d'Éthiopie' in *Atti del Convegno Int. di Studi Et.*, pp. 397–401. Lantschoot gives no fewer than thirteen separate references in Ethiopic literature to Abba Salama's activity as a translator. Cf. also Cerulli, *Storia della letteratura etiopica*, p. 68.

[1] '... primum locum obtinent Biblia Aethiopica, quae omnium literarum Abyssinicarum fundamentum sunt et norma, ad quam reliqui scriptores suum dicendi scribendique genus conformaverunt' (Dillmann, *Lexicon*, v).

[2] I am indebted to Professor Löfgren for sending me a copy of this paper.

[3] This proposal did not, in fact, come before the Conference at Addis Ababa, but it is hoped that the 1969 Conference to be held at Warsaw will initiate practical steps to deal with this problem.

[4] Löfgren, op. cit.

[5] *Alphabetum seu potius syllabarium literarum Chaldaearum, Psalterium Chaldaeum* . . . opera Joannis Potken, Rome, 1513.
See also A. Rahlfs, 'Nissel und Petraeus, ihre äthiopischen Textausgaben und Typen' in *Nachr. von d. K. Gesellschaft d. Wissensch.*, Göttingen, 1917.

[6] *cum duobus impressis et tribus MSStis codicibus diligenter collatum et emendatum*, Frankfort, 1701.

[7] *Biblia Veteris Testamenti aethiopica.*

were J. Bachmann[1] (Isaiah, Lamentations, Obadiah, Malachi), O. Boyd[2] (Genesis to Leviticus), Pereira,[3] Löfgren,[4] Mercer,[5] Gleave,[6] and one or two others. Some books of the Old Testament have not been edited at all: Jeremiah,[7] Ezekiel, Proverbs, Hosea, and Micah, while others are in urgent need of re-edition in the light of earlier or better manuscripts now available.[8]

We are even worse off as regards the edition of the Ethiopic New Testament, for here we have virtually no critical studies at all. The *editio princeps* was published at Rome in 1548 and is owed to the endeavours of three Ethiopian monks who had come to Rome from Debra Libanos, via Jerusalem, and had brought with them some Ethiopic Biblical manuscripts.[9] The senior monk, Täsfa Ṣəyon, was a well-educated man and attained, under the name of 'Petrus Aethiops' (or 'Pietro Indiano'), a good deal of local fame. His New Testament text gained a dominant position in Europe and in all subsequent study of the Ethiopic Gospels.

There is, however, an important exception to the gloomy picture of lacking or inadequate editions: the books of Enoch,[10] Jubilees[11] and, to a somewhat lesser extent, Ascension of Isaiah[12] have for long enjoyed excellent critical treatment. This is no doubt due to the fact that their full versions were extant in Ethiopic but not in other languages, which accorded to the Ethiopic text a critical value it did not possess in the case of the canonical books of the Bible.

The translation of the Bible into Ethiopic thus comprises all

---

[1] *Der Prophet Jesaia nach der aeth. Bibelübersetzung*, Berlin, 1893.

[2] *Bibliotheca Abessinica*, Genesis (Leiden and Princeton, 1909), Exodus and Leviticus (1911).

[3] Job (1907), Esther (1913), Ezra-Neh. (1919), Amos (1917)—in *Patrologia Orientalis*.

[4] Daniel (1927), Jona, Nahum, Habakuk, Zephaniah, Haggai, Zechariah, and Malachi (1930).

[5] Ecclesiastes (1931). Cf., however, the reviews by Löfgren, *MO* 1933, and Littmann, *OLZ* 1933/6.

[6] Song of Songs (1951).

[7] We possess, however, a preliminary study by Joseph Schäfers, *Die äthiopische Übersetzung des Propheten Jeremias*, Freiburg, 1912.

[8] Da Bassano's Ethiopic Old Testament (Asmara, 1922–6) is a complete edition, though scarcely a critical one, and will be discussed below.

[9] *Testamentum Novum cum Epistola Pauli ad Hebraeos* . . . quae omnia Frater Petrus Aethiops . . . imprimi curavit, Rome, 1548.

[10] Cf. Dillmann, *Liber Henoch Aethiopice*, Leipzig, 1851; Charles, *The Eth. Version of the Book of Enoch*, Oxford, 1906; idem, *The Book of Enoch*[2], Oxford, 1912; Flemming, *Das Buch Henoch*, Leipzig, 1902; Goldschmidt, *Das Buch Henoch* (transl. from Ethiopic into Hebrew), Berlin, 1892; Ullendorff, 'An Aramaic *Vorlage* of the Ethiopic Text of Enoch?', in *Atti del Convegno Int. di Studi Et.*, Rome, 1960.

[11] Dillmann, *Liber Jubilaeorum*, Kiel, 1859; Charles, *The Ethiopic Version of the Hebrew Book of Jubilees*, Oxford, 1895; idem, *The Book of Jubilees*, London, 1902; Baars and Zuurmond, 'A New Edition of the Eth. Book of Jubilees' in *JSS*, Spring 1964; Rönsch, *Das Buch der Jubiläen*, Leipzig, 1874.

[12] Dillmann, *Ascensio Isaiae*, Leipzig, 1877; Tisserant, *Ascension d'Isaïe*, Paris, 1909.

canonical and apocryphal[1] books in addition to some pseudepigrapha that were accepted as genuine in Abyssinia. It represents
the foremost literary achievement of the Aksumite period and
was probably a gradual process extending over a century or two.
During the literary renaissance which occurred in the reign of
king 'Amda Ṣəyon (mid-fourteenth century) some attention appears to have been devoted to a revision of the existing Bible
translations, and it is this activity which is usually connected
with the name of the Metropolitan Salama,[2] 'Translator of the
Holy Scriptures'.

Large numbers of Ethiopic Biblical manuscripts, either of the
whole canon or of individual books, are preserved in European
libraries and in Ethiopian monastery collections. Some of these
are splendid specimens, beautifully illuminated and magnifi-
cently written, often requiring as many as 100–50 goats to
provide the parchment. Very few Ethiopic manuscripts can
be securely attributed to the earliest period of the 'Solomonic
restoration' (thirteenth century). Most of them are later copies,
for it must be assumed that the number of those which fell
victim to Aḥmad Grañ's destructive fury was very large. Also,
the dating of Ethiopic manuscripts presents considerable problems. The conditions in which many of them are kept in Ethiopia
are liable to expose them to damp as well as to damage of other
kinds and thus tend to give them an appearance of greater
age than they actually deserve. The most reliable indications
in determining the approximate date of manuscripts are still
furnished by palaeographical criteria,[3] although these have to
be employed with much caution and qualification. Fortunately,
however, a number of fourteenth- and fifteenth-century manuscripts have survived in the monasteries of Debra Libanos,
Debra Bizen, Gunda Gundie, St. Stephen of Hayq, the islands
of Lake Tana, and some others.

The treasures of Ethiopic Biblical manuscripts in the Bibliothèque Nationale[4] and the British Museum (Dillmann and
Wright) are of exceptional range and quality, but fine collections also exist in the Vatican Library (Grébaut–Tisserant),
the Bodleian Library (Dillmann and Ullendorff), Cambridge

---

[1] Edited by Dillmann in 1894 (appearing shortly after his death in the same year)
and including Baruch, Epistola Jeremiae, Tobit, Judith, Ecclesiasticus, Sapientia, Esdrae
Apocalypsis, Esdras Graecus.   [2] See pp. 32–33, above.

[3] Cf. Wright, B.M. Catalogue, p. x; and especially the important observations by Conti
Rossini, Collection d'Abbadie, pp. 556–65.

[4] Catalogues by Zotenberg, d'Abbadie, Chaîne, Conti Rossini, Grébaut–Strelcyn.

Details in this and the following instances will be found in the Bibliography under the
name of the cataloguer.

University Library (Ullendorff and Wright), Berlin (Dillmann), Leningrad (Turaiev), Vienna (Rhodokanakis), Windsor Castle (Ullendorff), Frankfurt (Goldschmidt), the John Rylands Library, Manchester,[1] and a few other places.[2]

Time, authorship, and Vorlage *of Ethiopic Bible translations*

We must now address ourselves to the questions raised at the beginning of this chapter: at what time was the Bible translated into Ethiopic? Was it a work accomplished simultaneously with the introduction of Christianity in the middle of the fourth century or did it extend over a prolonged period? And what was the identity of the translator or translators? Were they Syrian monks or Greek-speaking Ethiopians or teams of translators who were able to handle the Greek, Syriac, and Hebrew texts, possibly with the aid of some local Jews who might have had a traditional knowledge of Hebrew? And what kind of revision was carried out in the fourteenth century? Was it based on Arabic alone? How profound was it and did it seriously interfere with the original translation?

All these questions, and more, have been asked and conjecturally answered at one time or another, but it would be hazardous to assert that we have reached conclusions which have been adequately tested. Not only—as has been shown earlier—is the work of editing far from being complete, but it need scarcely be emphasized that *Vorlagestudien* are notoriously risky and have led respectable scholars to very different inferences and diametrically opposed results. It might be useful to begin by reviewing the opinions of some of the principal scholars in this field.

As is so often the case in the sphere of Ethiopian studies, the first important recognitions come from the pen of Ludolf:

Habessini cum religione Christiana etiam Sacram Scripturam acceperunt. Illa in linguam Aethiopicam (quam Tigrensibus quondam vernaculam fuisse diximus) ex versione LXX interpretum translata fuit . . . secundum exemplar quoddam in Ecclesia Alexandrina usitatum. . . .

De autore et tempore versionis nihil certi compertum habeo; probabile tamen est, eam tempore conversionis Habessinorum, vel paulo post, . . . concinnatam fuisse. . . .

---

[1] A catalogue of this fine collection was begun by the present writer, but had to be interrupted owing to more pressing commitments. It is not now expected to be completed before the early 1970s.

[2] Gregory, *Prolegomena* (1894), pp. 900–11, lists no fewer than 101 Ethiopic Biblical manuscripts in European libraries—and this is far from being an exhaustive inventory.

Novum Testamentum ex textu Graeco authentico versum quidem habent. . . .[1]

Ludolf thus finds that the Old Testament was translated from the Septuagint, according to a version used by the Church of Alexandria, probably either at the time of the conversion to Christianity or a little later. And the New Testament was likewise rendered from a Greek text. In his *Commentarius* (pp. 295 ff.) Ludolf rejects the view[2] that the Bible was translated into Gəʻəz from Arabic ('. . . Aethiopica tam Veteris quam Novi Testamenti versio . . . ex Arabica lingua nullo modo facta dici potest').

Dillmann, writing 150 years later, was able to form his judgement on the basis of a good deal of text-critical work, mostly accomplished by himself. He divided Ethiopic Old Testament manuscripts into three groups:[3] (1) those in which the original translation, derived from the LXX, is fairly well preserved; yet even here we have to reckon with large numbers of variants (cf. Zotenberg, *Catalogue*, pp. 3, 5, 7, 8); (2) those which contain a later text, generally revised according to the LXX, and one that is linguistically smoother and more modern; (3) those which have been revised on the basis of the Hebrew text (cf. Zotenberg, *Catalogue*, pp. 9–11). Nöldeke has expressed the view[4] 'daß es blos Juden gewesen sein können, welche die zahlreichen Korrekturen der Geezbibel nach dem Hebräischen vorgenommen haben'. Nobody seems to have hazarded a guess as to the identity and period of those Jews. Nöldeke, loc. cit., realized, of course, that the Falashas have no knowledge of Hebrew, yet he seems to have toyed with the idea that in earlier times they possessed 'sicher auch größere litterarische Bildung'. I think there is no evidence to substantiate the identification of the Falashas with those elements who might have assisted with their knowledge of Hebrew in the translation of the Gəʻəz Old Testament.[5]

Dillmann (loc. cit.) has averred that the old Ethiopic translation was very faithful and rendered the Greek text in a most literal manner—often to the point of following the Greek order of words. At the same time, however, it is 'recht lesbar und . . .

---

[1] Ludolf, *Hist. Aeth.*, Lib. iii, Cap. 4, 2–7.   [2] Cf. p. 32, above.
[3] *Bibl. V.T. aeth.*, vol. ii, fasc. 1, app. crit., pp. 3 ff. See also Herzog's *Realencyclopaedie*[3], iii. 87 ff.   [4] *GGA* 1884, p. 581. See also footnote (2) to p. 27, above.
[5] In a letter to me, dated 29 Jan. 1967, M. Rodinson says: 'Il est bien possible aussi qu'ils [les Juifs] aient fourni des conseils techniques pour la traduction de l'Ancien Testament en guèze.' In these general terms, and in the absence of any more detailed information, this proposition seems quite feasible.

fließend und trifft mit dem Sinn und den Worten des hebräischen Urtextes im A. T. oft auf *überraschende* [my italics] Weise
zusammen'. I, too, find it 'surprising' that there should be this
frequent congruence, in sense and expression, with the Hebrew
original when the Ethiopic text is supposed to be a direct derivative of the LXX without the intervention of any Hebrew or other
Semitic *Vorlage*. This will need further probing. At the same
time, Dillmann declares that the Ethiopian translators were not
very learned and, as it seems, 'auch der griechischen Sprache
nicht durchaus mächtig', which inevitably led to many mistakes and misunderstandings. There would, therefore, appear to
be at least a prima facie presumption that with their inadequate
knowledge of Greek they might well have had recourse to a
second *Vorlage* which would also account for the existence of
Hebrew or Semitic correspondences that cannot be explained
from the Septuagint alone.

As to the time of the translations, Dillmann and Praetorius[1]
have argued that they were not necessarily made at the time
of the introduction of Christianity in the fourth century. They
have assumed a gradual process extending over two or even
three centuries and obviously involving a number of translators.
This last point had already been made by Ludolf[2] who conjectured that different renderings of the same word presupposed
different authorship—in itself by no means a safe inference. Both
Dillmann and Praetorius accept (loc. cit.) that the Old Testament and New Testament versions were later modified to some
extent by individual scribes and readers and made to conform
with Arabic[3] or Hebrew models (Zotenberg, op. cit., p. 11*b*, is
a case in point).

An equally complex problem is the determination of the
identity of the Septuagint recension from which the Ethiopic
Old Testament is derived. In view of the dependence of the
Ethiopian Church on that of Alexandria it has often been tacitly
assumed that the Ethiopic version must be based on the Hesy-
chian recension then current in Egypt.[4] But different scholars
have thought that they were able to identify different recensions—
Alexandrinus,[5] Vaticanus,[6] or Sinaiticus[7]—underlying the Ethiopic text.

---

[1] Herzog's *RE*[3] iii. 88.   [2] *Commentarius*, p. 296.
[3] Cf. Rahlfs, *Septuaginta-Studien*, ii. 166–7.
[4] Cf. Rahlfs, *Septuaginta-Studien*, i. 87; ii. 235; Praetorius, loc. cit.; S. Reckendorf, *ZAW* vii
(1887), 68.   [5] Cf. Hackspill, *ZA* xi (1896), 125.
[6] Rahlfs, op. cit. i. 84: 'Aeth. ist in den Königsbüchern B's nächster Verwandter.' Similarly
Roupp in *ZA* xvi. 329.
[7] Schäfers, *Äth. Übers. Jer.*, pp. 156–7, feels justified in excluding Alexandrinus altogether

As to the translation of the Gospels, Hackspill (whose 'study deservedly acquired authoritative standing'[1]) came to the following conclusions which merit to be quoted in full:[2]

1. Der äthiopische Evangelientext ist eine Übersetzung aus dem Griechischen.
2. Dieser griechische Text ist nicht der Alexandrinische, sondern ein Syro-occidentaler.
3. Als Zeitalter dieser Übersetzung ist ungefähr das Jahr 500 anzunehmen.
4. Unter dem Einflusse der vermittelst der Alexandrinischen Vulgata in den äthiopischen Text eingedrungenen koptisch-syrischen Elemente nahm die Gǝ'ǝz Übersetzung die Form an, die uns heute, natürlich mit vielen Varianten, in allen gedruckten Exemplaren und den meisten Handschriften vorliegt.

These important recognitions had been anticipated, in substance, by Dillmann,[3] Guidi,[4] and Zotenberg,[5] but Hackspill's paper is the most detailed and is based on the extensive sample of B.N. MS. 32 (the first ten chapters of Matthew).

Praetorius (loc. cit., p. 89), reverting to the Old Testament, draws attention to the fact that Ethiopia was converted to Christianity 'durch aramäische Missionare'. Hence:

Der tiefgehende litterarische Einfluß dieser Aramäer zeigt sich in den sehr zahlreichen aramäischen Fremdwörtern für die neuen Begriffe der christlichen Lehre,[6] die einfach ins Äthiopische herübergenommen

and asserting that 'der Altäthiope steht in nächster Verwandtschaftsbeziehung zum Typus des Sinaiticus'.

[1] So Polotsky in *JSS* 1964, p. 9.

[2] *ZA* xi (1896), 126. Hackspill's study had been preceded by Guidi's 'Le traduzioni degli Evangelii in arabo e in etiopico', *Mem. R. Acc. Linc.* 1888, to which H. pays tribute. In fact, H.'s conclusions tally with those of Guidi—except that he refines the determination of the Greek prototype. It was Guidi who had drawn attention to the importance of MS. 32 in the Bibl. Nationale, Paris, and who, as H.'s teacher, had advised him in the preparation of his study. I would respectfully differ from Polotsky who thinks (in a most detailed paper read to the 2nd Int. Conf. of Eth. Stud. at Manchester—*JSS* 1964, pp. 9–10—to which frequent reference will be made in the following) that Guidi had misunderstood H.'s 'syrisch-occidental' (*ZA* xi. 132). In fact, H. also uses 'syro-occidental' (op. cit. 126), and it is this which G. correctly turns into 'siro-occidentale'. The addition of 'di S. Luciano' (*Storia della lett. et.* (1932), p. 13) is redundant rather than wrong, and Guidi's position is quite clear from his own paper, esp. pp. 13, 33, 35, 37. Polotsky is right in his strictures upon the present writer (p. 10), but Guidi may safely be exculpated from misunderstanding Westcott and Hort's اصولهٔ (he specifically refers to their classification on p. 33—*MRAL* 1888).

[3] B.M. *Catalogus*, p. 7b.   [4] *MRAL* 1888.   [5] *Catalogue*, pp. 24 ff.

[6] Polotsky (op. cit.) has cogently argued that these Aramaic words belong 'to the Judaic leaven in Christianity' (p. 10). Yet to say that '*none* of these words is distinctively Christian in meaning' (ibid.) is, perhaps, a little too definite. Nöldeke, *Neue Beiträge*, p. 37, describes ቀሲስ: 'priest' as 'ein spezifisch christliches Wort'; the same is true of a few others such as ተእኅ: (p. 35), ሕርበ:, and possibly ይድምፅት: (p. 35) despite the justifiably cautionary note sounded by Polotsky (pp. 4–7) and the remarks on p. 40, below. While Polotsky has convincingly shown that the overwhelming number of such words are derived from Jewish-Aramaic and belong to the pre-Christian Jewish sediment in Ethiopia, this does not, of

und daselbst dauernd beibehalten wurden. Es wäre wohl denkbar, daß schon in jener frühesten Zeit mindestens einzelne Bücher des AT's durch die Aramäer oder ihre nächsten Schüler ins Äthiopische übertragen worden sind. Dann aber ist die Annahme einer ägyptisch-griechischen Vorlage so gut wie ganz ausgeschlossen.

Praetorius' view is supported by Guidi and Conti Rossini.[1] The former thinks[2] that the translators have to be sought among the Syrian monophysite monks who came to Ethiopia after the Council of Chalcedon in 451 to escape the persecutions of members of their persuasion:

... che ad essi o ai loro discepoli si debba la traduzione della Sacra Scrittura ... si puo inferire dal fatto che il testo in essa seguito non è già quello di Esichio, ricevuto nel Patriarcato alessandrino, cui certamente avrebbe seguito Frumenzio, ma bensì il siro-occidentale di S. Luciano, ricevuto nel vasto Patriarcato di Antiochia ed oltre; onde è che in questa traduzione figurano parole aramaiche e nominatamente siriache: come *haymanot*.

Guidi is in error, however, in supposing that *haymānūṯā* in the sense of πίστις 'faith' is limited to the Christian faith and peculiar to Syriac from the New Testament onwards (op. cit., p. 14). In fact, it occurs in the Targum of Psalm 33: 4, the Peshitta of Deuteronomy 32: 20, and in the Ethiopic Old Testament as well. Polotsky has shown (op. cit., p. 7) that these twin claims are not borne out by the documents. However, this does not, in my understanding, necessarily invalidate Guidi's assertion that Syrians introduced this term into Gǝ'ǝz—except that they applied it to pre-Christian sources as well and did not confine it to a narrowly circumscribed use: 'sono queste chiare indicazioni qual fosse la provenienza degli autori delle versioni colle quali comincia la letteratura gǝ'ǝz' (op. cit., p. 15). Guidi may well

course, invalidate the entire argument advanced by Guidi, Praetorius, Gildemeister (*apud* Gregory) and others; for there might still be Syriac-mediated loanwords that belong to a later linguistic layer. And it seems that the linguistic and especially historical evidence favours such an assumption of two independent strands of Aramaic loanwords deriving from different Aramaic dialects and different periods. This question will be further discussed in the linguistic excursus to Chapter II.

[1] Gildemeister (in Gregory's *Prolegomena*, p. 896) argues that the formation of ecclesiastical Ethiopic and the translation of the Bible belong to different periods, for the 'Syriac' vocabulary must have acquired home-rights before the translation was made. Polotsky has shown that, while G.'s conclusion may be correct, his reasoning is unacceptable: 'it seems hardly possible that the Aramaic words should have been introduced by Syriac-speaking missionaries or Bible translators; some of the words are characteristically non-Syriac . . .' (*JSS* 1964, p. 10). It is, however, arguable that the existing Aramaic stock owed its preservation and survival to the Aramaean missionaries, even though their dialect differed from the Jewish-Aramaic of the earlier layer.

[2] *Storia della letteratura etiopica*, pp. 13 ff.

be right in this conclusion, but the linguistic evidence by itself falls short of offering the 'clear indication' which he postulates.[1]

Conti Rossini[2] thinks that the diffusion of Christianity in the fourth century was insufficient to have warranted a translation of the Bible into Ethiopic at so early a period. By the middle of the fifth century, however, Ethiopia had become a decidedly Christian state, thanks largely to the missionary activities of 'ecclesiastici Siri'.[3] He adduces a list of Aramaic terms which, he believes, cannot be of Jewish provenance;[4] these, together with the well-known Syrian commercial activities over the entire orient, offer an adequate explanation for the presence of those Syrian nuclei in Ethiopia. Yet Conti Rossini avers that it is 'indiscutibile' that the Scriptures were translated into Gə'əz from Greek, for Greek was the official language of the 'Impero d'Oriente', commonly used in the Church of Syria, Asia Minor, and Egypt, and also of such general use in the Aksumite kingdom that inscriptions on monuments and legends on coins were written in Greek. When the Bible was rendered into Ethiopic from Greek, 'i suoni greci, la cui corrispondenza in etiopico poteva apparir dubbiosa, furono trascritti secondo il sistema siriaco'.[5]

The first work to be translated was naturally that of the Gospels, but the translator (according to Conti Rossini) did not follow the text adopted in the Church of Egypt but the recension common in the Syrian[6] Church. The foreign words in the language of the Ethiopian Bible are almost always Greek, 'ma talora i nomi ebraici sembrano assumere una forma mista greco-semitica' (loc. cit.). Conti Rossini quotes no examples of this type of mixed Greek–Semitic forms. But despite his firm statement that the Scriptures were translated from Greek, he concedes that there exist indications of 'scritti[7] passati direttamente dal siriaco in etiopico' (loc. cit.). Conti Rossini's own rehearsal

---

[1] There are, of course, other factors which Guidi mentions in his article in *MRAL* 1888, p. 34 (footnote): 'Se per l'A.T. vi poterono aver parte gli Aramei ebrei, per il Nuovo non vi ebbero parte che gli Aramei cristiani cioè, senza dubbio, i Siri. Quindi l'antica trascrizione dei nomi propri in etiopico segue la regola aramea, $\Phi = \kappa$, $\hbar = \chi$, $\mathfrak{m} = \tau$, $\dagger = \theta$. Quest'influenza aramea potè esercitarsi nell'Abissinia non dal solo Egitto, ma anco dall'Arabia meridionale. . . . Resta quindi assai probabile che monaci siri giacobiti siano penetrati in Abissinia.'

[2] See especially 'Note per la storia letteraria abissina', *RRAL* 1899, pp. 3–5; *Storia d'Etiopia*, pp. 155–6, 223 ff.

[3] *Storia*, p. 155.

[4] See Chapter II, linguistic excursus.

[5] Op. cit., p. 156. See above note 1.

[6] Polotsky (*JSS* 1964, p. 9) has pointed out the misunderstanding implied in Conti Rossini's 'nelle chiese siro-occidentali'.

[7] No doubt meant to be non-Biblical writings.

of the evidence does not seem to me to add up to so confident a belief in an exclusively Greek *Vorlage*.[1]

Zotenberg's splendid *Catalogue*, so full of precious observations and detailed documentation, contains important information relevant to our present survey (see especially pp. 5–11, 25, etc.). He accepts, it would appear, Dillmann's division into ancient translations made from the LXX and revisions on the basis of later Hebrew-inspired elaborations (see p. 37, above). As an example of the ancient version, translated from the text of the Septuagint, he cites (p. 5) his MS. 3 (= Éth. 102). As an instance of 'la version corrigée' (p. 9) may serve MS. 6 (= Éth. 9). This contains the book of Jeremiah and related writings: according to Zotenberg the chapter division of the Ethiopic text follows that of the Hebrew original; in a large number of passages Ethiopic roots are employed which correspond to the Hebrew ones in the original, and in some instances Hebrew words have been taken over without translation: ፍዘብ: נגב (Jer. 13: 19), ኩታራት: כתרת (52: 22). Zotenberg adds, however:

Mais la traduction primitive a été exécutée, comme celle des autres parties de la Bible, d'après le texte des Septante, comme le montre un passage du chap. XXV, vers. 10, où la traduction primitive መዓዛ: (መዐዛ) ዐፍራት:, qui rend l'expression ὀσμὴν μύρου des Septante, se trouve à côté des mots ቃል: መግረዐ: qui correspondent plus exactement au sens de l'hébreu קול רחים.[2]

Other manuscripts, such as those on which da Bassano based his edition (see below), have the equivalent of the Hebrew text only.

In a manuscript of the Book of Job (Zotenberg 7 = Éth. 11) we find marginal notes penned by one Marqoryos[3] who appears to have collated the Hebrew text and an Arabic version. That he used the Masoretic text can be seen from his gloss to Job 22: 15: ዝየ: መንፈቅ: በእብራይስጥ.:: He clearly possessed a knowledge of Hebrew, though it is hard to assess its precise extent. Unfortunately, we know nothing about this Mercurius whom Zotenberg describes as 'un savant indigène' (op. cit., p. 11). His *floruit* might have been crucial to our assessment of this Hebrew evidence. Zotenberg describes the manuscript as belonging to the fifteenth century; it came from the 'bibliothèque de Séguier'. One Marqorewos or Marqoryos was a disciple of

---

[1] In *Note*, p. 4, and *Storia*, pp. 223–4, Conti Rossini affirms that the translation of the New Testament was made from a Syro-occidental recension, while the Old Testament derives from the LXX. He then proceeds to offer a brief evaluation of the merit of the translations of individual books of the canon, but these indications carry too little detail to be of much help.

[2] Zotenberg, *Catalogue*, p. 9.

[3] Cf. Löfgren, *Daniel*, p. xxiv; Conti Rossini, *Note*, p. 208.

the famous Ewosṭatewos; he was the founder of the monastery of Debra Demaḥ and died in 1419; his *gadl* was edited and translated by Conti Rossini.[1] It is, perhaps, rather improbable that he should have possessed a knowledge of Hebrew. The position is different with regard to one Marqorewos who is mentioned among the Ethiopian pilgrim communities abroad;[2] he would have had an opportunity of studying Hebrew and Arabic. On the other hand, Marqorewos is not an uncommon name, and without further information on this glossator his time and place must remain within the realm of speculation.

R. H. Charles[3] considers it 'unquestionable' that the Ethiopic version was made *in the main* from the Greek—in the main, 'for there are certain phenomena in the MSS. which cannot be explained from this hypothesis alone'. Charles adduces some evidence to show that the Hexapla of Origen was used by the Ethiopian translators. As to Dillmann's view (and thenceforth almost universally accepted) that the Greek text was later on corrected from the Hebrew, Charles regards it as 'just as likely' that the transliterations of Hebrew words, which are found in some Ethiopic manuscripts but not in the LXX, as well as other divergences from the Greek text 'may be survivals of the earliest form of the text made directly in many cases from the Hebrew'. If all these Hebraisms were to be ascribed to medieval glossators, how could we account (Charles argues) for their appearance in all manuscripts? Cases in point are Lamentations 3: 12, where the Ethiopic text reflects the Hebrew[4] most closely (and against the LXX), or Ezek. 30: 5 (cf. p. 7, above). Charles believes that the theory of the primitive Ethiopic version containing a large number of words taken directly from the Hebrew is supported by the fact that the Abyssinians received Christianity 'through Aramaean missionaries, and that very many Aramaic words were actually naturalized in order to express the new doctrines of the Christian faith.' He adds, cautiously and rightly, that it will not be possible to settle these questions with any degree of finality until we possess a complete critical edition of the Ethiopic version.

For the New Testament Charles accepts the views associated with Dillmann, Guidi, Hackspill, Conti Rossini, and others: the original version was made from the Greek text which received

---

[1] *C.S.C.O.*, vols. 33 and 34 (= Aeth. 16 and 17), 1904.
[2] Cerulli, *Etiopi in Palestina*, ii. 398, 402.
[3] In Hastings's *Dictionary of the Bible*, i. 791 ff.
[4] The resemblance is not confined to መሰረ፡ (Zotenberg, op. cit., p. 10, no. 3) but is patent throughout this verse—and indeed elsewhere.

a series of revisions and corrections on the basis of Arabic versions. These Arabic revisions are principally connected with the activities of Abba Salama 'the translator'[1] whose period has been authoritatively fixed by A. van Lantschoot[2] as 1348–88. His corrections were undoubtedly made 'sur la recension arabe alors la plus en vogue en Egypte'.[3] Lantschoot finds the evidence insufficient to decide the extent to which this revisionary work was associated with Abba Salama in person. It is not even entirely clear which books of the canon were subjected to at least some revision, for in the absence of external testimony we have to rely exclusively on the results of internal criteria which are not always as unambiguous as is desirable. The full complexity of the situation is revealed when one recalls that some ancient codices of the Arabic translation of the Gospels correspond fairly closely to the text of the Peshitta: 'sia che la traduzione in essi contenuta fosse fatta direttamente sul siriaco, o sia che la primitiva traduzione dal greco fosse poi corretta secondo la Peshitta.'[4]

Charles follows his predecessors in assigning the Ethiopic Bible translations to the fourth–sixth centuries. Since it was only during the first period of Ethiopic literature that translations were made from the Greek, it may safely be taken for granted that none of the original renderings was later than the end of the sixth century.

Schäfers (op. cit., pp. 170 ff.), on the basis of his work on the Ethiopic text of Jeremiah, came to the conclusion that the Ethiopians received their Bible not from Syria but from Egypt. The reasons which persuaded Schäfers to adopt this view had already been questioned, rightly I believe, by Rahlfs.[5] In a manuscript in the Berlin Library (Orient. Fol. 3067) chapters 46–52 of Jeremiah appear in a rather peculiar form which betrays an inadequate command of Greek. Moreover, Schäfers noticed that the translator used the preposition *'əm* to render both 'to' and 'from': 'Mir ist nur eine einzige Sprache bekannt, wo *'əm* beide Bedeutungen haben kann: die koptische.'[6] In fact, however, the same is true of Amharic *kä-*, and it seems at least as likely that the Ethiopian translator was influenced by his native tongue, Amharic. Schäfers now deduces from these data

---

[1] See p. 32, above.
[2] *Atti Convegno Int. di St. Et.*, pp. 397–401. [3] Lantschoot, op. cit., p. 399.
[4] Guidi, *MRAL* 1888, p. 13, which also contains further details as well as samples of an Arabic text derived from a Syriac one.
[5] *Aeth. Bibelübersetzung*, pp. 677–8. While I agree with Rahlfs, his objections do not coincide with those adduced by me in the following. [6] Schäfers, op. cit., p. 171.

that the translator 'must' have possessed a smattering of Greek, Coptic, and Ethiopic (Gəʿəz). He 'must', however, have had a different native tongue, and here Schäfers decides in favour of Syriac, mainly because Christianity was introduced into Ethiopia by Syrian (Aramaean) missionaries. Whence did these originate? Not from South Arabia, for Syrians in South Arabia would not have possessed a knowledge of Coptic; hence they must have come from Egypt, and the translator of the Ethiopic version was thus 'ein in Ägypten wohnender Syrer' (Schäfers, p. 170).

The entire reasoning hinges on the inferences to be drawn from the translator's peculiar use of Gəʿəz 'əm; if Coptic influence is excluded, the entire edifice collapses. Moreover, Schäfers postulates that those last seven chapters must represent the original and ancient version, while the remainder of the book is the result of later revision and elaboration (p. 177). But—as Rahlfs (op. cit., p. 678) has justifiably objected—the last seven chapters of Jeremiah in the Berlin manuscript are a singular phenomenon, confined to only one known manuscript, and do not allow of far-reaching conclusions as regards the entire Bible.

Rahlfs, in his posthumously published article on the Ethiopic Bible translations, took issue with Gildemeister and others who held that the Aramaic loanwords in Gəʿəz possessed a specifically Syriac form. Like Polotsky later on,[1] Rahlfs shows that most of these words are 'großenteils gar nicht echt syrisch, sondern erst von den Juden zu den Syrern gekommen' (p. 675). Not equally cogently argued is Rahlfs's opinion that it was Frumentius himself, in the middle of the fourth century, who began the Ethiopic translation (p. 673). True, I am not aware of any convincing argument that militates against the view that Frumentius may have commenced this long and arduous enterprise, yet Rahlfs does not adduce any positive evidence in support of his position. His article has, however, remained a fragment, and had he himself looked after its publication he might have presented his arguments in a somewhat different manner.

Littmann, in the early years of his career, took a great interest in the problems of the Ethiopic Bible translation.[2] In common with most scholars he thinks that the Gospels were the first books to have been rendered into Gəʿəz. This seems to me a very

---

[1] *JSS* 1964.
[2] It was Littmann who had inspired, and in part supervised, the Octateuch ed. by Boyd of which Genesis, Exodus, and Leviticus only were completed. The excellent chapter on the Bible in his *Geschichte der äthiopischen Litteratur*, pp. 223 ff., bears witness to direct preoccupation with these problems.

reasonable assumption, but I know of no specific evidence to support this view which by way of constant repetition has acquired the status of an established fact. The authors of the translation were 'perhaps' Syrian monks who had reached Aksum from South Arabia. Littmann has no doubt that the basis of their rendering was a Greek text, probably in a 'syrisch-okzidentalen' recension current in the region of Antioch. The Gospels were followed by the other books of the New Testament and, eventually, the entire canon of the Old Testament. The translation of the Old Testament was made from a Greek version as well, i.e. the Lucianic recension of the Septuagint: 'sie liegt aller Wahrscheinlichkeit nach der altäthiopischen Übersetzung zugrunde. Daß die äthiopische Version auf die griechische zurückgeht, steht außer Zweifel.'[1] I find it a little difficult to account for the varying degrees of certainty ascribed to these two statements, especially since critical examination of the Ethiopic Bible translations is still not sufficiently advanced to establish beyond reasonable doubt whether the same type of *Vorlage* is common to the entire canon of the Old Testament.[2]

There are many indications, Littmann finds, to suggest that Aramaeans took part in these translations, i.e. the introduction of Aramaic loanwords, especially in the case of theological concepts, and the transcription of proper names. It remains, however, to be established whether these Aramaic loanwords in Gə'əz express 'wirklich speziell christliche Ideen'.[3]

Littmann declares that the individual books of the Bible were translated in quick succession[4] by a number of translators clearly distinguished from each other by their varying attainments. Some books of the Old Testament were, he says, successfully rendered into Gə'əz, others much less so; some translations are literal, others merely reflect the general sense; some translators had a good knowledge of Greek and Ethiopic, others showed many deficiencies in this respect. It would have been important to know to which books of the canon[5] these comments refer and to have them exemplified by at least a few instances. The tenuousness of such generalities is high-lighted by the fact—readily conceded by Littmann—that we are unable to form any

---

[1] Littmann, op. cit., p. 224.
[2] Cf. Ullendorff, *The Ethiopians*[2], p. 139.
[3] Cf. p. 39, note 6, above, and Chapter II (excursus), below.
[4] I do not know on what evidence this is based.
[5] Conti Rossini, *Note*, p. 4, identifies some of the books, but—as has been pointed out above—proffers no detailed documentation.

valid judgement on the detailed nature of these old translations, as we possess no manuscripts going back to that period or, indeed, to any time prior to the thirteenth century.

Littmann surmises that in the interval between the composition of the old translation (fifth century?) and the thirteenth century many mistakes and textual corruptions must have entered our versions. When, in the fourteenth century, Abba Salama began to revise the Ethiopic text of the Gospels on the basis of an Arabic recension, this movement of revision is likely to have extended beyond the Gospels. Littmann further avers that, since virtually the entire Ethiopic literature since the thirteenth century was under the impact of Arabic, this Arabic influence must also be directly felt in the revision of the text of the Ethiopic Old Testament. One would readily concur with Littmann's doubt that an Ethiopian[1] should have acquired a sufficient command of Hebrew in order to revise the Gə'əz text on the basis of the original. The Hebrew evidence is not, however, confined to a few isolated Hebrew words, but is mainly attested in agreements with the Hebrew original as against the Greek versions, correspondences which Littmann justly describes as 'unzweifelhafte Anklänge an das hebräische Alte Testament' (op. cit., p. 226).

If the Hebrew elements are held to be associated with the period of scriptural revision in the Middle Ages (and I know of no conclusive evidence which forces us to assume so late a date), we are naturally hard put to identify the authors of this Hebraic revision. Littmann is inclined to follow a suggestion by I. Guidi[2] that the Ethiopian translators may have used the Arabic rendering by Sa'adya Ga'on which follows the Hebrew original very closely[3] and which would account for textual and even etymological correspondences with the Masoretic text. While this is an attractive proposition that would remove at least some difficulties (not, of course, those concerned with Hebrew transliterations),[4] it has to be realized that we possess no evidence in support of Guidi's suggestion. It would, of course, be possible to

---

[1] Littmann should have added 'in the thirteenth or fourteenth century', for he does not appear to have considered the possibility of direct Hebrew aid during the Aksumite period, either by Judaized elements or by Aramaic-speaking missionaries with a smattering of Hebrew.

[2] Repeated in *Storia della lett. et.*, p. 25. I cannot at present put my finger on the place where Guidi made this suggestion first—if he made it at all in print and not just privately to Conti Rossini (*Note*, p. 208).

Cf. also Graf, *Geschichte d. christl. arab. Lit.* i. 101–3.

[3] Despite paraphrases. It also employs untranslated Hebrew expressions on occasion—no doubt with a view to Sa'adya's Jewish readers.   [4] See p. 32, above.

study Sa'adya's text and compare it with the Ethiopic version. This remains to be done.

Some of the most recent observations on Ethiopic Bible translations come from the magisterial pen of the great Enrico Cerulli:[1] 'che queste traduzioni siano state fatte dal greco in etiopico è un fatto[2] che indica bene l'influenza del greco cristiano agli albori della letteratura etiopica.' The period of this work is given as fourth to seventh centuries by Cerulli who suggests that the Ethiopic translations 'hanno interesse per gli studi di letteratura greca cristiana in quanto conservano testi più antichi, generalmente, dei manoscritti greci che noi oggi abbiamo a disposizione'. This last point is not entirely clear to me in view of the fact that we possess the fourth-century Codex Sinaiticus[3] and Codex Vaticanus as well as the fifth-century Codex Alexandrinus.[4]

Cerulli finds that the Old Testament was rendered into Ethiopic from the Greek of the Septuagint, but neither all at once nor by the same translator. The method of translation and its value differ in the various books of the canon. The New Testament was, according to Cerulli and most of his precursors, translated from the Lucianic text received in the Patriarchate of Antioch. This translation is, 'molto verisimilmente', the work of Syrian monophysite ecclesiastics who had taken refuge in Ethiopia during the fifth and sixth centuries. Cerulli thinks that the books of both Testaments were, after the first translation, subjected to revisions on various occasions, particularly from the fourteenth century onwards. He adds, significantly, that this was done with the aid of 'testi arabo-*cristiani* [my italics] accolti nel Patriarcato di Alessandria'. Again, I am unaware of the specific evidence for this assumption, but if it were correct it would exclude Guidi's suggestion of Sa'adya's Arabic version having served as a *Vorlage*. However, Cerulli concludes judiciously: 'uno studio sistematico non è stato ancora fatto'—and this applies to a good deal of the '*ḥadīt*' which has attached itself, without adequately tested '*isnād*'s', to the subject of the Ethiopic Bible translations.

No contemporary scholar has rendered greater and more

---

[1] *Storia della lett. et.*, pp. 23–25.

[2] To what extent this can be considered a fully established 'fact', for the Bible as a whole and in all circumstances, will be discussed in the concluding part of this chapter.

[3] 156 leaves (besides the whole New Testament) in the British Museum.

[4] For other early Greek texts as well as further details cf. the Grant–Rowley revision of Hastings's one-volume *Dictionary of the Bible*[2] (1963), p. 350.

It is true, of course, that we have no manuscripts of very early 'pure' Lucianic texts; cf. Rahlfs, *Septuaginta-Studien*, ii, § 66.

meritorious services to the cause of Ethiopic Bible translations than O. Löfgren (see bibliography). In a still unpublished paper,[1] written in 1966, he states: 'Owing to its great antiquity and to the *indisputable fact* [my italics] that it was originally translated from the Greek, this [Ethiopic] version presents a good deal of interest for the critical study of the text of the Bible, especially that of the Old Testament.' Löfgren further declares that the old Gǝ'ǝz Old Testament is a good witness to the LXX text 'as it was found in uncial codices about the middle of the first millennium'. Yet, the translators were not always able to do justice to their difficult task and, apart from their own short-comings, many corruptions crept into the text at later periods. Löfgren cites the example of Daniel (which was edited by him) where, in 11: 13–45, eight older manuscripts present a poor text and sizable lacunae, while seven younger manuscripts have a virtually complete text in two different recensions.

It is customary to distinguish two later revisions[2] of the Old Testament text: one has been called the 'vulgar' text and is derived from work on the Arabic version current in Egypt; this is the fourteenth-century revision attributed to Abba Salama and already referred to before.[3] The other has been termed 'academic' and is, according to Löfgren, 'probably younger' and incorporates corrections from the Hebrew original. Löfgren adds that 'nothing is known with certainty about its origin and purpose'. This is, indeed, an understatement of our ignorance, for we know absolutely nothing about this revision—nor, in fact, whether it is a revision at all or, perhaps, part of the original translation process. It is a pity that Löfgren has not, to my knowledge, expressed a detailed opinion on Guidi's Sa'adya conjecture;[4] nor does he appear to have dealt with the objection, raised by Littmann, Guidi, and others, that the Middle Ages can scarcely be described as an era propitious to the exercise of Hebrew learning in Ethiopia.

As to the New Testament, Löfgren accepts the verdict of Guidi and Hackspill that the Gǝ'ǝz Gospels were originally translated

---

[1] See bibliography and p. 33, above.

[2] Löfgren (loc. cit.) accedes to this custom and terminology; cf. also Schäfers, op. cit., p. 178. A. Heider appears to have introduced this nomenclature (*Die aethiopische Bibelüberset-zung*, Leipzig, 1902, p. 5). Heider is, incidentally, remarkably precise about dates: according to him, the old Ethiopic translation was made about A.D. 330, the 'vulgar' revision in the sixteenth century and the 'academic' text at the end of the seventeenth century (op. cit., p. 6). I think it can be shown without much difficulty that all three dates are likely to be in-accurate. Heider's views on the Ethiopic Bible translations are set out summarily on pp. 3–8 of his opuscule and lack nothing in confident assurance.

[3] See esp. pp. 32, 44, above.

[4] Apart from a brief reference in his splendid Daniel edition, p. xlvi.

from Greek: 'This fundamental thesis was fully confirmed as regards *Acts* by Montgomery's study[1] in 1934, the only textual-critical investigation of any New Testament book in Gǝ'ǝz carried out in this century.' Löfgren pronounces as 'quite unsuccessful' Vööbus's recent attempt (see presently) to find a Syriac original as the basis of the primitive text of the Gospels in Ethiopic.

Löfgren is inclined 'to trust in the indigenous tradition that Frumentius, alias Abba Salama senior, was the first translator'. It seems to him 'utterly improbable' that the ordinary Christian in the Aksumite kingdom could have been content (or indeed able) to use Greek texts in the divine service for well over a century. To this Löfgren adds a very important observation: 'It is also difficult to explain why Syrian monks would have used Greek texts and not their own Syriac Bible in translating. In this respect I agree with Vööbus.' Löfgren thus appears to accept the proposition that, if it were shown that Syrian monks were the translators (and that is the view of the great majority of scholars), the almost axiomatically held view of a Greek *Vorlage* would become much more doubtful. We shall have to revert to this point in some detail.

Löfgren's position on dating and *Vorlage* is thus one of considerable consistency. He is not 'convinced' that the text of the famous Paris codex of the Gospels (Zotenberg no. 32) is identical with the primitive translation of the fourth century, for 'secondary readings and harmonizing additions' seem to have found their way into the text during the following dark centuries. Löfgren finally urges that in any future work account should be taken—besides some of the early manuscripts in European libraries—of recently discovered early manuscripts in Ethiopia (such as the Hayq Gospel codex) and of old Gǝ'ǝz texts in Biblical polyglots executed in Egyptian monasteries.

H. J. Polotsky has recently spoken[2] on the subject of Ethiopic Bible translations. His pronouncement seems to me of such importance that it should be quoted in full:

In the complete absence of direct documentary evidence a given literary text can be attributed to the Aksum period only on internal criteria or on *a priori* grounds. Chief among the former is direct translation from a Greek original: it is assumed, probably rightly, that direct translation from the Greek is out of the question in the Second Period of Ethiopic literature. This applies also to the Ethiopic Bible. On *a priori* grounds it is unlikely that the Bible should have been translated

[1] J. A. Montgomery, *The Ethiopic Text of the Acts of the Apostles.*
[2] At the Manchester Conference of Ethiopian Studies, 1963 (*JSS* 1964, p. 2).

very much later than the introduction of Christianity; and on internal evidence it is clear that the Ethiopic Bible was, in the first instance, translated directly from the Greek. I am aware that some scholars[1] are not yet convinced that such was really the case. I can only say that all the evidence known to me leads to this conclusion, and that no evidence to the contrary has come to my knowledge. But the researches of Dillmann, Guidi, and many others, have made it clear that the old translation is heavily overlaid with the results of different revisions from other sources, including the Syriac Peshitta, as a rule through the medium of Arabic. Therefore, the mere fact that an Aramaic word occurs in our ordinary editions, especially as regards the New Testament, does not yet prove that it formed part of the old translation.

This is, of course, a model of a clear and well-presented argument, and it would be churlish to dissent from the principal conclusions reached by Polotsky. There are, however, one or two points which give rise to some worry: it is argued that the Ethiopic Bible was translated direct from the Greek, at least *in the first instance*; and again: it is *heavily overlaid* with the results of different revisions (e.g. Syriac, probably by way of Arabic). While all this *may* be true, it seems to me wellnigh impossible— at least in the present conditions of manuscript studies and lacking critical editions—to disentangle the various layers, reveal the seams, and assert categorically that the one must be original and the other the result of revision. And on internal grounds, syntax, vocabulary, calques, etc., the situation is often confusing and contradictory—as the conflicting results obtained by scholars demonstrate and as I hope to have shown in my work on the Ethiopic text of Enoch. Polotsky is, of course, right in saying that the mere fact that an Aramaic word occurs in our editions does not yet prove that it formed part of the old translation, but it seems to me that the onus is on him to show that it did not. For in the Aksumite kingdom of the fifth and sixth centuries direct translation from an Aramaic original should not have encountered any insuperable obstacles, while this can scarcely be claimed as regards the fourteenth century, especially as translations at that time were mediated through Arabic. I would not, at this stage, express a preference for any particular stance in this argument, but I venture to suggest that things are not quite so cut and dried as is sometimes averred.

Finally, we must turn to the position taken by A. Vööbus[2]

[1] I imagine Polotsky is here thinking of Vööbus (see bibliography) and the present writer's 'Aramaic *Vorlage* of the Ethiopic Text of Enoch?' and *The Ethiopians*[2], pp. 139, 143.

[2] See the two relevant writings mentioned in the bibliography, abbreviated in the following as *Spuren* and *Early Versions*, respectively.

who favours a Syriac *Vorlage* to replace the customary view of a Greek original underlying the Ethiopic translation of the Gospels. This is a minority opinion, though by no means a completely isolated one.[1] F. C. Burkitt had already reached the conclusion that an old Syriac version had also been used for the Ethiopic translation.[2] Vööbus maintains, not altogether unfairly, that for many years now no independent examination of the evidence has been carried out, and scholars have usually been content to rehearse the results at which Dillmann or Hackspill had arrived close on a century ago. Even the most favourable circumstances, i.e. the collection of all variants peculiar to the Ethiopic translation, will not necessarily bring about a solution, for even if we are able to detect in those variants a good deal of old Syriac material, the protagonists of the Greek thesis can point to many instances (as Vööbus concedes) which follow the Greek text so slavishly that they reflect even the Greek order of words. The problem is not only to draw the right conclusions from this complex and seemingly irreconcilable state of affairs, but to extend the range of internal as well as external criteria and to seek fresh clues which may help us to break out from what appears to be a vicious circle.

Vööbus argues—and here he follows the majority view—that Christianity under Frumentius had not spread very far by the second half of the fourth century. Ethiopian sources, and in particular the Synaxarium,[3] testify to the great impetus which the young Christian faith received from the advent of the famous Nine Saints. They brought about the full christianization of the country by the late fifth or early sixth century. That they were Syrian monks has been generally assumed,[4] and it is likely that they came to Ethiopia by way of South Arabia,[5] possibly as a consequence of the anti-Christian excesses by Du Nuwas.[6] They founded monasteries, were instrumental in the

---

[1] Vööbus claims that Gildemeister 'nahm eine syrische Herkunft an' (*Spuren*, p. 8; *Early Versions*, p. 250), but as far as I can see from Gildemeister's letter to Gregory (cf. p. 40, above), Gildemeister speaks of Syrian translators and Syriac linguistic influences—yet he assumes an original that is predominantly Greek.

[2] *Encyclopaedia Biblica*, vol. iv, col. 5012. Vööbus (*Spuren*, p. 8) claims much more than Burkitt, in fact, suggested: 'The translation was from the Greek. . . . A few traces survive of a yet older Ethiopic version of the Gospels made from the Syriac . . . and the text now and again agrees with Syriac against almost all other authorities, though it usually follows the Greek or the Arabic . . .' (*Encycl. Bibl.* iv, col. 5012).

[3] Cf. Guidi, *Synaxaire*, 17 Sane; Budge, *Book of the Saints of the Ethiopian Church*, index in vol. iv (under names of the Nine Saints); Dillmann, *Zur Geschichte* . . ., pp. 24 ff.

[4] Guidi, 'La chiesa abissina', *OM* 1922, p. 126.

[5] Vööbus, *Early Versions*, p. 247; Hackspill, op. cit., p. 155.

[6] These were apparently directed at monophysites in particular; cf. J. Ryckmans, 'Le Christianisme en Arabie . . .', p. 448.

spread of Christianity, and are generally credited with the translation of the Scriptures into Gəʿəz.[1]

Vööbus inveighs against Hackspill's theory[2] that the Syrian monks carried with them the Holy Scriptures in Greek and not in their own language. On the face of it, this does seem a trifle improbable, but Hackspill has three fairly weighty arguments: (1) proper names exhibit the Greek and not the Aramaic forms; (2) there are a number of words which have entered the Ethiopic version in their Greek and untranslated garb; (3) some mistranslations can only be traced back to a Greek source. Vööbus counters these strong propositions by querying the notion that Hackspill's arguments lead us to assume, necessarily, a Greek *Vorlage* for the *original* translation. Instead, he claims that a Greek text may have been used for the revisions which we know to have been carried out at much later periods.

Vööbus's point does, however, meet some serious obstacles: it seems highly improbable that fourteenth-century revisions were undertaken on the basis of a Greek original. The linguistic and cultural conditions of medieval Ethiopia scarcely favour such a proposition. Moreover, we possess at least some indications that Arabic texts were employed for much of this work; and even the closest Arabic approximation to the Greek original could not have produced some of the Ethiopic peculiarities noticed by Hackspill.

It seems to me likely that neither Hackspill's nor Vööbus's (see presently) positions do justice to the complexities of the situation. Hackspill's manuscript (Zotenberg 32) is probably the oldest Gəʿəz Gospel text known to us at present (thirteenth century); but this does not mean, of course, that it represents a particularly ancient recension or, for that matter, that the work of translation was necessarily carried out on one *Vorlage* only, that not more than one attempt was made, and that any given manuscript may not incorporate the results of varying strands and translational traditions.

Vööbus invites attention to specifically Syriac translation techniques[3] and modes of transliteration;[4] he also refers to textual corruptions which can best be explained from a Syriac version. Löfgren has said[5] that, if the Bible translations were made by Syrian missionaries, it would indeed be hard to explain why they would not use their own Syriac texts. Vööbus makes the same point by showing the great attachment of Syrian

[1] Guidi, loc. cit. For other sources cf. Vööbus, op. cit. [2] Op. cit., p. 156.
[3] *Early Versions*, p. 253.   [4] See p. 41, above.   [5] p. 50, above.

divines to their own language and writings[1] and refers to a passage in the *Maṣḥafa Məṣṭir* (Zotenberg MS. 113, fol. 63a) which relates that the Syrian monks had brought along መጽሐፈት፡ ሕገሙ፡ ወሥርዓተሙ፡ 'the books of their rites and service'. That these clerics produced translations of their own literature which had at times little relevance to conditions in Ethiopia had already been demonstrated by Guidi[2] who drew attention to the *Qerillos* which is aimed against the Nestorians in particular, although there were no Nestorians in the Aksumite kingdom. Vööbus infers from this, fairly, that these Syrians 'simply translated works and writings which suited their interests'.[3]

Vööbus also deals with a number of specific instances in the Gospels[4] which, he maintains, can be elucidated only from a Syriac original. More important, perhaps, is an examination which Vööbus has pioneered and which may well open up valuable vistas: Since we possess no Ethiopic manuscripts prior to the thirteenth century and few, if any, that have not been subject to later revisions, it is just conceivable that some old readings and quotations may accidentally have been preserved in non-Biblical Ethiopic manuscripts which have escaped the hands of the revisers. This seems indeed a promising line; one example must suffice:

Matthew 23: 13 (14):

እለ፡ ተአጽዉ፡ ቅድመ፡ ገጸ፡ ሰብእ፡ አንቀጸ፡ መንግሥት፡ ሰማያት ፡፡[5]

You who close before the face of man the gate of the kingdom of heaven.

With this one should compare the usual text:

እስመ፡ ተዐጽዉ፡ መንግሥት፡ ሰማያት፡ ውስተ፡ ገጸ፡ ሰብእ ፡፡

ὅτι κλείετε τὴν βασιλείαν τῶν οὐρανῶν ἔμπροσθεν τῶν ἀνθρώπων

Vööbus claims that the reading preserved in the Ethiopic hagiographic text 'ist den altsyrischen Handschriften, die noch mehr altertümliches Gut enthielten, nicht fremd gewesen'.[6] Unfortunately, he does not cite the actual Syriac text, which would have been helpful and instructive.[7]

Vööbus thus avers that in these Ethiopic hagiographa we encounter remnants of a textual type which have otherwise been removed by the various revisions. The Ethiopian monks who

[1] Op. cit., p. 255. [2] OM 1922, pp. 126–7. [3] Early Versions, p. 256.
[4] Op. cit., pp. 257 ff. [5] Conti Rossini, Acta S. Baṣalota Mika'el (C.S.C.O.), p. 22.
[6] Spuren, p. 25. [7] For other examples of this kind cf. Spuren, pp. 23–29.

composed these writings must, however, have used Gospel manuscripts of an early vintage which have now disappeared: 'Eine Phase der Textgeschichte tritt vor unsere Augen, die uns etwas von der älteren Periode und Entwicklung bloßlegt.'[1] In the list of variants, Vööbus maintains, will be found readings which one seeks in vain in the sphere of Greek manuscripts but which can be encountered in the fertile soil of old Syriac manuscripts. All these indications, cumulatively, favour the assumption of a Syriac *Vorlage* of the Ethiopic Bible translations. We shall see in the following to what extent Vööbus's claims can be accepted.

We shall now summarize the findings of this section and set out some tentative conclusions for the Old Testament, New Testament, and Apocrypha and Pseudepigrapha.

Tentative conclusions

The Old Testament adds at least one complication which is absent from the formulation of the problem as regards the New Testament: in the case of the latter we may have to reckon with a Greek or possibly a Syriac *Vorlage*, but the former was written in Hebrew, and in addition to the Greek and Syriac translations—Septuagint, Peshitta, and other versions—we may have to take into account either passages of direct translation from the original into Ethiopic (or, possibly, by way of Arabic) or revision and correction from a Hebrew text. With this important exception, the questions which are posed by the Gəʿəz rendering of both Testaments are not markedly different, and many of the conclusions reached for the one will frequently apply to the other as well.

It has been said before, and must be reiterated once more at this point, that no views on the time, authorship, and *Vorlage* of the Ethiopic Bible translations can lay claim to any measure of finality. The work of editing remains incomplete, and even the best manuscripts in our possession do not go back beyond the thirteenth century—and most of them are of much more recent date. External sources are almost completely silent, and internal criteria are frequently open to widely varying interpretations.

I am aware of no historical or linguistic aspects that would preclude us from assuming that some work of translating the Scriptures into Ethiopic followed soon after the introduction of

---

[1] *Spuren*, p. 29.

Christianity into Ethiopia in the fourth century. In so far as translation from Greek can be proved, it is likely to have occurred in the first century after the Christian conversion in Aksum—and probably not later than the end of the fifth century A.D. Modern scholars are unanimous that the standard of Greek shown by the translations is not impressive, and the conditions which would have maintained even those minimum linguistic requirements for any moderately successful translation rapidly deteriorated. This is not to assert that Greek was no longer used for translational work after the end of the fifth century, but it does seem likely that it was not then taken as the sole and exclusive basis. The evidence certainly encourages the opinion that, with the advent of the Syrian missionaries in the fifth and sixth centuries, Syriac translations were employed in conjunction with the Greek text.

I fail to understand the position of those who claim either an exclusively Greek or an exclusively Syriac *Vorlage*. It seems to me that the historical circumstances and a linguistic analysis of the texts already edited rule out such a dogmatic option for either posture. Some respectable pieces of evidence can be adduced in favour of each of several hypotheses, but it seems that reality was a good deal more complex and eclectic than is sometimes conceded, and the linguistic facts refuse to fall into neat patterns. If the same book—or even chapter—offers clear evidence of, say, Greek, Syriac, and Hebrew elaborations, nothing that has so far come to my notice would prevent us from assuming that all three might have been employed, in one form or another, directly or indirectly, by a team of translators. On the face of it, work on one single linguistic *Vorlage* was, perhaps, the exception rather than the rule in the peculiar circumstances that obtained in the Aksumite kingdom of the fourth–sixth centuries.

It seems to me that only such a view of the situation can do justice to the intrinsic facts as well as to their varying interpretation by scholars. When Dillmann speaks of the translators' poor knowledge of Greek or of some surprising correspondences of words and sense as between the Hebrew and Gə'əz texts; when Conti Rossini refers to writings that have passed direct from Syriac into Ethiopic, and Zotenberg and Littmann find in the Gə'əz rendering remarkable reflections of the Hebrew of the Old Testament; when Charles speaks of survivals of the earliest form of the text made directly in many cases from the Hebrew, though the bulk of the translation was made 'in the main' from the Greek (Polotsky: 'in the first instance'), then the general impression inexorably emerges that any one hypothesis is unable to carry the full burden of all these qualifications and reservations. Nor, I would submit, can these difficulties all be relegated to the period of revisions from the thirteenth or fourteenth centuries onwards.

That such revisions did take place is not in question, but they were, I believe, nearly all due to the influence of Arabic. Direct Syriac or Hebrew influences (from different quarters, of course) can readily be accounted for in the period from the fourth to perhaps the seventh century; they cannot be made credible in the fourteenth or fifteenth centuries. Löfgren has rightly said[1] that, if Syrian monks were the translators, it would be difficult to see why they would not have used the Scriptures in their own language as a basis. The disagreement between Löfgren and Vööbus, on one hand, and the *Vorlage*-discrepancies which may even occur in the same chapter, on the other, can be explained and resolved on the assumption of dual original texts—used to varying degrees and no doubt in accordance with the difficulty or smoothness of the passages concerned. In purely statistical and quantitative terms, Greek must probably be considered the source *par excellence*.

Nöldeke and Rodinson have pointed out[2] that the translators must have had the assistance of Jews in all those cases where a Hebrew original is reflected in the Ethiopic translation. There is no difficulty in seeking such helpers among the Jewish or Judaized immigrants from South Arabia in any period till about the seventh century. On the other hand, the conditions cannot possibly be adjudged suitable for large-scale Hebrew revisions or corrections in the late Middle Ages. Hence I find it impossible to accept the so-called 'academic' revision. The elements which the latter is alleged to contain are either old or part of an isolated freak phenomenon which can never be excluded, but which is far removed from a systematic re-examination of the Scriptures. The mysterious Mercurius[3] who had some knowledge of the Masoretic text may well have been such a freak.

In contrast to this, we possess good evidence, internal as well as external, of revisions on the basis of Arabic texts. The originator of this movement appears to have been the fourteenth-century Abba Salama, 'the translator'.[4] In this context it is an

---

[1] It will be recalled that Löfgren favours very early translation activity under Frumentius on the basis of a Greek original.
[2] See p. 37, above.
[3] See pp. 42–43, above.
[4] Cf. pp. 32 and 44, above.

urgent desideratum to examine Sa'adya's Hebrew-Arabic version and to find out whether it was ever used as a base-text
which might also account for any of the Hebrew approximations. I would hazard the guess that Löfgren's doubts about
this are likely to be confirmed.[1] As during the Aksumite period
Gə'əz drew its literary strength from Greek models, scriptural or
otherwise, so during the Middle Ages Arabic provided the
material from which translations and adaptations were made.
Among the Christians of Egypt Coptic had gradually been replaced by Arabic, and it was in this language that a fresh
blossoming of literary activity occurred in Egypt at a time when
the restoration of the Solomonic dynasty had prepared the
ground for a high degree of cultural receptiveness in Ethiopia.
No doubt the arrival of the Coptic archbishops (and Abba
Salama and his retinue offer a notable example) had at times
a salutary effect in keeping Ethiopia in touch with literary
trends in other parts of the Christian Orient.[2] Coptic monks of
the Abuna's suite assisted in the interpretation and translation
of such writings. The oral influence of Coptic priests, who acted
as 'accoucheurs' in the delivery of these renderings, can be
detected—as Guidi, Cerulli, and others have recognized—in
cases where the Ethiopic version deviates from the Arabic *Vorlage* and approximates more closely to the Coptic original. In
those instances the Coptic passage was remembered, but the
actual text used for the preparation of the Gə'əz version was in
Arabic. There is no evidence that Coptic texts had any *direct*
part in the rendering of the Gə'əz Bible.

The complexities of Greek, Syriac, Hebrew, and Arabic
originals, used either for translation or revision, have been
magisterially sketched by Löfgren in his justly renowned Daniel
edition (pp. xliii–l) which may serve as a model of this type of
text-critical study. Much of what Löfgren has found out for
Daniel will, *mutatis mutandis*, apply to many other Biblical books
as well, though the quality and coherence of these translations
do exhibit very marked variations and distinctions. In paying
sincere tribute to the excellence of Löfgren's editions, one need
not be committed to accepting all of Löfgren's views as to the
genesis and later development of these translations. If Löfgren's
rejection of the 'Annahme zweier Vorlagen' (op. cit., p. xliv) is
limited to the idea of simultaneous work on an Arabic and
a Syriac text, I would readily concur; but if this repudiation is

---

[1] *Daniel*, p. xlvi.
[2] Cf. Cerulli, *Storia della lett. et.*, pp. 31–33.

meant to apply to all work on dual sources (e.g. Greek and Syriac), I would not feel able to follow him in this.

A few words must be said about the four-volume Asmara edition of the Ethiopic Old Testament prepared by Francesco da Bassano[1] (well known for his earlier Tigrinya dictionary) with the help of several Ethiopian clerics, chief among them Abba Kidanä Maryam Kasa (p. xi), later on Bishop of the Catholics of Ethiopian rite. The title-page states (in Gǝ'ǝz) that the edition is based on collation with ancient manuscripts and with editions in Syriac, Greek, and Arabic, while the dedication to Pope Pius XI includes the information: '. . . Vetus Testamentum aethiopico idiomate conscriptum ex vetustioribus optimisque codicibus in Erythraea, Abyssynia, Parisiis, Londinis . . . collectis. . . .' This is not, of course, a critical edition with an apparatus of variant readings but a practical tool intended for the use of the Ethiopian people. Beyond that, the edition represents the first complete publication of the Gǝ'ǝz Old Testament and is thus also of inestimable value to scholars.[2]

On p. ix of his Ethiopic preface da Bassano explains that it was his aim to publish the type of text which appears in the finest and oldest manuscripts from the time of Frumentius and the Nine Saints—certainly an ambitious undertaking which is unlikely to have been capable of fulfilment. For this purpose he collected not only printed texts but also the oldest manuscripts available in the churches and monasteries of Ethiopia. Unfortunately, he does not tell us from which places he obtained those manuscripts and what their approximate dating was. In addition, da Bassano also used photographic reproductions of Ethiopic Old Testament manuscripts in the British Museum and the Bibliothèque Nationale. In all this work he had the aid of indigenous priests who were versed in Gǝ'ǝz and in the study of the Holy Scriptures. However, his principal object was the collection of manuscripts and their comparison with መጽሐፈ፡ ሰብዓ፡ ሊቃውንት፡ ወምስለ፡ ካልአት፡ መጻሕፍት፡ ሶርያ፡ ወዓረብ፡ 'the Septuagint and with other Syriac and Arabic texts'. He paid particular attention to those manuscripts which in the sixteenth century were revised according to Syriac[3] and Arabic texts. Since the Books of Maccabees were composed after the translation of the LXX (so da Bassano declares), he himself had

[1] ብሉይ፡ ኪዳን፡፡ Asmara 1922/3–1925/6.
[2] Cf. Löfgren's excellent review in MO 1929, pp. 174–80.
[3] I do not know why da Bassano singled out the sixteenth century in particular and, above all, what evidence he possesses for revision on the basis of Syriac texts at that period.

to translate them from Greek into Ethiopic, using some British
Museum Ethiopic manuscripts which contain a Vulgate-based
text of these books.[1]

Löfgren (loc. cit.) describes da Bassano's work as largely
based on old manuscript tradition offering an eclectic or con-
flate text. Chapter and verse division follows the Vulgate, 'sonst
aber habe ich keine Beeinflussung durch diese Quelle bemerkt'.
Löfgren has carried out a detailed comparison of the Asmara
edition with his own manuscripts used for his work on Daniel
and some of the minor prophets. His results coincide with my
own conclusions which are derived from less detailed—yet more
extended—comparisons, the fruit of a quarter of a century's
desultory reading. Da Bassano's principal aim was to produce
a readily comprehensible text which would be of practical
benefit to the people of Ethiopia. Hence it was essential to
remove, as far as possible, all *lectiones difficiliores* and to replace
them by readings which made 'good sense'. For this purpose the
editor adjusted, according to Löfgren, 'die alte Übersetzung
dem *textus receptus*'. I agree with Löfgren that the result of this
procedure was a 'Mischtext', but I would find it hard to detect
any real evidence that da Bassano's version stands somewhere
half-way between the 'vulgar' and 'academic' recensions. In any
event, considering its limited and specific object the Asmara
Old Testament was a fine achievement.

As for the New Testament, I have little doubt that the massive evidence mustered by Hackspill is sufficient to prove a predominantly Greek *Vorlage*, at least for the famous M.S. B.N. 32.
This does not, of course, establish beyond reasonable doubt that
other manuscript traditions must necessarily have a similar provenance. Nor does the fact that MS. 32 appears to be the oldest
Gə'əz Gospel manuscript at present in our possession accord
to it *as such* a position of precedence, for it is perfectly feasible
that younger manuscripts might derive from a more ancient
filiation. Vööbus has undoubtedly shown up a number of loop-
holes and difficulties, but even cumulatively they seem to me to
fall short of statistical certitude. The most important and promising aspect of Vööbus's work concerns the occurrence of
Biblical quotations in Ethiopic literature. A systematic exploita-
tion of this vast mine may well bring to light further divergences
from the received text which may go back to an earlier pre-
revision version. If most of those variants can be shown to

---

[1] Probably Wright, B.M. xv. 8; xxviii. 4; xxxi, 1. Wright (p. 14) describes the text as
translated (in modern times) from the Vulgate.

derive from an old Syriac recension, as Vööbus claims, then our views will inevitably have to undergo some modification. But that stage has not been reached yet.

Vorlage-problems naturally affect the Apocrypha and Pseudepigrapha as well. New editions of Jubilees[1] and Enoch[2] are at present under preparation, and both will benefit from the discoveries of Hebrew and Aramaic fragments, respectively, at Qumran. These fragments—and the Aramaic ones in particular—may have a direct bearing on the vexed question of the language(s) from which the translators into Gəʿəz worked. On the basis of a pilot study[3], carried out on the Ethiopic version and the Greek and Aramaic fragments extant, the likelihood of direct translation from Aramaic was increasingly pressed upon me by the evidence proffered by vocabulary (especially in the case of mis-translations)[4] and syntax. Yet, it will be prudent to await the results accruing from the new edition as a whole.

In presenting the arguments for direct Ethiopic translation from the Aramaic text of Enoch it was not part of my case to claim that no Greek text was available to the translators or that there exists no passage of the Ethiopic text which can, in fact, be most conveniently explained by assuming a Greek basis. One need only think of the misreading in Enoch 22: 2 where the context seems to require 'hollow places' and where the Ethiopic version is likely to have mistaken κοῖλοι for καλοί (ሠናያት). But in the few instances of this type the Greek text appears to have been primarily invoked as a translation aid, perhaps in obscure

---

[1] See the fine paper on the projected new edition of the Ethiopic Book of Jubilees by W. Baars and R. Zuurmond in *JSS*, Spring 1964, pp. 67–74.

[2] By M. Black and Edward Ullendorff. Cf. my 'An Aramaic *Vorlage* of the Ethiopic Text of Enoch?'

In that article I also touched briefly upon the 'son of man' problem (p. 265), and there seemed to exist at least a remote possibility that the Ethiopic phrasing might shed some light on this expression. On re-examining the question in conjunction with G. Vermes's important study on 'The Use of Bar Nash/Bar Nasha in Jewish Aramaic', it now appears to me that the Ethiopic evidence has little or nothing to contribute and that it remains essentially an Aramaic (Hebrew) issue.

[3] See preceding footnote.

[4] Two fairly typical examples:

In Enoch 5: 9 the context and parallelism obviously require the sense: 'And they shall not again transgress, nor shall they *sin* all the days of their life.' This is indeed what the Greek text renders by the verbs πλημμελήσουσιν and ἁμάρτωσιν. The Ethiopic version, however, translates the second verb ኢይትኴነኑ፤ 'they shall not be judged' = οὐ κριθήσονται which can neither be a rendering nor a misreading of the common ἁμάρτωσιν. It is probable, therefore, that the error arose from the Semitic *Vorlage* in which the Gəʿəz translator seems to have mistaken *psq* 'to judge' for *pšʿ* 'to sin'. It is equally obvious that this mistake cannot be the result of a later revision but must be the product of the original version.

In chapter 27: 2, for 'this accursed valley' the Greek text simply transcribes Semitic נחל as γῆ (κατάρατος), while the Ethiopic understands correctly (surely not by way of Greek!) ቆላ፤ 'valley'.

or difficult places. Examination of the textual evidence has, however, led me to this tentative and provisional conclusion: the nature of some of the errors in the versions and attempts at a retranslation into the Semitic original have encouraged the view (now also reinforced by the Dead Sea fragments) that the bulk of Enoch was written in Aramaic but that there existed a number of passages or admixtures in Hebrew. And it was when encountering those Hebrew parts that the Syrian translators of Enoch had recourse to the Greek version, while the Aramaic bulk of the text could generally be rendered into Ethiopic without the intermediacy of Greek. Nor should one dismiss the possibility that the Aramaic-based translation was subsequently subjected to revision or retouching on the strength of the Greek version. The evidence in support of direct translation from Aramaic into Gə'əz is of necessity cumulative and can only be fully accepted if sustained throughout the entire work—as indeed I hope to demonstrate elsewhere in the not too distant future.[1]

Bible translations into some modern Ethiopian languages

Translations of the entire Bible have hitherto been published in Amharic and Tigrinya (*təgrəñña*) only. In Tigre we possess the New Testament, Psalms, and Isaiah, but it is reported that a Tigre translation of the complete Bible is now in an advanced state of preparation.[2] There is virtually nothing in the remaining *Semitic* Ethiopian languages. It is, perhaps, rather remarkable that, if one of our principal difficulties in discussing the Gə'əz Bible translations (made a millennium and a half ago) was the identity of the language on which the translation was based, a similar problem should be encountered as regards the modern Ethiopian languages whose rendering does not go back more than a century and a half. Of course, we do possess some external information, but we must also have recourse to internal criteria. Both together throw an interesting light on the problems with which we have been wrestling in the preceding pages.

The history of the first translation of the Bible into Amharic is a romantic and exciting story which deserves to be better known among *éthiopisants*. The fullest account is contained in

---

[1] The work on the new edition of Enoch has hitherto been held up by the failure of those in charge of the Aramaic Qumran fragments to arrange for prompt publication of those texts.

[2] This information has been confirmed by the British and Foreign Bible Society to whom I am much obliged for a good deal of helpful information.

William Jowett,[1] *Christian Researches in the Mediterranean* (London, 1822); this book has an extremely interesting and valuable chapter on 'Abyssinians', running to some sixty pages.[2] Jowett thinks that 'though the province which bears the name of Amhara is small, its dialect is spoken through at least half of Abyssinia' (p. 197). When Jowett visited Cairo, in about 1820, he met there the French Consul, M. Asselin de Cherville, who owned a translation, in manuscript, of the entire Bible into Amharic. M. Asselin had become friendly with an elderly Ethiopian from Gondar;[3] his name was Abu Rumi (at times it is also given as Abi Ruhh[4] or Abu Ruhh or Abba Rukh Habessinus)[5] which appears to be an Arabicized corruption of Abraham. According to Asselin, 'Abu Rumi', a master of the literature of his country, had been the instructor of James Bruce[6] and Sir William Jones.[7] Asselin, when he had become convinced of the knowledge and literary competence of his

---

[1] Of the Church Missionary Society; 1787–1855.

[2] Pp. 171–229, including sections on the early establishment of Christianity in Ethiopia; the dependence of the Church on the Coptic Patriarch; the ancient Confession of Faith (by Claudius); the modern Creed of the Abyssinian Church; the Ethiopic Scriptures; the Amharic Version of the Scriptures (pp. 197–204); the Tigre (i.e. Tigriña) Version of the Scriptures; on the encouragement of Abyssinian Learning; Thoughts on a Mission to Abyssinia.

The present writer, as the first incumbent of a Chair of Ethiopian Studies, may perhaps be forgiven for quoting a passage from Jowett's book which anticipates the foundation of this Chair by close on a century and a half (at a time when Oxford and Cambridge were the only two *English* universities): '. . . It is worthy of consideration, however, whether, in entering, with such ample means and such fair hopes, upon another Continent [i.e. Africa], it may not be expedient to contemplate some New Establishment, founded with an express view to those ends which have been already stated.

'The endowing of an Abyssinian Professorship, with Three Scholarships, in either or both of the English Universities, would display a generous and enlightened consideration of the wants of Africa.

'The amount of Literature already in our possession, with this view, is as follows: in Ethiopic (the Ecclesiastical Language) the whole Bible, and various Liturgies and Histories— in Amharic (the reigning modern dialect) the whole Bible.

'Eight dialects, as has been already noticed, (one of which, that of Tigre, has been in a considerable degree elucidated) will afford ample scope for the Researches of an Abyssinian Scholar . . .' (op. cit., p. 215).

Jowett goes on to express the hope that public opinion on this measure would ripen. Nor should his proposal be understood as 'deranging the admirable system of Classical and Scientific Education . . . by giving undue prominence to Oriental Studies. . . . We would gladly see the rewards of Hebrew, Arabic, and Abyssinian Scholarship presented . . . to the newly-graduated Student. . . .' This is a remarkably prescient disquisition on the place and value of Oriental studies at university level.

[3] According to Isenberg's informant, Däbtära Matewos, he was 'a native of Godjam' (*Dictionary of the Amharic Language*, p. iii).

[4] Isenberg, loc. cit.   [5] Cf. Fumagalli, *Bibliografia Etiopica*, p. 144.

It is amusing to note that the obituarist of Thomas Pell Platt (1798–1852; orientalist, librarian of the British and Foreign Bible Society, and editor of the Bible in Amharic) writes in the *Dictionary of National Biography* (p. 1296): 'in 1844 Platt edited an Amharic version of the Bible, using the translation of Abba Rukh for the O.T., and that of Abu Rumi Habessinus for the N.T.'

[6] I cannot recall Bruce mentioning an Ethiopian by some such name.

[7] 1746–94, the famous orientalist.

Abyssinian friend, set him to translate the entire Bible into Amharic. As an Ethiopic version was already in existence,[1] the new Amharic rendering was to become 'a point of comparison, in order to assign the differences between the Vernacular and the Ancient Language' (p. 199).

Fortunately, Asselin has left an account of the way the translation was executed:[2] the work occupied him and Abu Rumi for fully ten years (1808–18).[3] Every Tuesday and Saturday his door was shut to all visitors when he read with 'my Abyssinian, slowly, and with the utmost attention, every verse of the Sacred Volume, in the Arabic Version[4] which we were about to translate'. But we are not told from which Arabic version the rendering was made. However,

all those words which were either abstruse, difficult, or foreign to the Arabic, I explained to him, by the help of the Hebrew Original, the Syriac Version, or the Septuagint; as well as a few Glossaries and Commentaries, which I had gathered about me: but he also found often the key to them in the Ethiopic, or Gheez. . . .[5] After having finished the translation of one Book, we collated it once more, before we proceeded farther.

This is helpful as far as it goes and offers a lesson, I would suggest, for an assessment of the translation—*mutatis mutandis*—of the Scriptures into Gə'əz, particularly as regards the question of a single *Vorlage*. But there remain a number of doubtful factors: we possess no reliable information on the quality and level of Asselin's or Abu Rumi's knowledge of Arabic, nor, for that matter, on the standard of the Ethiopian's Gə'əz or the Frenchman's Hebrew, Syriac, and Greek. And critical study of the Amharic Bible is not sufficiently advanced to throw any light on this question. Asselin's account of the genesis of the Amharic translation is corroborated[6] by a note in the B. & F.B.S.'s catalogue which refers to the rendering having been made from Arabic, with external arrangement according to the Vulgate, and 'collateral help' from the Hebrew,[7] Greek, and Syriac.

---

[1] Not, of course, in print.   [2] Jowett, *Christian Researches*, pp. 199 ff.

[3] These dates (which I cannot find anywhere else) are given in an extensive footnote on p. 14 of Dr. G. Goldenberg's very brilliant Ph.D. thesis (Jerusalem, 1966—in Hebrew) on the Amharic tense-system.

[4] Cf. p. 91, note 1, below.

[5] We do not know, of course, what Gə'əz Bible manuscripts were available at Cairo at that time and to which of them Abu Rumi may have had access (cf. Zanutto, *Bibl. Etiop.*, p. 138). It is also possible that he may have known by heart at least some portions of the Ethiopic Bible.

[6] Though the independence of this confirmation must remain somewhat doubtful.

[7] Zotenberg, *Catalogue*, p. 21, avers that Platt's 1844 edition of the Amharic Bible (see below) had introduced changes 'en beaucoup d'endroits' and is now much closer to the

This collateral help was given by T. P. Platt[1] and Samuel Lee.[2]

M. Asselin de Cherville was quite lyrical in his description of the translation which

'respects a language almost unknown; and a translation absolutely unique, which unheard-of circumstances have combined to procure, and which doubtless will not present themselves a second time. For I must confess to you, that if unhappily a single Book were wanting, I should now find it impossible to supply the defect.

I owe this entire collection . . . to the kindness of Providence, . . . to the gratitude and strong attachment of this venerable Old Man [Abu Rumi] whom I had snatched from the arms of death, and who had devoted to me the remainder of a life which he considered to be mine . . .' (Jowett, op. cit., p. 200).

M. Asselin was anxious to dispose of the work 'on terms which would re-imburse his expenses', and he knew that both the Church Missionary Society and the British and Foreign Bible Society would 'justly deem the Manuscript in question of the highest importance'. In these circumstances Jowett was entrusted by the B. & F.B.S. with discretionary powers to bring negotiations to a successful conclusion. 'This was happily effected, on the 10th of April 1820; on terms which appeared to be equitable to all parties.' These terms involved the payment to Asselin of £1,250[3]—a truly prodigious sum 150 years ago, especially in a low-cost area such as Egypt. Jowett, however, was extremely pleased with the result of his mission and declared that 'the publication of the Amharic Scriptures will be as the lighting of a Pharos on the inhospitable shores of the Red Sea!' (p. 203).

The manuscript which Jowett had acquired contains 9,539 pages in small octavo, written in the fine hand of 'Abu Rumi', and covers the entire Bible. It was submitted for scrutiny to Professor Samuel Lee, and Thomas Pell Platt prepared it for publication with commendable speed: the Gospels were published in 1824,[4] the entire New Testament in 1829,[5] and the

Hebrew text. This is undoubtedly the case, as comparison with the Abu Rumi manuscript shows.

[1] See above, note 5 on p. 63.

[2] 1783–1852, Professor of Arabic at Cambridge (from 1819) and later Regius Professor of Hebrew (1831), a renowned polyglot.

[3] So Goldenberg, loc. cit. The B. & F.B.S. have kindly confirmed from their records that £1,250 was, in fact, the sum paid to M. Asselin.

[4] *Evangelia Sancta*, sub auspiciis D. Asselini, rerum gallicarum apud Aegyptios procuratoris, in linguam amharicam, vertit Abu Rumi Habessinus; edidit Th. Pell Platt, London, 1824.

[5] *Testamentum Novum* Domini Nostri . . . ed. Th. P. Platt, London, 1829.

complete Bible in 1840.[1] Thus a printed edition of the whole Bible existed in Amharic some eighty-five years before the same could be said for Gəˤəz. Moreover, an improved reprinting was carried out by L. Krapf and published in three volumes in 1871–3.[2] It is this edition which was used by F. Praetorius for his *Amharische Sprache* (p. 11), a work 'of which Semitic linguistics can be proud'.[3] Every edition of the Amharic Bible issued by the B. & F.B.S. has been based on Abu Rumi's version, and it was not until the appearance of the Emperor Bible (see presently) in 1960/1 that a new translation formed the basis of the publication of an Amharic Bible.

The Ethiopian, whose translation thus acquired a long and memorable life, possessed a 'perfectly Abyssinian countenance' (Jowett, p. 201). Abu Rumi was born in about 1750.[4] He left his country when he was about twenty-eight, visited Cairo and Jerusalem, traded in Syria, and went to India by way of Armenia and Persia. In India he resided in Sir William Jones's house and was said, by Asselin (p. 201), to have been Sir William's instructor. We are not told what he is supposed to have taught that great orientalist, but presumably it was a smattering of Gəˤəz and Amharic poetry. After a brief return to Ethiopia he went once more to Cairo where he was discovered, desperately ill, by M. Asselin. The Amharic translation of the Bible occupied him for ten years. Upon completion of this monumental labour he visited Jerusalem and died, shortly after his return to Cairo, of the plague—in about 1819. Abu Rumi did for Amharic and Bible studies what his compatriot Abba Gregory had done for the great Ludolf a century and a half earlier.

Abu Rumi's version, with some changes and amendments, held sway until the Emperor Haile Sellassie I ordered a new translation of the entire Bible which appeared in 1960/1. The emperor's preface to this work is dated 1955 and coincides with the silver jubilee of his accession to the throne. He describes the genesis and background of this work in terms which command attention

---

[1] *Biblia sacra amharice*, sub auspiciis D. Asselini . . . ed. T. P. Platt, London, 1840.

[2] The New Testament was reprinted in 1870, but the changes are confined to the Old Testament: *The Books of the Old Testament*, translated into the Amharic Language by Abba Rukh, an Abyssinian Learned. For the first time corrected and edited in England by the Revd. Thomas Platt. Now improved after the Hebrew Original by the Revd. Dr. Krapf in Germany. Printed at the expense and by the request of the B. & F.B.S. in London at the Mission-Press of St. Chrishona, near Basle, Switzerland, 1871–3. 3 vols.

[3] So H. J. Polotsky in his article 'Semitics' in *The World History of the Jewish People*, i. 107. Polotsky also refers ibidem to the Semitic languages of Ethiopia as an 'inexhaustible and exceptionally fascinating' field.

[4] Jowett reports (p. 201) that he was 'about 22 when he interpreted for Mr. Bruce at Gondar'.

and interest:[1] he first refers to the Gǝ'ǝz translation which was made 'at the time when Ethiopia received the Pentateuch in O.T. times and the Gospels in N.T. times'. Ethiopia thus possesses 'priority over most countries—as is attested by history —in accepting first the Old Testament and subsequently the New'. H.I.M. thus appears to adhere to the traditional notion (see p. 31, above) of the Old Testament having been introduced into Ethiopia first and that translation into Gǝ'ǝz took place simultaneously with the acceptance, respectively, of the Old Testament and the New Testament.

However, in the course of time Amharic came to replace Gǝ'ǝz, and knowledge of the classical tongue became increasingly confined to clerics, while ordinary people could no longer understand it. This state of affairs induced the emperor, so he explains, to commission—even while still regent and heir to the throne—a translation of the Holy Scriptures into Amharic to be carried out by scholars selected by him. He also imported, out of his own purse, printing presses from Europe and set up a printing establishment at Addis Ababa. When the task of translating had been accomplished and the new version was in the press, the Italo-Abyssinian war broke out and the work was held up indefinitely. After the liberation of Ethiopia the emperor set up a committee of experts to correct the Amharic version of the Scriptures and to collate it with the Hebrew and the Greek texts, respectively. This undertaking was carried out 'with care and accuracy', and the results were presented to H.I.M. in 1951/2.

I have not made a systematic comparative study of the 'Abu Rumi' and 'Emperor' translations, but from desultory reading of both versions the following picture seems to emerge: I can find no evidence that the new recension has been subjected to any perceptible collation with the Hebrew and Greek originals. The Amharic has certainly been modernized and 'up-dated'; the order of words, in particular, has been brought into conformity with contemporary stylistic tastes in Amharic. The use of Abu Rumi's text can be clearly discerned, even where the changes that have been introduced are by no means negligible.

The first known translation of any part of the Bible into Tigriña[2] is the rendering of St. John's Gospel commissioned, in

---

[1] The full Amharic text of the Imperial preface appears in photographic reproduction on p. 68.

[2] For the failure to distinguish between Tigriña and Tigre see Praetorius, *Tigriñasprache*, pp. 8–9; Ullendorff, *Semitic Languages of Ethiopia*, pp. 18–23, 227.

መቅድም ፨

ሞን ፣ አንበሳ ፣ ዘእምነገደ ፣ ይሁዳ ፨
ቀዳማዊ ፣ ኃይለ ፣ ሥላሴ ፣
ሥዮመ ፣ እግዚአብሔር ፣ ንጉሠ ፣ ነገሥት ፣ ዘኢትዮጵያ ፨

የክርስቲያን ፣ ደሌት ፣ የሆኑች ፣ ኢትዮጵያ ፣ አስቀ
ድሞ ፣ ብሉይ ፣ ኪዳንን ፣ ቀጥሎም ፣ ሐዲስ ፣ ኪዳንን ፣
በመቀበል ፣ ከአብዛኞቹ ፣ አገሮች ፣ ቀዳሚነት ፣ ያላት ፣
መሆንዋን ፣ በታሪክ ፣ እንዱ ፣ ተመሰከረ ፣ በመኖ ፣
ብሉይ ፣ ሕገ ፣ አሪትን ፣ በመኖ ፣ ሐዲስ ፣ ሕገ ፣ ወንጌልን ፣
በተቀበለች ፣ ጊዜ ፣ ቅዱሳት ፣ መጻሕፍት ፣ በጥንታዊ ፣
ቋንቋዋ ፣ በሕግ ፣ እንዲተረጐሙ ፣ አደረገች ፣ ከዚያም ፣
ወዲህ ፣ ለመንፈሳዊና ፣ ለሥ ጋግ ፣ አውቀት ፣ በ ቋ
ዎች ፣ የሆኑ ፣ አያሌ ፣ መጻሕፍት ፣ በየ ዚ ዜው ፣ የተደረ
ሱትና ፣ የተጻፉት ፣ በግዕዝ ፣ ቋንቋ ፣ ነው ፨ ጊዜ ውረ
ዘመኑ ፣ በሚፌ ቀ ደ ው ፣ መጠን ፣ በብዙ ፣ ትጋትና ፣ ድ ካም ፣
ሠር ተው ፣ ለ ዛ ግ ማ ኖች ፣ መ ጠ በቂ ያ ፣ ለተምሀር ትና ፣ ለአ
ውቀት ፣ ማሰፋ ፌ ያ ፣ የሚ ሆኑ ፣ መ ጻ ሕ ፍ ት ን ፣ ላ ቄ ዮ ል ን ፣
ለተ ድ ሞ ዎ ቹ ፣ አ ባ ቶ ች ፣ ከ ፍ ፣ ያ ለ ፣ ም ስ ጋ ና ፣ ይ ደ ረ ሰ
ቸ ው ፣ እ ያ ል ን ፣ እ ና ስ ታ ው ሰ ቸ ዋ ለ ን ፨

በፌተኞቹ ፣ ዘ መ ና ት ፣ ግ ዕ ዝ ፣ ያ ገ ረ ቱ ፣ ቋ ን ቋ ፣ ስ ለ ፣
ነ በ ረ ፣ ሕ ገ በ ሱ ፣ ያ ለ ፣ አ ስ ተ ር ጓ ሚ ፣ የ መ ጻ ሕ ፍ ት ን ፣ ም ሥ
ጢ ር ፣ ለ መ መ ር መ ር ና ፣ ለ መ ረ ዳ ት ፣ ቸ ግ ር ፣ አ ል ነ በ ረ
በ ት ም ፣ ነ ገ ር ፣ ግ ን ፣ ዘ መ ና ት ፣ በ ዘ መ ን ፣ ሲ ታ ደ ሱ ፣
እ ን ዲ ሚ ኖ ሩ ፣ ሁ ሉ ፣ ቋ ን ቋ ም ፣ በ ቋ ን ቋ ፣ መ ታ ደ ሱ ፣
ል ማ ዱ ፣ ስ ለ ፣ ሆ ነ ፣ ከ ግ ዕ ዝ ፣ የ ተ ወ ለ ደ ፣ አ ማ ር ኛ ፣ ቀ ስ ፣
በ ቀ ስ ፣ እ ያ ለ ፣ አ ድ ጎ ፣ ወ ዲ ያ ው ፣ የ ሕ ገ ቡ ፣ መ ነ ግ ገ ር ያ ፣
ሆ ነ ና ፣ የ ግ ዕ ዝ ን ፣ ስ ፍ ራ ፣ ወ ሰ ደ ፣ በ ዚ ህ ም ፣ ጊ ዜ ፣ የ ግ
ዕ ዙ ን ፣ ቋ ን ቋ ፣ ም ሁ ራ ን ፣ የ ሆ ኑ ት ፣ የ ቤ ት ፣ ክ ር ስ ቲ
ያ ን ፣ ሰ ዎ ች ፣ እ ን ጂ ፣ ተ ራ ው ፣ ሕ ዝ ብ ፣ በ ቀ ላ ል ፣ የ ማ
ያ ስ ተ ው ለ ው ፣ ሆ ነ ፨ ከ ዚ ህ ም ፣ የ ተ ነ ሣ ፣ ሊ ቃ ው ን ቲ ፣
የ ግ ዕ ቱ ን ፣ ቃ ል ፣ በ አ ማ ር ኛ ፣ እ የ ተ ረ ጐ መ ው ፣ በ ማ ስ ረ ዳ ት ፣
ሲ ሰ ብ ኩ ና ፣ ሲ ሠ ሩ ፣ ብ ዞ ፣ ዘ መ ና ት ፣ አ ለ ፋ ፣ ዶ ኸ ው ፣
ሁ ና ቱ ፣ እ ስ ከ ፣ እ ኛ ፣ ዘ መ ን ፣ ድ ረ ስ ፣ የ ነ በ ረ ፣ ነ ው ፨

በ እ ግ ዚ አ ብ ሔ ር ፣ ቸ ር ነ ት ፣ ለ ኢ ት ዮ ጵ ያ ፣ ዙ ፋ ን ፣
ከ ተ መ ረ ጥ ን ፣ ጀ ም ሮ ፣ ሕ ገ ባ ች ን ፣ በ ተ ም ህ ር ት ና ፣ በ አ
ው ቀ ት ፣ እ ን ዲ ያ ድ ግ ፣ ስ ን መ ረ ው ፣ በ መ ፌ ሳ ዊ ው ፣
በ ሥ ጋ ግ ም ፣ ት ም ህ ር ት ና ፣ እ ው ቀ ት ፣ እ ን ዲ ያ ድ ግ ፣ አ ስ
በ ን ፣ በ ተ ቻ ለ ን ፣ ሁ ሉ ፣ ደ ከ ም ነ ለ ት ፣ ወ ደ ዚ ህ ም ፣
ግ ብ ፣ ለ መ ድ ረ ስ ፣ አ ስ ቀ ድ ሞ ፣ ቅ ዱ ሳ ት ፣ መ ጻ ሕ ፍ ት ን ፣
በ አ ማ ር ኛ ፣ ማ ስ ተ ር ጐ ም ና ፣ አ ብ ዝ ቶ ፣ ማ ሰ ተ ም ፣ የ ሚ ያ
ስ ፈ ል ግ ፣ መ ሆ ኑ ን ፣ ስ ለ ፣ ተ ረ ዳ ን ፣ በ 1925 ፣ ዓ . ም . ግ ር ገ
በ አ ል ጋ ፣ ወ ራ ሽ ነ ት ና ፣ በ እ ን ደ ራ ሴ ነ ት ፣ ሳ ለ ን ፣ ከ ኢ ት
ዮ ጵ ያ ፣ ሊ ቃ ው ን ት ፣ መ ክ ክ ለ ፣ መ ር ጠ ን ፣ መ ጻ ሕ ፍ ት ን ፣
እ ን ዲ ተ ረ ጐ ሙ ፣ አ ደ ር ገ ን ፣ ን በ ቡ ን ፣ ከ ነ ማ ረ ኛ ው ፣
በ ት ር ጓ ሚ ፣ አ ስ ወ ጣ ን ለ ት ፣ ቀ ጥ ሎ ም ፣ በ ግ ል ፣ ገ ን ዘ ብ
ች ን ፣ ማ ተ ሚ ያ ፣ መ ኪ ና ፣ ከ አ ው ሮ ፓ ፣ አ ስ መ ጥ ተ ን ና ፣
ማ ተ ሚ ያ ፣ ቤ ት ፣ አ ቋ ቋ መ ን ፣ መ ጻ ሕ ፍ ቱ ን ፣ ማ ስ ተ ም ፣

ጀ መ ር ን ፨ በ ዚ ያ ን ፣ ጊ ዜ . በ ግ ዕ ግ ና ፣ በ አ ማ ር ኛ ፣ ያ ለ
ት ም ና ቸ ው ፣ ጥ ቂ ቶ ቹ ፣ መ ጻ ሕ ፍ ት ፣ በ አ ብ ያ ተ ፣ ክ ር ስ ቲ
ያ ና ት ና ፣ በ የ ሕ ዝ ቡ ም ፣ ቤ ት ፣ እ የ ተ ነ በ ቡ ፣ የ ነ ይ ማ ኖ ት ፣
ማ ጽ ኛ ፣ የ መ ን ፈ ሱ ፣ መ በ ረ ታ ቻ ፣ ሆ ነ ው ፣ ተ ገ ኝ ተ
ዋ ል ፨ ከ ዚ ያ ም ፣ በ ኋ ላ ፣ የ ሕ ገ ቡ ፣ አ እ ም ሮ ፣ በ ማ ስ ተ
ዋ ል ፣ እ ያ ደ ገ ፣ መ ሄ ዱ ን ፣ ተ መ ል ክ ተ ን ፣ በ ኢ ት ዮ ጵ ያ ፣
ቤ ት ፣ ክ ር ስ ቲ ያ ን ፣ ሥ ር ዓ ት ፣ ቋ ዳ ፣ (ቋ ወ ፅ ፋ .) ተ ብ
ለ ው ፣ የ ሚ ቄ ጠ ሩ ት ፣ የ ብ ሉ ይ ና ፣ የ ሐ ዲ ስ ፣ ኪ ዳ ን ፣ መ ጻ
ሕ ፍ ት ፣ በ ነ ጠ ላ ፣ ዘ ይ ቤ . በ አ ማ ር ኛ ፣ እ ን ዲ ተ ረ ጐ መ ው ፣
አ ደ ረ ግ ን ፨ ሊ ቃ ቀ ረ በ ል ን ፣ ት ር ጐ ሙ ን ፣ ፈ ጽ
መ ው ፣ በ1933 ፣ ዓ . ም . ስ ላ ቀ ረ በ ል ን ፣ እ ን ዲ ታ ተ ም ፣
አ በ ን ፣ መ ጽ ሐ ፉ ፣ በ ማ ተ ሚ ያ ፣ ቤ ት ፣ ስ ለ ፣ ያ1935
ዓ . ም ፣ የ ጠ ላ ት ፣ ወ ረ ራ ፣ የ ሥ ራ ው ፣ መ ሰ ና ክ ል ፣ ሆ ነ ፨
ይ ሁ ን ፣ እ ን ጂ ፣ በ ስ ደ ት ፣ ዘ መ ን ፣ ሉ ን ዶ ን ፣ ሳ ይ ፣ ሳ ለ ን ፣
ይ ሽ ው ፣ መ ጽ ሐ ፍ ፣ ቅ ዱ ስ ፣ በ ሮ ች ፣ አ ፍ ፣ ሴ ት ፣ እ ን ዱ ፣
ታ ተ ም ፣ ስ ለ ፣ ፈ ቀ ድ ን ና ፣ ታ ት ም ፣ ስ ለ ፣ ወ ጣ ፣ የ ኢ ት
ዮ ጵ ያ ን ፣ መ መ ለ ስ ፣ በ ተ ስ ፋ ፣ እ የ ተ ጠ በ ቁ ፣ በ ያ ኑ ፣ በ ስ
ደ ት ፣ የ ነ በ ሩ ት ፣ ኢ ት ዮ ጵ ያ ው ያ ን ፣ ዜ ጎ ች ን ፣ ዘ ጎ ች ን ፣ በ ዚ ህ ፣
መ ጽ ሐ ፍ ፣ ቅ ዱ ስ ፣ ሃ ይ ማ ኖ ታ ቸ ው ን ፣ እ ን በ ቁ ፣ ሁ ሉ ን ፣
ወ ደ ሚ ች ል ፣ አ ም ላ ክ ፣ ጸ ሎ ት ፣ ያ ቀ ር ቡ ብ ት ፣ ነ በ ር ፨

ለ እ ግ ዚ አ ብ ሔ ር ፣ ክ ብ ር ፣ ም ስ ጋ ና ፣ ይ ድ ረ ሰ ው ና ፣
የ ኢ ት ዮ ጵ ያ ን ፣ ነ ጻ ነ ት ፣ አ ስ መ ል ስ ን ፣ ከ ን ን ው ፣ ነ ገ ሥ ት ፣
መ ን ግ ሥ ታ ች ን ፣ ከ ገ ባ ን ፣ በ ኋ ላ ፣ የ መ ጽ ሐ ፍ ፣ ቅ ዱ ስ ፣
ት ር ጐ ም ፣ ከ መ ሠ ረ ታ ዊ ፣ ቋ ን ቋ ው ፣ ከ ዕ ብ ራ ይ ስ ጥ ና ፣
ከ ዕ ር ቆ ፣ ጋ ር ፣ እ የ ተ ያ የ ፣ ሊ ታ ረ ም ፣ እ ን ዲ ሚ ገ በ ው ፣
ስ ለ ፣ ተ መ ለ ክ ተ ን ፣ በ ቅ ዱ ሳ ት ፣ መ ጻ ሕ ፍ ት ፣ ት ም ህ ር ት ፣
ለ ዚ ህ ፣ ሥ ራ ፣ ተ ገ ቢ ፣ የ ሆ ኑ ት ን ፣ ሊ ቃ ው ን ት ፣ መ ር ጠ ን ፣
በ የ ካ ቲ ት ፣ ፳ ፯ ፣ ቀ ን ፣ 1939 ፣ ዓ . ም . እ ን ዴ ፣ የ መ ጽ
ሐ ፍ ፣ ቅ ዱ ስ ፣ ከ ሚ ቴ ፣ በ ቤ ት ፣ መ ን ግ ሥ ታ ች ን ፣ ግ ቢ ፣
እ ን ዲ ቋ ቋ ም ፣ አ ደ ረ ግ ን ፣ ከ ሚ ቴ ው ም ፣ ፮ ፣ ዓ መ ት ፣
ያ ሀ ል ፣ በ ት ጋ ት ና ፣ በ ቁ ን ነ ት ፣ ሠ ር ቶ ፣ በ ሚ ያ ገ ያ ፣ ፲ ፱
ቀ ን ፣ 1948 ፣ ዓ . ም . አ ቀ ረ በ ል ን ፨ በ ዚ ህ ፣ ሥ ራ ፣
ላ ይ ፣ ለ ረ ዱ ን ና ፣ ላ ገ ለ ገ ሉ ን ፣ ሁ ሉ ፣ ከ ል ብ ፣ የ ሆ ነ ፣ ም ስ
ጋ ና ፣ እ ን ሰ ጣ ቸ ዋ ለ ን ፨

በ መ ዳ ን ት ና ፣ መ ጻ ሕ ፍ ት ፣ በ ሚ ሰ ጡ ት ፣ መ ጽ ና
ና ት ፣ ተ ስ ፋ ፣ ይ ሆ ን ል ን ፣ ዘ ን ድ ፣ የ ተ ጻ ፈ ው ፣ ሁ ሉ ፣
ለ ት ም ህ ር ታ ች ን ፣ ተ ጽ ፎ ል ል ፣ ከ መ ጻ ሕ ፍ ት ም ፣ የ ሚ ገ
ኘ ው ፣ ብ ር ሃ ን ፣ ለ ሁ ሉ ፣ እ ን ዲ ያ በ ራ ፣ ስ ለ ፣ ተ መ ኘ ን ፣
ይ ህ ፣ መ ጽ ሐ ፍ ፣ ቅ ዱ ስ ፣ በ ኛ ፣ ት ክ ዛ ዝ ና ፣ ፈ ቃ ድ ፣
ታ ር ሞ ና ፣ ተ ዘ ጋ ጅ ቶ ፣ በ ጀ መ ኖ ፣ መ ን ግ ሥ ታ ች ን ፣ በ ሀ ይ ፣
አ ም ስ ተ ኛ ው ፣ ዓ መ ት ፣ ታ ተ መ ፨

ሐ ም ሌ ፣ ፲፱ ፣ ቀ ን ፣ 1948 ፣ ዓ . ም .
ቀ ዳ ማ ዊ ፣ ኃ ይ ለ ፣ ሥ ላ ሴ ፣ ን . ነ .

the 1830s, by Samuel Gobat.[1] It was written on paper, consists of 140 pages, and was given by E. Rüppell to the Frankfurt municipal library.[2] There are two Tña versions of the four Gospels (also made in the 1830s), both allegedly translated by Däbtära Matewos of Adwa, though Praetorius (*Tigriñasprache*, p. 10) has shown that they are marked by profound differences as 'zwei von einander ganz unabhängige Versionen'. The first manuscript was owned by E. Rödiger,[3] and the first chapter of St. John according to this version was printed in Praetorius' *Tigriñasprache*. The other manuscript (ወንጌል ፡ ቅዱስ ፡ ናይ ፡ ጉይታና ፡ ናይ ፡ መድኃኒትና ፡ ናይ ፡ የሱስ ፡ ክርስቶስ ፡ ብትግራይ ፡፡) is in the Berlin library[4] and contains the following note on the title-page: 'Die 4 Evangelien ins Tigrische übersetzt durch Debtera Mateos, revidirt durch C. W. Isenberg, Missionar in Adoa in Abessinien, in den Jahren 1836 u. 1837. Der Königl. Bibliothek in Berlin ehrfurchtsvoll geschenkt. C. W. I.' It is this version which underlies the Krapf edition of the Gospels of 1866.[5] And it is also this text which exists in manuscript in the B. & F.B.S. as part of the entire New Testament, Genesis, and Psalms.

The Frankfurt and Rödiger manuscripts, though independent of each other, have both been translated from a Gəʿəz original. Praetorius (*Tñaspr.*, p. 11) had no hesitation in arriving at this conclusion. The Berlin manuscript has been written in a European hand (Praetorius, op. cit., p. 10)—probably Isenberg's—though Dillmann, in his Berlin catalogue entry, does not refer to this fact but notes that the text is arranged in the European manner, without division into columns. Praetorius (p. 11) has also shown that 'der Version Berlin und Chrischona irgend ein europäisches Original zu Grunde lag'. Such European models were henceforth increasingly used and must be reckoned with in Amharic, Tigriña, and Tigre translations of the Bible.

Praetorius has established that the Frankfurt and Rödiger manuscripts are to such an extent under the influence of Ethiopic that they contain much that is quite alien to Tigriña proper. Not only do we encounter entire phrases in Gəʿəz as well as

---

[1] 1799–1879, later Bishop of Jerusalem.
[2] Rüppell, *Reise in Abyssinien*, ii. 408, erroneously thought that this was St. Luke's Gospel. It was, incidentally, the only composition in Tña seen by Rüppell. Cf. also L. Goldschmidt, *Abess. Handsch. . . . zu Frankfurt*, p. 22; Praetorius copied this manuscript when he worked on his *Tigriñasprache* (p. 10).
[3] 1801–74, a pupil of Gesenius. Cf. also my *Amharic Chrestomathy*, p. 3, note 4.
[4] See Dillmann's *Verzeichniss*, pp. 14–15 (MS. or. fol. 445).
[5] *Evangelia sacra . . . in linguam tigricam vertit Debtera Matheos Habessinus*, Adoae, Tigriae oppido, natus, nunc primum in lucem edita per J. L. Krapf . . . Basileae . . . in officina typographica Chrischonae. MDCCCLXVI.

chapter and section headings, but proper names appear in archaic forms, and pronominal suffixes and auxiliary verbs are used in an Ethiopic rather than a Tňa manner. In contrast, the Berlin and Chrischona texts reflect the language spoken in the region of Adwa[1] and appear to be a great deal more idiomatic.

I have not mentioned an earlier 'translation' of St. Mark and St. John into Tňa undertaken by Nathaniel Pearce[2] who had accompanied Henry Salt and lived in Ethiopia from 1805 to 1819. His rendering was written 'in English characters' and conforms with the notions of traditional English spelling.[3] It is a most singular composition written in an idiom of which Praetorius charitably said (*Tňasprache*, p. 12): 'vielleicht wird man denselben gar nicht mehr zum Tňa rechnen dürfen'. The *spiritus movens* behind Mr. Pearce's Tňa (and also Amharic) attempts was William Jowett who met Pearce while at Cairo in 1819 (*Christian Researches*, pp. 204–13):

. . . as it appeared desirable to have the greatest variety possible of specimens of Abyssinian Languages, it was resolved to employ Mr. Pearce in attempting both dialects, those, namely, of Amhara and Tigre. The Gospel of St. Mark was, in consequence, translated by him, from the English Version, into these two dialects; and subsequently he added that of St. John, in Tigre.[4] These three Versions are now in the possession of the British & Foreign Bible Society.

Jowett, despite his admiration for Pearce's talents, concedes that, since Abu Rumi's Amharic rendering has become available, Pearce's Gospel of St. Mark in Amharic 'may be considered as entirely superseded. It cannot even serve as a criterion by which to correct anything that may appear to us faulty in the Version of Abu Rumi; this latter having paramount claims to be esteemed as a Standard Version' (pp. 205/206). Jowett also maintains that 'had he [Pearce] possessed the advantages of a Classical Education, he would have combined many of the chief qualifications requisite in a Translator'.

One brief specimen of Pearce's Tňa translation (*St. Mark*, 4: 8):

[1] There is no Adwa dialect in the narrow sense, and the language spoken there has wide currency over the entire Tňa area. Cf. on this point my *Semitic Languages of Ethiopia, passim.*

[2] Cf. *The Life and Adventures of Nathaniel Pearce*, written by himself, London, 1831. See also items 146 and 2335 in Fumagalli; H. Salt, *Voyage to Abyssinia, passim.* Wright, *B.M. Catalogue*, ccccv; and *Sem. Langg. of Ethiopia*, p. 39, note 13.

[3] For a specimen of Pearce's Tňa 'orthography' see Wright, loc. cit., who calls Pearce 'an illiterate man, who had not studied the native languages scientifically'.

[4] i.e. Tňa.

Wer[1] calle woddock ov subbuck muddre, wer gebber

ወካልእ ወደቅ ኣብ ጽቡቅ ምድሪ ወገበረ

fruhe ter larl wer ter chummerhu; wer wolledhu

ፍሬ እተሳዐሰ ወተጨመሪ ወወሰደ

eddeta serlasser eddeta sidser wer eddeta merete.

ሕደታ ሠሳሳ ሕደታ ስድሳ ወሕደታ ምእቲ

This is, I think, about the most successful passage in Pearce's rendering;[2] I hope that my interlinear transcription into Tña corresponds to Pearce's intentions.

To revert to the mainstream of Tña Bible translations: the 1866 Krapf edition of the Gospels was not followed by a rendering of the entire New Testament until 1909 when Dr. C. Winquist of the Swedish Evangelical Mission and Aläk'a Täwåldä Mädhən of Aksum[3] collaborated on such a version.[4] The entire Tña Bible was published as recently as 1956: the Old Testament was printed by Petros Silla at Asmara and the New Testament by the Eritrean Government Press; both together were then printed by offset process in Great Britain.

The first instalment of the Scriptures in *Tigre* was printed in 1889 at the Swedish Mission Press at Monkullo,[5] some ten miles from Massawa. It was the Gospel of St. Mark and had been translated into Tigre by Täwåldä Mädhən and Dawit Emmanuel, under the supervision of Dr. C. Winquist. In 1902 the entire New Testament in Tigre was printed at the Swedish Mission Press at Asmara. It was the work of the same two indigenous scholars, now working under the guidance of K. G. Roden.[6] In this first edition of 1902 it is stated that it was translated 'dal Greco, basandosi specialmente sull'ultima versione Inglese ed anche Etiopica'. From perusal of this work it becomes quite clear that the English and Gə'əz versions were principally used for the Tigre translation. A second and improved edition (ካልእ፡ ሕታም፡ እፉም፡) was produced at Asmara in 1931 and was followed by some fifty pages of ተወስክ፡ ስሕዳስ፡ ገሰይ፡

---

[1] On the occurrence, in Pearce's rendering, of the conjunction ወ Praetorius (*Tñaspr.*, p. 12) had already remarked with astonishment.

[2] Cf. Jowett, p. 207.   [3] See J. Kolmodin, *MO* 1910/13, p. 236.

[4] A second and improved edition was printed by the Swedish Evangelical Mission at Asmara in 1933.

[5] *Evangelium enligt Markus på Tigre-Språket*, tryckt på Missionspressen i Monkullo, 1889, in 16°, 52 pp.

[6] The Swedish Missionary to whom we are indebted for the Tigre text and Italian translation of the history, law, and customs of the Mensa tribes (Asmara, 1913).

እግል ፡ ማርሐት ፡ ጸሎታት ፡ ቤት ፡ ክስታን ። 'appendix to the New Testament for the guidance and prayers of the Church'.

Two parts—and hitherto the only ones—of the Old Testament in Tigre, Psalms and Isaiah, were printed at the Swedish Mission Press at Asmara in 1925. In both, the Revd. G. R. Sundström[1] is stated to be the translator; the names of his indigenous assistants are not indicated.

The Gafat version of *Song of Songs* (Dillmann, *Bodleian Catalogue* XXIII = MS. Bruce 94) is more in the nature of a linguistic curiosity. Cf. W. Leslau, *Gafat Documents*, New Haven, 1945.

[1] 1869–1919. The 1925 Tigre edition of Psalms and Isaiah is posthumous. Cf. Littmann's obituary in *Der Neue Orient*, 1920 (reprinted in *Ein Jahrhundert Orientalistik*, Wiesbaden, 1955, pp. 26–30). Sundström was also the author of a Tigre grammar, the manuscript of which I inspected at Asmara in the early 1940s but which has still not been published. According to Littmann (loc. cit.), Sundström also left Tigre translations of Genesis and Exodus; these may conceivably be incorporated in the planned Tigre edition of the Bible.

II

THE IMPACT OF THE OLD TESTAMENT

Introductory

In the historical section of the Introduction we have seen how early Jewish influences, deep-rooted Old Testament practices, and a widespread *imitatio Veteris Testamenti* have combined to bring about the syncretistic nature of Ethiopian civilization. In the following it will be our task to examine certain selected facets of this civilization and to identify those which can be traced back to the world of the Old Testament.[1]

The present chapter is, therefore, devoted to a study of the impact of Hebraic and Old Testament elements on the peculiar form of indigenous Abyssinian Christianity. It does not aim at exhaustiveness, and the following notes are more in the nature of prolegomena to a fuller examination that ought to be undertaken in the future.[2] The present writer cannot claim expert knowledge in each of the dozen or so subjects to be touched upon in the ensuing investigation. It is hoped that specialists in the various fields will subject my summary observations to critical scrutiny and expand them in both extent and depth.

No doubt some of the connections to be studied here may, in some instances, turn out to be either fortuitous or to be part of the general Semitic heritage. In other cases, the parallels may seem too tenuous or, perhaps, capable of a different interpretation, but these hesitations scarcely detract from the need and value of such a pilot study. Travellers from the earliest times to the present day[3] have detected in Ethiopia and her people the

---

[1] Rathjens, *Juden in Abessinien*, pp. 42 ff., has discussed the view (expressed by Kromrei, *Glaubenslehre und Gebräuche der älteren abessinischen Kirche*, and some others) that the alleged Jewish influences in Ethiopia are, in fact, simply the common heritage of the old Christian Church. He goes on to show that 'die alttestamentlichen Relikte in dem Kultus der abessinischen Kirche nicht nur Erscheinungen sind, die in der altchristlichen Kirche überall vorhanden waren, sondern daß es sich um Beeinflussung des übernommenen christlichen Kultus durch Beibehaltung vorher vorhandener jüdischer Gewohnheiten handelt'.

[2] Such a study has also been demanded by M. Rodinson (*Bi Or*, 1964, p. 245, 1st col.). See above, p. 15, note 1, where I have paid tribute to the profound learning and gratifying urbanity of M. Rodinson's criticisms of my position as outlined in *JSS* 1956. The present chapter will take up, in a revised and expanded form, the points made in my 1956 article; it will also take account of M. Rodinson's observations without necessarily entering into detailed argument and debate at every juncture.

[3] In an article in *Encounter*, Feb. 1962, M. J. Lasky reports a conversation with a Jew living in Addis Ababa who told him *inter alia*: 'When I first came here—from Eastern Europe

authentic flavour of the Old Testament and thus—according to their view or bias—have praised or condemned them for it: 'In generale, chi esamina le credenze e le pratiche della chiesa abissina vi rivela maggiori punti di contatto col giudaismo. . . .'[1]

The Kebra Nagast

The *chef-d'œuvre* of Ethiopic literature is the *Kebra Nagast* ('Glory of the Kings') which has as its centre-piece the legend of the Queen of Sheba (based on the narrative in 1 Kings 10: 1–13 and liberally amplified and embellished), how she visited Solomon, accepted his religion, bore him a son (Menelik I), and how the son visited his father and abducted the Ark of the Covenant which was taken to Aksum, the new Zion. Chapter III will be devoted in its entirety to a study of this famous cycle of legends. In the present context we shall refer only to such aspects of the *Kebra Nagast* as can be discussed independently of the Sheba story.

Among the Magdala manuscripts in the British Museum were two copies of the *Kebra Nagast*, Oriental 818 and 819 (= Wright, *Catalogue*, cccxci), but Orient. 819,[2] written in the reign of Iyasu I (1682–1706), was returned to Ethiopia in circumstances which throw a dramatic light on the paramount importance of this work. The Emperor Yohannes of Ethiopia wrote to Earl Granville, the British Foreign Secretary, and requested the return of the *Kebra Nagast* which had been taken to England by the Napier expedition in 1868. According to Budge (*Queen of Sheba*, pp. xxxiv–xxxv),[3] the emperor's letter includes the following passage:[4]

—I was simply overwhelmed at how 'Jewish' everything was. Have you been to one of the traditional religious services—what does it remind you of if not a Sabbath morning in an orthodox *shul*! I found among the various Ethiopian amulets things very close to my own phylacteries and *mezuza*. I was exhilarated to discover the high holy days also falling in September, the Sabbath being celebrated on Saturday, and time reckoned from sunset . . .' (p. 24).

[1] Conti Rossini, *L'Abissinia*, p. 83.

[2] A short description of this manuscript was published in *ZDMG* xxiv. 614–15. See also Wright, *Catalogue*, p. 297, footnote.

[3] See also Budge's *Amulets and Talismans*, pp. 197–9.

[4] In fact, the Emperor Yohannes wrote two letters on the same day (8 Nahase 1864 = 14 [not 10 as Budge states] August 1872), one addressed to Queen Victoria and the other to Lord Granville. While some passages are virtually identical, there are nevertheless large parts of these letters which differ from each other considerably. The scribe who penned these two missives was remarkably careless leaving out letters and even numerals in the date. The language represents an interesting specimen of nineteenth-century Amharic with peculiarities that might well reflect the habits of the native speaker of Tigrinya. I hope to publish the originals of these two letters on an early occasion. They have never been accurately translated.

Since Budge published the following extract on several occasions and as many scholars copied it in good faith, I ought to mention that I have long had some doubt about the authenticity

Again there is a book called Kebra Nagast which contains the Law of the whole of Ethiopia; and the names of the chiefs, churches, and provinces are in this book. I pray you will find out who has got this book and send it to me, for in my country my people will not obey my orders without it.

The trustees of the British Museum complied with the emperor's request, and the manuscript was 'returned to the King of Ethiopia by order of the Trustees on Dec. 14th, 1872'.

Bezold[1] had already drawn attention, in 1905, to the need for a thorough examination of the literary sources of the *Kebra Nagast*, but fifty years were to elapse before this task was successfully accomplished in a mature and competent doctoral thesis by D. A. Hubbard.[2] Apart from numerous quotations and paraphrases from the Old and New Testaments, we find generous borrowings from apocryphal literature, the book of Enoch (of which, even after the discovery of Aramaic Dead Sea fragments, the Ethiopic version still offers the only complete text), the legend of the Pearl,[3] from the christological and patristic writings in Coptic, Syriac, Arabic, and Greek, from the *Testamentum Adami*,[4] from Jewish-Rabbinical literature as well as from parallels to material incorporated in the Qur'an.

When the *Kebra Nagast* was committed to writing, early in the fourteenth century, its purpose no doubt was to lend support to the claims and aspirations of the recently established Solomonic dynasty. Its author, the *nəburä 'əd* Yeshaq of Aksum, was thus mainly redactor and interpreter of material which had long been known but had not until then found a co-ordinating hand, an expository mind, and a great national need. The *Kebra Nagast* is not merely a literary work, but—as the Old Testament to the Hebrews or the Qur'an to the Arabs—it is the repository of Ethiopian national and religious feelings.

In the present context, however, we are only concerned with

---

of the final clause ('for in my country my people will not obey my orders without it'). Study of the original Amharic text has now shown that there is no Amharic phrase in those letters which would correspond to that 'translation'. The Public Record Office reference is F.O. 95/731, and I should like to acknowledge, gratefully, the courtesy of the P.R.O. officials.

[1] *Kebra Nagast*, p. xxxviii.

[2] St. Andrews University, 1956. Dr. Hubbard, who is now President of Fuller Theological Seminary in California, has unhappily still not prepared this work for publication. In a recent letter (Jan. 1967) he informs me, however, that he now expects to return to this task at an early date. Meanwhile, his thesis can be consulted in the University Library at St. Andrews.

[3] Cf. the gnostic story of the Pearl in chapter 68 of the *Kebra Nagast* as well as the *Life of Hanna*, ed. Sir E. A. W. Budge, pp. 86 ff. (= pp. 164 ff. of the translation). See also the references to the pearl in the Syriac *Hymn of the Soul*, ed. A. A. Bevan, p. 12. Cf. Bezold, *Kebra Nagast*, pp. xl–xli; Hubbard, op. cit., pp. 267 ff.; and especially Cerulli, *Lett.*, pp. 50–58.

[4] Cf. C. Bezold, 'Das arabisch-äthiopische Testamentum Adami', *Nöldeke Festschrift* (1906).

such of its elements as are traceable to Old Testament sources, forms, style, and genre. As the carriers of those influences we have to envisage both the Jews of South Arabia,[1] who are the obvious link between Old Testament and Rabbinic writings and their reflections in Qur'an and *Kebra Nagast*, and the profound tendency towards imitating Israel and the Old Testament—a trend which is strong among Ethiopians but is by no means confined to them. M. Rodinson has invited attention to

la conception de l'Église . . . comme successeur authentique d'Israël, comme *Verus Israel*, l'idée moins fréquente que les pratiques vétéro-testamentaires conservent leur validité pour les Chrétiens, l'idée enfin d'une connexion historique entre une communauté chrétienne donnée et Israël.[2]

A glance at the list of passages[3] from the Old and New Testaments quoted in the *Kebra Nagast* shows the vast preponderance of Old Testament references, and this indicates accurately the sediment of Hebraic lore which underlies this great storehouse of traditions and legends. It is, however, not only the contents with their Biblical and Rabbinical allusions, but especially the Midrashic form of narrative which is strongly reminiscent of Jewish literature. In chapter 13 of the *Kebra Nagast*, for instance, we encounter the story of Abraham selling his father's idols, making fun of them, and finally destroying them. This is clearly borrowed from the identical Midrash[4] and, as the Qur'an[5] shows, was probably a legend frequently told by the Jews of Arabia. Chapter 100, about the angels who rebelled, is no doubt connected with the concluding part of section 11 of *Midrash Deuteronomy Rabba*.[6] In addition to some direct borrowings and a greater number of indirect ones, we may thus detect in the *Kebra Nagast* the reflections of Hebraic motifs, style, genre, and above all of that elusive, yet very real, thing: literary atmosphere.

Hubbard (op. cit., pp. 14 ff.) has called the Old Testament the primary source of the *Kebra Nagast*, not only on account of the sheer bulk of the Old Testament material incorporated in it but also because of the strategic place it occupies in the struc-

---

[1] 'Des traditions juives ont donc pu traverser la Mer Rouge avec les marchands et les autres émigrants partis de la Judée . . . la fidélité aux coutumes judaiques et judéo-chrétiennes a duré jusqu'aux temps modernes . . .' (J. Deramey, *Revue de l'Histoire des Religions*, xxiv, 1891, 359–60).

[2] *JSS* 1964, pp. 17–18; *Bi Or*, 1964, p. 240.

[3] Budge, *Queen of Sheba*, pp. 242–3; Hubbard, op. cit., pp. 447 ff.

[4] *Midrash Haggadol on Genesis*, éd. Schechter, Cambridge, 1902, col. 189.

[5] *Surah*, xix. 42 ff.   [6] Cf. also Ginzberg, *Legends of the Jews*, v. 153 ff.

ture of the work: the Sheba cycle, the *tabot* cycle, the voluminous concatenations of prophecies beginning with chapter 102, the numerous typological interpretations—are all rooted in the Old Testament. These materials can be divided into quotations and references; the former reflect fairly accurately the text of the Ethiopic Old Testament, while the latter merely refer, with varying degrees of accuracy, to subjects treated in the Old Testament. There is no point in going once more over the ground which has been covered so competently by Hubbard whose study should soon appear in print.

A point of particular interest in the present context is the identity of the version from which the *Kebra Nagast* derives its quotations. A systematic study of this aspect might well be helpful for an elucidation of the problems discussed in the previous chapter, i.e. the translation of the Bible into Ethiopic, the *Vorlage* used, and the possible survival, in works like the *Kebra Nagast*, of pre-revision materials. Hubbard found that 'for all practical purposes' it may be said that the *Kebra Nagast* is not acquainted with any text of the Old Testament apart from that represented in da Bassano's Asmara Ethiopic Old Testament (p. 52). This verdict would corroborate da Bassano's claim of having made use of the oldest and best manuscripts available in Ethiopia (see above, pp. 59–60). The large number of quotations, especially from the Psalms, which agree verbatim (or virtually verbatim) with the da Bassano text, would appear to suggest some widely accepted text-model from a fairly early period. This question will, however, require more detailed study. The tendency of the *Kebra Nagast* to amplify, condense, or paraphrase makes it difficult—as Hubbard has pointed out—to subject to critical scrutiny the Old Testament text used by the *Kebra Nagast*.

Hubbard has rightly said (op. cit., pp. 53 ff.) that the Old Testament quotations in the *Kebra Nagast* fulfil two principal tasks: to serve as proof-texts and to play a didactic role. The former occur predominantly in chapters 102–11 where the Messianic office of Jesus is 'proved' from Old Testament prophecies. The latter can be observed particularly in chapters 40–42 where Zadok teaches Menelik the essentials of the law which is to be enforced in the kingdom of Ethiopia. Both show the high regard and the crucial importance which the Ethiopian Church attaches to the Old Testament.

The manner in which the *Kebra Nagast* uses Old Testament quotations is apt to be rather cavalier at times: passages may be altered to make them more suitable as proof-texts, and the context may be ignored for the sake of some superficial verbal resemblance. Hubbard finds that 'for the *Kebra Nagast*, as for the Alexandrian Fathers, the rabbinic tradition, and general Oriental practice, the text has tremendous elasticity. The meaning of a passage may be stretched to fit any subject the wording will bear' (op. cit., p. 55).

References to Old Testament material are, of course, even more numerous and pervasive than direct quotations. They are often woven into the fabric of the *Kebra Nagast* and appear as allusions to narratives, legal material, genealogies, and allegories. A good example of this type of reference is the story of Judah and Tamar (Gen. 38); this is embodied in the *Kebra Nagast*, chapter 77, which deals with the descent from Shem of the king of Persia. The connexion is established by the Septuagint transcription of Perez as *Fares* which leads to the rather far-fetched linking of Persia (*Fars*) with Perez (*Fares*). The Ethiopic Old Testament frequently follows the LXX forms of proper names. At times the *Kebra Nagast* conflates elements from disparate Old Testament stories: thus Lot's drunkenness (Gen. 19) is put together with Noah's (Gen. 9) to form one version in chapters 78–79. For further details see Hubbard, op. cit., pp. 61 ff.

It must not, of course, be thought that there are no New Testament quotations and references in the *Kebra Nagast*. There are, in fact, very many, but they are outnumbered by the Old Testament at a ratio of about 5 : 1 (according to Hubbard, op. cit., p. 111). The reasons for this Old Testament preponderance are not far to seek: the Queen of Sheba cycle, the central narrative of the *Kebra Nagast*, is derived from the Old Testament, at least in its basic features. The Old Testament is the ambience of the Solomonic legend and dynasty, of the Ark of the Covenant, and of most of the framework within which its characters move. Also, while the *Kebra Nagast* uses its New Testament material in an orthodox way in conformity with the accepted contextual interpretation, it allows much greater freedom in its treatment of the Old Testament; hence the Old Testament offers far more scope and literary usefulness and latitude for the compilers of the *Kebra Nagast*. Moreover, Hubbard avers that the Semitic affinities of the Ethiopian Church predispose it somewhat towards the Old Testament and its *Weltanschauung*:

There can be little doubt that the Ethiopians were acquainted with substantial portions of the O.T. before they knew anything about the N.T. This early deposit of O.T. material on Ethiopian soil is reflected in the vast preponderance of O.T. quotations and references, especially in the collections of O.T. commandments (op. cit., p. 112).

Magic

One of the most notable features in Abyssinian Christianity is the survival of magical practices and prayers as well as a whole body of superstitious beliefs.[1] Many of these magical prayers combine their pagan substratum with a hastily and belatedly superimposed layer of divine invocations or references to the Virgin Mary and the Saints. It is likely that the majority of superstitious and magical practices are derived from the old Cushitic pagan beliefs, but there are indications also of a different kind. Demonology and magic were widespread in the ancient East (and elsewhere), and in most cases it is quite impossible to determine any precise national origin. A very large body of magical craft, contrivances, and prayers was common to most peoples of the ancient Semitic world. Even so, a few hints may here be thrown out where it seems possible to detect some specifically Hebraic and Old Testament elements.[2] How serious a danger sorcery, witchcraft, and magic constituted in the religion of the Hebrews may be gathered from Leviticus 20: 6. There is little doubt that many magical practices formed so integral a part of the pagan folklore of Canaan that they were taken over into the Hebrew religion and given a fresh and sublimated significance.[3] One need, in this connection, think only of the *Urim* and *Thummim*,[4] phylactery,[5] and *məzuza*.[6] The last two, being the literal interpretation of the command in Deuteronomy 6: 8–9, were originally no doubt meant to avert demons and other evil spirits and may be compared to the amulets worn by Ethiopians for the same purpose.

Amulets and *təfillin*, shield of David, and seal and net of Solomon are accompanied, among both Hebrews and Ethiopians, by spells to scatter demons (שׁדים–አጋንንት) and to avert disease. The

[1] Cf. Strelcyn's important *Prières magiques éthiopiennes* and the literature cited there; also his 'Quelques éléments du vocabulaire magique éthiopien' in *GLECS* v. 41–45; Budge, *Amulets and Talismans*; W. H. Worrell, 'Studien zum abess. Zauberwesen', *ZA* 1910; D. Lifchitz, *Textes éthiopiens magico-religieux*; Hammerschmidt, *Kultsymbolik*, pp. 232–3. See also the literature referred to by M. Rodinson in *Bi Or*, 1964, p. 240.

[2] M. Rodinson, whose knowledge of magic, the *zar* cult, etc., is unrivalled, thinks that even these clearly expressed reservations do not take sufficient account of the fact that 'il s'agit d'un fond commun, d'usages répandus dans tout le monde hellénistique oriental . . .' (*Bi Or*, 1964, p. 240).

[3] Cf. Benzinger, *Hebräische Archäologie*³, pp. 188–9.
[4] Cf. Benzinger, op. cit., pp. 344–5; de Vaux, *Ancient Israel*, p. 352.
[5] Benzinger, op. cit., p. 377; Lifchitz, op. cit., pp. 2–3.
[6] Benzinger, op. cit., p. 383. Cf. also Isa. 57: 8.

long list of illnesses is headed, in Hebrew as well as Ethiopian tradition, by diseases of the eye (שברירי–ሕማም፡ ፱፻፸፡). The importance of עין רעה–ዐይን፡ እኪት፡ need not be underlined. In Tigre *ta'ayyana* means 'to be obsessed, to become mad'. Wərzəlya,[1] the nighthag, is the most formidable female demon; she causes abortion and destroys children. That she is closely related to, and possibly derived from, Lilith, the night demon of the Hebrews, can scarcely be in doubt.

In post-Biblical times *Gematria* and *Notarikon* are the vehicles of magical calculations: and from here we get the disposition of letters in magic squares, the special patterns, the secret charms— all widespread in Ethiopia.[2] There is little doubt that the shield of David and the seal of Solomon have a similar origin. Among the countless magical names and words in use in Ethiopia *El*, *Elohe*, *Adonay*, etc., occur frequently.[3] Ludolf (loc. cit.) goes so far as to assert that 'tota ista detestabilis scientia a Judaeis originem habet . . .' and claims that Kabbalistic doctrines and practices brought about the abundance of magic and demons in Ethiopia.[4]

If this is, perhaps, a slightly extravagant assertion, Ludolf is on safe ground when he mentions the extraordinary importance Jews and Ethiopians alike attach to the effect of 'name'.[5] Of course, this is a general and widespread phenomenon, but there are certain features which may be held to be peculiar to Old Testament and Abyssinian folklore. To both, knowledge of the name means power over the person or the spirit. This is, of course, well known from the Old Testament: cf. Genesis 32: 30; Exodus 3: 13–14, 20: 7, etc. It appears that of all the sources, Near Eastern and African, which have left their imprint in Ethiopia the Old Testament impact has been the most powerful and enduring. One need only think of the command not to mention God's name in vain or the edict against mentioning 'out of thy mouth' the name of any other god (Exod. 23: 13). 'Tout les courants mystiques formés dans le monde hellénistique grâce au formidable brassage des croyances judéo-araméennes, grecques

---

[1] Budge, op. cit., p. 182.

[2] Cf. Strelcyn, op. cit.; Budge, op. cit.; and the very large number of magical manuscripts listed in Strelcyn, *Catalogue des MSS. éth.* (coll. Griaule), vol. iv, *passim*; Ullendorff, *Catalogue of Eth. MSS. in the Bodl. Libr.*, vol. ii, section E.

[3] Cf. Ludolf, *Commentarius*, p. 350; Littmann, *Gesch. d. aeth. Lit.*, p. 237.

[4] It is, of course, beyond the scope of this section to trace in detail the manifold points of resemblance between Hebraic-Old Testament and Ethiopian magical practices. The subject will need to be taken up by someone more versed in the field of magic than the present writer can claim to be.

[5] *Historia*, lib. iii, cap. iv.

et égyptiennes, ont hérité le culte du nom caché.'[1] The Qur'an, which is of course a product of the same tradition, says: 'To Allah belong the most beautiful names; so call upon Him by them, and pay no attention to those who make covert hints in regard to His names . . .' (*Surah* vii. 179).[2]

In Ethiopia, belief in the magical significance of the name is popular, widespread, and powerful. Knowledge of the name of a disease or of an evil spirit means power over them: 'connaître les noms cachés de Dieu, c'est acquérir en quelque sorte une parcelle du pouvoir divin.'[3] In some regions in Ethiopia children are given two sets of names, one for ordinary use and a secret one. The latter is being revealed to them only at a time when these children are able to protect themselves against the evil effects of magic.[4] When Jacob wrestles with God, in Genesis chapter 32, he does so in order to obtain knowledge of the divine name.

Apart from those already mentioned (*Adonay*, *Elohe*, etc.), there are many magical names in Ethiopia which have an obvious Hebrew origin and which can often be recognized despite the changes and distortions, frequently intentional, they have undergone. The element -*el* occurs as a component with great frequency. The linguistic composition of these *'asmat* has, to my knowledge, not yet been studied systematically, but they have been assembled by Strelcyn, op. cit., pp. 411–80, where they can be conveniently examined. Some random samples:

ሐናኤል፡	חנאל	ቤቴል፡	בית אל
ሳባ፡	Strelcyn compares *eli, eli, lama sabakhtani*		
መራኤል፡	מרעאל	አማኑኤል፡	עמנואל
መናኤል፡	מניאל	አዝርያል፡	עוריאל
ሱራፌል፡	סרפיאל	የሁኤል፡ (የሁኤል)	יהואל
ሼማሽ፡	שמש	ዳንኤል፡	דניאל
ሸማኤል፡	שמעיאל	ጹርኤል፡	צוריאל
በትሬ፡ ኤል፡	בתריאל	ፀባኦት፡	צבאות
	አኽየ፡ ሸራኽየ፡	אהיה אשר אהיה	

Other names are no doubt derived from the ancient Cushitic lore, but all have been brought into harmony, at least superficially, with the requirements of Christianity. However pagan the spirit may be, *Maryam*, *Krestos*, etc., are rarely missing. Christ himself has become the greatest of magicians, but he is closely

---

[1] Strelcyn, *Prières magiques*, p. xxviii.
[2] See *al-Asmā' al-ḥusnā* in *Encyclopaedia of Islam*[2].
[3] Strelcyn, op. cit., p. xxix.
[4] Littmann, *Gesch. d. aeth. Lit.*, p. 236.

C 5377   G

followed by Moses (cf. the miracles related in the Pentateuch) and by Solomon. Budge has remarked that according to Ethiopian tradition

the Abyssinians abandoned their pagan cults and all their various magical practices at the command of the Queen of Sheba who, under the influence of Solomon's teaching, had embraced Judaism, but this ... only means that they exchanged native for Judaic systems of magic. Solomon's power of working magic was, they thought, greater than that of any Abyssinian magician, and with the acceptance of Solomon's God, they adopted much that appertained to Hebrew magic and sorcery.[1]

Apart from magical names, there exist large numbers of words which are supposed to possess magical properties. They are either nonsense-creations or imaginary foreign words, especially k'alat əbrayəst or k'alat arabi.[2]

Of a very different kind is the technical vocabulary of Ethiopian magic. This, too, has been investigated by Strelcyn in a fine article[3] from which most of the following examples have been drawn:

dgm (Gə'əz and Amharic) 'to repeat, to whisper incantations'—lḥš (Hebr. and Aram.) 'to whisper incantations';
rgm (Gə'əz) 'to curse'—rgm (Hebr.) 'to stone, to imprecate';
ḥrm (Gə'əz, Hebr., Aram., Mand. ḥrm) 'to anathematize';
'sr (Gə'əz, Aram., Mand.) 'to bind by spells and charms';
ḥtm (Gə'əz)—ḥtm (Aram.) 'to seal' (in the magical sense); cf. also Mand. hatamta 'seal';
ftḥ (ptḥ) 'to untie, to absolve'.

The Ark of the Covenant

The Ark of the Covenant (Gə'əz tabot) which, the Kebra Nagast alleges,[4] was stolen from Jerusalem has formed the centrepiece of the Ethiopian Church service since time immemorial. The word tabot ('Noah's ark; the Ark of the Covenant; tablets of the Law') is derived, like تابوت, from Jewish Pal. Aramaic tēḇūtā (tēḇōtā) which in turn is a derivative of Hebrew tēḇāh.[5] The concept and function of the tabot represent one of the most remarkable areas of agreement with Old Testament forms of worship.

[1] History of Ethiopia, p. 582.
[2] Cf. Strelcyn, op. cit., p. xxxi.
[3] GLECS v. 41–45 (23 Nov. 1949).   [4] Chapters 48 ff.
[5] Cf. the detailed discussion in Rabin, Ancient West Arabian, pp. 109–10; Nöldeke, Neue Beiträge, pp. 37, 49; Polotsky, JSS 1964, p. 6; Rodinson, GLECS ix. 64–68 (28 Nov. 1962) which contains a most important discussion of the issues involved as well as a detailed critique of the views expressed by me in JSS 1956, pp. 233 ff.

Abu Ṣāliḥ (early thirteenth century) had already observed[1] that

the Abyssinians possess also the Ark of the Covenant, in which are the two tables of stone, inscribed by the finger of God with the commandments which he ordained for the children of Israel. The Ark of the Covenant is placed upon the altar, but is not so wide as the altar; it is as high as the knee of a man, and is overlaid with gold; and upon its upper cover[2] (غطاه الفوقاني) there are crosses of gold; and there are five precious stones upon it, one at each of the four corners, and one in the middle. The liturgy is celebrated upon the Ark four times in the year, within the palace of the king; and a canopy is spread over it when it is taken out from its own church to the church which is in the palace of the king: namely on the feast of the great Nativity, on the feast of the glorious Baptism, on the feast of the holy Resurrection, and on the feast of the illuminating Cross. And the Ark is attended and carried by a large number of Israelites descended from the family of the prophet David. . . . In every town of Abyssinia there is one church, as spacious as it can possibly be.

This description clearly shows the marked resemblance to the Old Testament Ark of the Covenant;[3] one need only compare such passages as Exodus 25: 10–22; 37: 1–9 or Deuteronomy 10: 8 where the honour of carrying the Ark is entrusted to the Levites. It is called the Ark of the Covenant because it contained the 'tablets of the Covenant' (luḥoṯ habbrīṯ).

The theme of the *tabot* is one of great prominence throughout the *Kebra Nagast*.[4] It serves as guarantor of the legitimacy of the Solomonic dynasty whose prestige is safeguarded by the transfer of the Ark from Jerusalem to Aksum. Chapters 103–4 of the *Kebra Nagast* stress the importance of the *tabot* as the focal point of Ethiopian worship[5] and appear to rebut criticisms levelled against the Ethiopians on account of their *tabot*-centred worship. Another important link between the first Zion (Jerusalem) and the second (Aksum) is the party of Israelites who accompanied the Ark and who, like the Levites, had the honour of carrying it (according to Abu Ṣāliḥ). 'Zion' is, in fact, the usual name given to the Ark by the *Kebra Nagast*:

Whereas in the O.T. Zion, the mount of God's holiness, is His special habitation, in the *Kebra Nagast* the Ark is the place of God's dwelling

---

[1] *Churches and Monasteries of Egypt*, ff. 105b, 106a. Arabic text on p. 133. See also p. 26, above.
[2] Evetts translates this as 'lid'.
[3] Cf. de Vaux, *Ancient Israel*, pp. 297 ff.
[4] Cf. Hubbard, op. cit., pp. 325 ff.
[5] Hubbard, op. cit., p. 327.

whether it is located in Jerusalem or Aksum. Hence, to the Ethiopians
Zion is not primarily a geographical location but is rather the name of
God's dwelling place localized by them in terms of the Ark.[1]

Ludolf (*Historia*, iii. 6, 62), after describing the *mänbär* 'table',
continues: 'Huic imponuntur sacra vasa, imprimis ፇባት Arca.
Tabella sic dicta. Cuius appellationis rationem, cum nusquam
reperiam, quia nihil commune cum arca habet; est enim tabula
quadrangularis oblonga. . . .' Ludolf's difficulty in explaining
how the tablets of wood or stone can be called *tabot* 'ark' appears to be shared by some scholars to this day. Dillmann (*Lexicon*) and Guidi (*Vocabolario Amarico*) provide two entries under
tabot: (1) The Ark of Noah and the Ark of the Covenant;
(2) 'pietra d'altare; è propriamente una tavoletta di pietra o di
legno duro come ebano, che si pone sull'altare . . .'.

I do not think there is any real difficulty here: the genuine
Ark is supposed to rest at Aksum; all other churches can only
possess replicas. In most cases they were not, however, replicas
of the whole ark but merely of its supposed contents, i.e. the
tablets of the Law or the Covenant. The description of these
stone or wooden tablets as *tabotat* would appear to be by way of
a *pars pro toto* referring to the most important part of the Ark, the
tables of the Covenant.[2] That the Ark contained these *luḥot
habbrīt* is, of course, expressly stated in Deuteronomy 10: 1–5,
1 Kings 8: 9, Hebrews 9: 4, etc.

It is this identification of the *tabot* with the tables of the Law
contained in the Ark that has incurred M. Rodinson's criticism.[3]
I have studied M. Rodinson's views with great care, but I cannot see that they differ, in any important and decisive aspect,
from the basic proposition which I have advanced. Thus I have
no great difficulty in assenting to at least the substance of M.
Rodinson's position as summarized in *Bi Or*, 1964, p. 243:

Il paraît donc clair que l'assimilation de la table d'autel chrétienne
à l'Arche de l'Ancien Testament, absurde du point de vue de la forme,
est une innovation due à un courant idéologique qui cherchait à faire de
l'Éthiopie un *verus Israel*, à la constituer héritière des privilèges du
peuple élu, transmission symbolisée par le passage en Éthiopie du pal-
ladium central des Hébreux.

[1] Hubbard, op. cit., p. 338.
[2] 'Das Tabot par excellence ist die alttestamentliche Bundeslade, die sich in Aksum
befinden soll; dann aber hat jeder Heilige sein eigenes Tabot (in Kasten- oder Plattenform),
das als sein Wohnsitz gedacht wird. . . . In größeren Kirchen pflegt man auch einen Altar
aufzumauern und eine wirkliche Lade daraufzustellen. Die gewöhnlichen Tabotat jedoch
sind einfache Holzplatten mit eingeschnitzten Verzierungen . . .' (Littmann in German
Aksum Expedition, iii. 47).   [3] *GLECS* ix. 64–68; *Bi Or*, 1964, p. 243.

I have no doubt that M. Rodinson is right in assigning to the altar table, in Christian worship, the function of the Old Testament Ark, but it seems to me that the *tabot* has an even closer parallel in Old Testament as well as in later Jewish worship: The Hebrew synagogue, as the Tent (Num. 9: 15) and the Temple (1 Kings 6: 19; 8: 1–9) before it, has the Ark (תיבה, ארון, תיבותא) as its principal item of furniture.[1] Inside the Ark were the tablets of the Covenant in Old Testament times, and in the post-Biblical era it contains the scrolls of the law. 'An ihrem Oberbau sind in der Regel die beiden Gesetzestafeln angebracht. . . .'[2] It seems to me more than likely that the *tabot* symbolizes the tablets of the Covenant and the scrolls of the law. The manner in which the *tabotat* are carried in procession around the churches[3] is strongly reminiscent of the carrying of the Torah scrolls, especially at *Simḥaṯ Tora*.[4]

M. Rodinson's objection that 'les tables de la Loi ne sont pas une décoration obligatoire, ni permanente des armoires synagogales'[5] is, of course, correct (though one would be hard put to find a synagogue without the two ornamental tablets of the Law), but my point is that the *tabot* represents the contents of the Ark, i.e. the tablets of the Covenant in Old Testament times and the scrolls of the Law in the post-Biblical period. The treatment of the *tabot* and its function within the church underline the aptness and cogency of this parallel. 'It is the *tabot* and not the church building which is consecrated by the bishop and gives sanctity to the church in which it is placed.'[6] The same is true of the Tent and the Temple[7] as well as the synagogue in which, for the purposes of public worship, there was only one essential requirement: the *Teba* or *Aron*.[8]

The veneration accorded to the *tabot* in Abyssinia[9] up to the present day, its carriage in solemn procession accompanied by singing, dancing, beating of staffs or praying sticks (መቋምያ), rattling of sistra, and sounding of other musical instruments remind one most forcefully of the scene in 2 Samuel 6: 5, 14–16, where David and the people are dancing around the Ark.[10] The entire spectacle, its substance, its atmosphere, and its musical

---

[1] See I. Elbogen, *Der Jüdische Gottesdienst*[2], pp. 469 ff.   [2] Elbogen, op. cit., p. 471.
[3] See pl. 32 in Buxton's *Travels in Ethiopia*.
[4] So already Ludolf (*Commentarius*, p. 381).   [5] *GLECS* ix. 66.
[6] Trimingham, *Islam in Ethiopia*, p. 27; Hyatt, *Church of Abyssinia*, p. 121.
[7] Cf. De Vaux, *Ancient Israel*, pp. 297, 299.
[8] Cf. Elbogen, op. cit., pp. 469 ff.
[9] 'The *Sanctum Sanctorum* is the receptacle of the ark, an object of the profoundest veneration, and again of evident Jewish origin' (Parkyns, *Life in Abyssinia*, p. 291).
[10] See also pp. 2–3, above.

instruments, has caused all who have witnessed it to be 'in die Zeiten des Alten Testaments zurückversetzt . . .'.[1]

As had already been shown by Ludolf in the passage quoted above, the *tabot* is placed on the *mänbär* 'seat' or 'throne'. This term is, of course, well known as the *minbar* or *mimbar* of the mosque and is an Ethiopic loanword in Arabic (cf. Nöldeke, *Neue Beiträge*, p. 49). From Arabic it was taken over into the terminology of Jewish worship as *Almemor* which is a corruption of *al-mimbar*. In Biblical times this elevated place was called *migdal* (Neh. 8: 4); in post-Biblical days it is *dukan* or *bimah* (βῆμα).[2]

E. Hammerschmidt (*Kultsymbolik*, pp. 216–17) mentions a description of the *tabot* by the late S. Euringer based on information supplied to him by G. Graf. Euringer notes[3] that the *tabot* ('im weiteren Sinne') possesses

> die Form eines Kastens mit Fächern, die mittels Flügeltüren ver-schließbar sind. Das mittlere Querbrett dient als Altartisch, während die zwei unteren Fächer Aufbewahrungsort für liturgische Geräte sind. Auf diesem Altartisch liegt das eigentliche Kleinod, das eigentliche Heiligtum, die Altartafel, der Tabot im vollen und hauptsächlichen Sinne. . . . Deshalb führt das Gehäuse, der Tabernakel, in dem er thront, den Namen *manbara tabot*, d. i. 'Thron des Tabot'. Der Thron ist mit Vorhängen, die man je nach den Kirchenzeiten und Teilen der Liturgie auf- und zuziehen kann,[4] wie mit einem Zelte umgeben, was an das Bundeszelt über der Bundeslade mit den Gesetzestafeln in der Wüste Sinai erinnert und erinnern soll. Diese Vorhänge heißen mit einem amharisch konstruierten Ausdruck jamanbar lebes [*yämänbär ləbs*], 'Verkleidung des Thrones' (äthiop. *manṭolā'et*).

Hammerschmidt adds that Euringer has established that 'der Tabot im engeren Sinne (also die Tafel) nach Zweck und Form dem abendländischen Altarstein, altare portabile, gleicht'. And, similarly, Rodinson finds that 'le caractère sacré de l'autel fixe latin réside dans sa table de pierre qui le communique à sa base tandis que l'autel mobile (la pierre d'autel) le garde exclusive-ment. Ce caractère sacré résidant essentiellement dans une partie mobile de l'autel est donc général dans le christianisme.'[5]

The fact that this is a widespread phenomenon in Christianity does not, of course, preclude the existence of a very special

---

[1] Rathjens, *Juden in Abessinien*, p. 48. See also Bent, *Sacred City*, pp. 55–57; and pls. 29, 30, and 32 in Buxton's *Travels*.

[2] Elbogen, op. cit., p. 473.

[3] Hammerschmidt derives this from Euringer's unpublished papers (*Kultsymbolik*, p. 216, note 32).

[4] Exactly as is the practice in the synagogue.   [5] *GLECS* ix (1962), p. 67.

relationship between the *tabot* and the Old Testament Ark of the Covenant. It is, in fact, a prominent part of what Rodinson justly calls 'cette tendance à l'imitation de l'Ancien Testament'.[1]

Church building

Ethiopia is a country of churches[2] and monasteries. Some of the latter have played a significant part in the cultural, ecclesiastical, and political development of the country. Among the most ancient and famous are Debra Damo[3] and St. Stephen on an island in Lake Hayq. Debra Libanos[4] and Debra Bizen[5] have at times wielded great influence, while some of the churches on the islands in Lake Tana have a beauty and romantic remoteness all their own. The rock-hewn churches of Lalibela[6] have long been acknowledged as celebrated masterpieces of Ethiopian architectural art.

The number of churches is immense, and their size varies from the little round village churches, usually perched upon a hill, to large rectangular and octagonal buildings or modern cathedrals built in most of the major centres of the Ethiopian empire. The rectangular churches are generally older, while the round[7] ones are considerably more numerous. The most famous rectangular sanctuary is that of St. Mary of Zion at Aksum[8] which has been known since the sixth century.

The way in which Ethiopian churches are traditionally constructed appears to be derived from the threefold division of the Hebrew temple. That had already been recognized by Ludolf:

> Quippe prisci Christiani, cum primum facultatem nacti sunt aedes ad usum sacrorum publicum aedificandi, Judaeos quam gentiles imitari satius rati, ad exemplum prisci templi Hierosolymitani, vel synagogarum Judaicarum eas construxere. . . .[9]

In his *Commentarius* (pp. 365 ff.) Ludolf speaks in some detail *de ritibus antiquis Christianorum a Judaeis derivatis* and also deals with the construction of Ethiopian churches on the model of the

---

[1] *Bi Or*, 1964, p. 243. See also Mercer, *Ethiopic Liturgy*, p. 152, note 15; and especially the excellent photographs in vol. iii of the German *Aksum Expedition*, pl. viii and ix.

[2] 'As for their religion, they are . . . Christian rather in profession than in practice, many of their observances being clearly Jewish. Their very churches . . . remind one of the altars and temples spoken of in the Old Testament, not only from their being mostly built on high places, and surrounded by groves, but also from their internal construction' (Mansfield Parkyns, *Life in Abyssinia*, pp. 289–90).

[3] See S. Pankhurst, *Cultural History*, pl. xxii.   [4] See ibid., pl. clvi.

[5] See Ullendorff, *The Ethiopians*, pl. ixb.

[6] See the excellent illustrations (but *not* the text!) in I. Bidder, *Lalibela*, London, 1959.

[7] See Hammerschmidt, *Symbolik, Tafelband*, p. 89.

[8] See Doresse, *Au pays de la reine de Saba*, p. 17.   [9] Ludolf, *Historia*, iii. 6, 19.

Hebrew temple (pp. 366 ff.). Rathjens (op. cit., pp. 48–50) emphasizes that the threefold arrangement of Ethiopian churches, universal and irrespective of size and period, follows the similar division of the Jerusalem Temple. And von Lüpke and Littmann (German *Aksum Expedition*, iii. 47 ff.) state that the Ethiopian church building 'umschließt in ihrer Grundgestalt drei Räume und folgt damit der Gliederung des altjüdischen Tempels, wie auch der abessinische Ritus noch stark mit jüdischen Bestand-teilen durchsetzt ist'.

These respectable and independent authorities would appear to warrant that the present writer's views on the relationship between the internal layout of the Ethiopian church building and that of the Hebrew Temple (first voiced in *JSS* 1956, pp. 235–6) do not represent so singular a quirk as M. Rodinson's important, and by no means captious, strictures (*Bi Or*, 1964, p. 243) might imply. It is, of course, true that both the threefold arrangement and its terminology are matters of the greatest complexity: cultural influences are rarely one-sided and straight-forward phenomena. But in the present case both the specific evidence and the general Hebraic background seem to favour a large measure of dependence on the Old Testament model.

The outside ambulatory of the three concentric parts of the round church or the vestibule, lobby, or porch of the rectangu-lar church is called *qəne maḥlet*, i.e. the place where hymns are sung and where the *däbtära* or cantors stand. To this part the populace at large has ready access. This outer part corresponds to the *ḥāṣer* of the Tabernacle or the *'ulām* of Solomon's Temple. The next chamber is the *qəddəst* or *'ənda ta'amər* ('place of miracles') which is generally reserved for priests but to which laymen have access for the administration of communion. This is equivalent to the *qodeš* of the Tabernacle or *hēkāl*[1] of the Solomonic Temple. The innermost part is the *mäqdäs* or *qəddusä qəddusan* where the *tabot* rests and to which only senior priests and the king are admitted. This corresponds, of course, to the *qodeš haqqodāšīm* of the Tabernacle and the *dəbīr* of the Temple.[2] This room is carefully guarded, and by its subdued light or virtual darkness the air of awe and mystery is greatly accentuated.

---

[1] Contrary to what M. Rodinson says (*Bi Or*, 1964, p. 243), I have *not* commented on the complex history of this term. In fact, I have referred to the Solomonic *hēkāl* (*JSS* 1964, p. 235; *The Ethiopians*, p. 109) without even mentioning the Ethiopic *haykal* (cf. Nöldeke, *Neue Beiträge*, p. 32) and the connexion between these words. See also Ludolf, *Comm.*, p. 367.

[2] Cf. Exod. 26: 33; 1 Kings 6; Ezek. 40, 41. See also the sketch in Trimingham's *Islam in Ethiopia*, p. 31, and the plans in *Aksum Expedition*, pp. 88 ff. Now also Hammerschmidt, *Tafelband*, pp. 90, 94.

It seems clear that the form of the Hebrew sanctuary[1] was preferred by Ethiopians to the basilica type which was accepted by early Christians elsewhere. The requirements of the Ethiopian cult, and particularly the *tabot* or Ark-centred type of worship, made the imitation of the Old Testament form of ecclesiastical building the most suitable choice. Similarly, churches throughout Ethiopia are usually built upon a small hill overlooking the village or, at any rate, at the most elevated place available. The Tosefta mentions the same requirement for the site of a synagogue[2] which is to be erected at the highest point of the town (בגובה של עיר).

Music

Ethiopian music and hymnography have not yet received the detailed study which they deserve.[3] Research into the history of Ethiopian music and examination of its contemporary manifestations will require the co-operation of a trained musicologist and a competent *éthiopisant*. While the musical notation of the *dɔggwa* can be studied in Europe (where some excellent manuscripts of this work exist), much of the material will have to be gathered and recorded in Ethiopia.[4] In 1959 I wrote: 'But time is pressing, for the day will come when jazz and rock 'n' roll present a serious challenge to the survival of traditional musical forms in Ethiopia.'[5] Since then the situation has become markedly

---

[1] 'Iudaeorum templum Hierosolymitanum tribus constabat partibus: אולם vestibulo spatiosissimo, in quo Iudaei ante fores aedis stabant: היכל ναῷ sive aede ipsa, quae solis sacerdotibus patebat, ut in ea sine tumultu populi tranquille sacris operari possent: דביר adyto, seu sancto sanctorum; in quod summus sacerdos semel tantum in anno ingrediebatur' (Ludolf, *Comm.*, p. 366).

[2] Cf. Elbogen, *Gottesdienst*, p. 453. See also Trimingham, op. cit., pp. 26 and 31.

[3] The following works are relevant: Marianus Victorius appended an excursus *De musica Aethiopum* to his 1552 *Chaldeae seu Aethiopicae linguae institutiones* in which he offered some musical transcriptions which have, to my knowledge, never been properly examined; Ludolf, *Commentarius*, pp. 263, 380–1; Guidi, *Vocabolario*, cols. 265, 607–8; C. Mondon-Vidailhet's *Musique éthiopienne* (see bibliography) remains the most detailed account of Ethiopian music hitherto published; M. Cohen, 'Couplets Amhariques du Choa', *JA* 1924; idem, 'Sur la notation musicale éthiopienne', *Levi Della Vida Festschrift*, Rome, 1956; E. Wellesz, 'Studien zur aethiopischen Kirchenmusik', *Oriens Christianus*, 1920; *New Oxford History of Music*, vols. i and ii; A. M. Rothmüller, *The Music of the Jews*, London, 1953; Guidi, 'Qene o Inni Abissini', *RRAL* 1900; E. Cerulli, 'Di alcune varietà di inni della chiesa etiopica', *Orientalia*, 1934; idem, 'Canti popolari amarici', *RRAL* 1916; Conti Rossini, *Proverbi, Tradizioni e Canzoni Tigrine*, Verbania, 1942; E. Littmann, *Abess. Klagelieder*, Tübingen, 1949.

[4] J. Tubiana (*Journal of African History*, ii, 1961) refers to German Odeon recordings, taken just before the Second World War, and to the records of the Collection Universelle de Musique Populaire de l'Unesco. In recent years quite a number of recordings have been made of both secular and ecclesiastical Ethiopian music, though not in any systematic form. Mrs. Jean Jenkins of the Horniman Museum, London, is now aiming at a collection of records covering as wide a geographical area of Ethiopia as possible and as full a typological representation as can be arranged: A first record, entitled 'Music of the Ethiopian Coptic Church', was published in 1967 by the UNESCO collection.

[5] *The Ethiopians*[2], p. 173.

more serious, for the impact of contemporary Western modes of musical expression has grown at a rapid pace.

While the importance of music, song and dirge, dance and accompanying instruments, is common to most peoples of the East, we are, I suggest, able to recognize certain specifically Old Testament elements in the musical manifestations, largely of a religious character, of the Ethiopians. The fact as such had been recognized as long ago as Ludolf (*Commentarius*, pp. 380–1) and as recently as Rathjens (*Juden in Abessinien*, p. 48). How powerful the impression of Abyssinia as a living representative of Old Testament times is,[1] the present writer can attest from his own experience and may also be gathered from one of the last of E. Littmann's writings (*Abessinische Klagelieder*):

> Abessinien ist ein Land kultureller Fossilien. Was sich in Sitte und Brauch, in sprachlicher Ausdrucksweise und in Formen der Dichtkunst bei den Völkern, die in Afrika und Asien den Abessiniern verwandt sind, nur teilweise erhalten hat oder durch gelehrte Arbeit erschlossen worden ist, konnte ich vor 40 Jahren im nördlichen Abessinien noch mehrfach in *lebender* Gestalt beobachten (p. 3).

Littmann also speaks (p. 4) of the 'Vergleichsmaterial' which Ethiopia offers in this sphere for Old Testament studies and for an examination of the survival of ancient customs. His particular interest had been engaged by the metric and rhythmic form of Ethiopian poetical texts, 'da sie genau der entspricht, wie sie in den hebräischen Liedern des Alten Testaments gebräuchlich war'. Littmann even encountered here the 'Klagelieder-Rhythmus' which had been recognized in Old Testament Hebrew poetry only during the last century.

Professor Gavino Gabriel, an authority on Ethiopian music, says (in an unpublished note): 'L'Abissino parla e canta in "falsetto" o "voix de tête" . . . esso rappresenta una economia di fiato; si che l'abissino può cantare tutta la vita senza dare segno di stanchezza.' A similar tireless capacity seems to have been attributed to the Levites in 1 Chronicles 23: 30.[2] It is likely that the falsetto element was prominent in the vocal parts of the

---

[1] M. Rodinson sounds a note of warning (*Bi Or*, 1964, pp. 243–4) against the acceptance of comparisons based on impression. This caution is, of course, wholly justified. At the same time, comparisons and influences, in the nature of things, do not yield to the type of precise analysis which is otherwise so desirable. Of course, many facets are not peculiar to the world of the Old Testament and that of Ethiopia but extend beyond that to the ancient Orient in general. In such cases we can do no other than examine these features and their development and assess the probabilities of borrowings and influences in the light of the special circumstances obtaining in Ethiopia.

[2] Cf. Benzinger, *Hebr. Arch.*[3], pp. 245–53, and esp. p. 252; de Vaux, *Ancient Israel*, pp. 391, 457; Rothmüller, op. cit., index under 'Levites' and 'singing'.

Hebrew Temple services, and it would appear that the occasional indications to that effect in the Old Testament may not always have been properly understood. Among obscure musical terms in the Hebrew Bible (especially in Psalms and Chronicles) occurs על עלמות (Ps. 46: 1; 1 Chron. 15: 20). Koehler (*Lexicon*, p. 709) considers this an 'unexplained term of [musical] execution', but Gesenius–Buhl had already advanced the view 'mit Mädchenstimmen, mit hoher Stimme, im Sopran'. And Ben Yehuda (*Thesaurus*, p. 4527) renders this expression 'Soprano, falsetto'. In Chronicles (loc. cit.) על עלמות occurs in connexion with an instrument (*nəḇālīm*) rather than the human voice, and Rothmüller (op. cit., p. 26) has explained this, correctly I think, as 'high-pitched *nəḇālīm*'.

There is another expression which has not, perhaps, been accurately understood: *qōl rām* (Deut. 27: 14) is not, I would tentatively suggest, 'with a loud voice' (for that invariably is *qōl gādōl*),[1] but this singular combination is likely to refer to high-pitched, falsetto voice. Similarly, *hērīm qōl* may have a musical connotation, though I do not claim that this is invariably the case. In Deuteronomy 27: 14 it is the Levites who are reciting with *qōl rām*. They, as the Temple singers and choristers[2] (1 Chron. 16: 4, 23: 30; 2 Chron. 8: 14), were eminently qualified to produce the high pitch required. We have here, therefore, a number of technical musical terms (addressed to the skilled Levite Temple musicians 'die eine große und wohlorganisierte Zunft bildeten'[3]—1 Chronicles 25: 1 ff.) rather than indications of mere volume of voice.

The Levites[4] had been set apart for the service of the Ark and for choral functions. The twofold division of the Israelite priesthood is paralleled in Ethiopia by the categories of *kahən* and *däbtära*.[5] The office of the latter is in most respects comparable to the tasks entrusted to the Levites, particularly in their role as cantors and choristers. That had already been recognized by B. Tellez (L. i, c. 39, fol. 95) who is quoted by Ludolf[6] as stating: *däbtära*: 'vulgo etiam sic vocatur *Canonicus*, qui ex Levitis originem ducit, ut putant, quorum officium in templis Aethiopicis est cantare et crotala pulsare.' Ludolf himself also sees this

---

[1] The LXX employs the same φωνῇ μεγάλῃ, without change of adjective, for *qōl rām* and *qōl gādōl*; so does the Gə'əz Bible, but the Amharic version, following the Arabic text (see p. 64, above), distinguishes clearly between *rām* and *gādōl*.

[2] De Vaux, op. cit., pp. 391–2.   [3] Benzinger, *Hebr. Arch.*[3], p. 252.

[4] De Vaux, op. cit., pp. 358–71.

[5] Cf. Pollera, *Stato etiopico e la sua chiesa*, p. 193. *Däbtära* is probably derived from διφθέρα (*Sem. Langg. of Ethiopia*, p. 110).

[6] *Lexicon Aethiopico-Latinum*[2], Frankfort, 1699, col. 504.

connexion and envisages the *däbtära* 'tanquam imitando Davidi ante arcam foederis salienti'.[1] To his ear, however, 'non multo jucundior est musica sacra: insuavi satis voce canunt illorum Canonici, quos ደብተራ፡ vocant . . .'.

The *däbtära* occupies in the Ethiopian Church an 'intermediate' position 'between the clergy and laymen'.[2] 'Though the *däbtära* are not ordained . . ., no service can properly be held without their presence. It is their chief duty to chant the psalms and hymns' (ibid.). The profession or class of *däbtära* ('die sich aus dem Levitenstand herleiten'[3]) have as their principal function the 'Besorgung des Kirchengesanges und gewisse Lese- und Schreibobliegenheiten' (ibid.). This differs very little from the duties with which the Levites were charged. According to 1 Chronicles 23: 3–5, David's census established that Levites were employed as Temple-supervisors, as clerks and judges, as orderlies, and as musicians and singers.[4] Similarly, the *däbtära* look after the administration of the larger churches and their musical and liturgical requirements. They are trained in the study of Amharic and Gǝ'ǝz, but their attainments in the latter in particular are apt to vary widely. They undergo instruction in ቅኔ፡ 'poetry or sacred hymns', ዜማ፡ 'song', አቋቋም፡ 'dancing and rhythmical movements', and, at least in theory, also in Bible, *Fǝtḥa Nagast,* and canon law. Pollera is, perhaps, a trifle too pessimistic when he says that 'in realtà questo programma è più ipotetico che effettivo e l'insegnamento si riduce a ben poca cosa'.[5]

Of particular interest are the musical instruments described in the Old Testament and their counterparts in modern Ethiopia. Rodinson has rightly said (*Bi Or*, 1964, p. 243) that instruments of a similar type are known to have been used in many parts of the ancient Near East. That is not, of course, in doubt—one need only glance at the excellent illustrations in Benzinger's *Hebr. Arch.*[3], pp. 245 ff., or in Hastings's *Dictionary of the Bible* (article 'Music') to appreciate the cosmopolitan character of ancient oriental music. But the veneration of the Bible in Ethiopia and its imitation have brought about a relationship also in this sphere which is closer and more meaningful than the rather general connexions that exist over the Near Eastern and North African region as a whole.

---

[1] *Historia*, iii. 6, 88–89. [2] Hyatt, *Church of Abyssinia*, p. 59.
[3] Hammerschmidt, *Kultsymbolik*, p. 218. See also *Tafelband*, pp. 105–6; and Buxton, op. cit., pls. 29, 30.
[4] Cf. de Vaux, op. cit., p. 393.
[5] Op. cit., p. 200.

We might take as our starting-point 2 Samuel 6: 5 which refers to some of the main musical instruments:[1]

ודוד וכל בית ישראל משחקים לפני יהוה בכל. עצי ברושים
ובכנרות ובנבלים ובתפים ובמנענעים ובצלצלים.

And David and all the house of Israel were playing before the Lord on . . . and on lyres and on harps and on drums and on castanets and on sistra.

The lacuna in the translation relates to the cypress-wood mentioned in the text; the parallel verse in 1 Chronicles 13: 8 has, instead, בכל עז ובשירים which most commentators have accepted as the correct reading also in 2 Samuel 6: 5. This is, indeed, probably the case, but it seems to me just within the realm of possibility that עצי ברושים, as a musical instrument, might refer to cypress-wood prayer-sticks, the *mäqwamiya*,[2] which play so prominent a part in marking the beat, accompanied by rhythmic hand-clapping, at all religious ceremonies. It is, incidentally, interesting to note that the Gəʿəz text in the Asmara Old Testament is sadly defective in its reading of 2 Samuel 6: 5, while the Amharic version of Abu Rumi reflects the Arabic text (which follows the Hebrew fairly closely) and the Amharic 'Emperor' Bible conflates with the reading of 1 Chronicles 13: 8:

ዳዊትና፡ የእስራኤልም፡ ቤት፡ ሁሉ፡ በፊኑ፡ በበገና፡ በመሰንቆም፡ በከበሮም፡ በነጋሪትና፡ በጸናጽል፡ በእግዚአብሔር፡ ፊት፡ በሙሉ፡ ኃይላቸው፡ ይጫወቱ፡ ነበር ።

In this rendering *qəne* reflects the *šīrīm* of 1 Chronicles 13: 8, and the Ethiopian instruments are probably meant to correspond as closely as possible to those in the original text. *Kinnōr*[3] has its parallel (probably also etymologically[4]) in the Abyssinian *kərar* 'lyre' of six strings.[5] According to Josephus (*Antiquities*, vii. 12, 3), the *kinnōr* had ten strings, but on some Bar Kokhba coins the lyre is shown to possess six (or at times three) strings[6]—like its Ethiopian counterpart. Both the Hebrew and the Ethiopian instruments possess a bowl-shaped sounding-box made of wood or skin. *Nebel*[7] is probably the Ethiopian *bägänä*[8] 'harp' of eight

---

[1] See already p. 3, above.
[2] See Hammerschmidt, *Tafelband*, p. 106.
[3] LXX simply uses κινύρα.
[4] Cf. Syriac *kenra* and Arabic *kirān* (H. G. Farmer, *History of Arabian Music*, pp. 15–16).
[5] See Buxton, *Travels*, pl. 21; Mondon-Vidailhet, *Musique éthiopienne*, p. 3187.
[6] *Dict. of the Bible*, iii. 459.
[7] LXX transcribes νάβλα.
[8] See Buxton, op. cit., pl. 20; Hyatt, op. cit., p. 135; Mondon-Vidailhet, op. cit., p. 3188.

or ten strings; it is of much greater size than the *kərar* and usually rests on the floor beside the player's chair. There does not seem to be a Biblical string instrument which corresponds to the *mäsänqo*,[1] the one-stringed fiddle.

Tof[2] is a type of kettledrum which, like its Ethiopian counter-part, the *käbäro*,[3] is probably one of the earliest and most ubiquitous musical instruments. The *käbäro* is made of a hollowed-out tree-trunk and its size will vary accordingly. Its primary function, in the ceremonies of Temple and Church, is to indicate rhythm. The *mənaʿanʿīm*, rendered by the Amharic version as *nägarit*, is certainly not the 'drum' which the Amharic text would suggest. The Revised Version's translation 'castanets' is possibly near the truth, and the Septuagint's 'cymbals' de-serves serious consideration because the clashing movements of the two brass plates might reflect the meaning of Hebrew *mənaʿanʿīm* (perhaps it should be vowelled as a dual?). *Ṣəlṣəlīm* corresponds, no doubt also etymologically,[4] to *ṣänaṣəl*[5] 'sistrum'. The monotonous but highly effective hypnotic sound of this rattle plays an important part in all church services—as no doubt it did in ancient Israelite worship: Psalm 150: 5 dis-tinguishes two types of *ṣəlṣəlīm*, *šemaʿ* and *tərūʿā*, among the for-midable orchestral array mentioned in that psalm, but we have no knowledge at all in what way they differed.

The scene which this verse (2 Sam. 6: 5) depicts may still be witnessed in Ethiopia today in substantially the same form and atmosphere. Ethiopians themselves are deeply conscious of the Old Testament flavour with which many of their contemporary religious ceremonies are imbued: there is the dancing,[6] the beat-ing of the drums, the rattling of the sistra, the plucking of lyres and harps. There is nothing in this scene[7] that would compel us to place it in the twentieth century A.D. rather than the tenth century B.C.

---

[1] See Buxton, op. cit., pls. 19 and 22; Hyatt, op. cit., p. 135; Mondon-Vidailhet, op. cit., p. 3186.

[2] LXX τύμπανον is probably related, either etymologically or possibly onomatopoeically, to *tof*.

[3] Buxton, op. cit., pl. 30.

[4] Cf. Barth, *Nominalbildung*, § 138, 2; Brockelmann, *Grundriß*, i, 247; Nöldeke, *Neue Beiträge*, p. 42.

[5] See Hammerschmidt, *Tafelband*, p. 115. This is, of course, a plural form, and its proper rendering is 'sistra'.

[6] Littmann, in a personal letter to the present writer, dated 11 June 1956, wrote: 'When we were at Aksum sitting before the "Church of Sion" and watched the dances of the priests, we thought that we were sitting with King Solomon before the temple of Jerusalem watching the Israelite priests dancing.'

[7] Cf. the illustrations in Doresse, op. cit., p. 65; Ullendorff, *The Ethiopians*, pls. viib, viiib, xiia.

The Ethiopic *dəggwa*[1] or hymnary exhibits an elaborate system of musical notation (*mələkət*) which marks the liturgical chant (*zema*) and which reminds us in many ways of the Biblical *ṭaʿāmīm* and *nəgīnōt* or τρόπος. On the whole it would seem rather unlikely that there could exist any direct connexion between these two systems of cantillation. They were both introduced in medieval times, but it is probable that the tradition on which they are based goes back a good deal further. We are still not quite certain when the Biblical 'accents' came into use, but this development is bound to have occurred during the second half of the first millennium A.D. Similar uncertainty surrounds the Ethiopian system, but I. Guidi (*Vocabolario Amarico*, col. 265, note 1) has supported the view that the signs of the *dəggwa* were introduced under the Emperor Claudius (1540–59). Ethiopians themselves attribute the invention of the *zema* notation to Yared who is said to have conceived the idea under the inspiration of the Holy Ghost.[2] It is the Ethiopian view, however, that not the *zema* or plain-song as such was evolved at that time but merely its graphic expression. The musical recitation of the psalms, as preserved in Ethiopia, is alleged to have an Hebraic origin and to reflect the modes of chanting practised in the days of David and Solomon.[3] While the traditional view is somewhat extravagant in its claims, it would be wrong to dismiss it out of hand and to deny that there might be certain aspects of the received recitation and its notation which are old and which have retained some authentic elements. It is not altogether impossible that South Arabian Jews were the carriers of such a musical or recitative tradition which took root in Ethiopia.

The Hebrew structure[4] appears to derive its origin, at least in part, from the neume notation of the Greek gospels—as Praetorius (op. cit.) has shown with some cogency. The original function of the Biblical signs was almost certainly syntactic; a correct distribution of the syntactical elements had hermeneutical significance and, in the nature of things, also established the sentence rhythm. This gave rise to the musical phrasing of the scriptural passage concerned. There exist different modes of cantillation for the Pentateuch and the Prophets; and

---

[1] The finest *dəggwa* manuscript known to me is the eighteenth-century *Dəggwa* in the Bodleian Library (cf. Ullendorff, *Catalogue*, no. 52). See also pl. xviii in Grébaut–Tisserant's catalogue of Vatican Ethiopic MSS.

[2] Cf. Dillmann, *Chrestomathia*, pp. 34 ff.; Mondon-Vidailhet, op. cit., pp. 3189 ff.

[3] This view is also reported by Mondon-Vidailhet, op. cit., p. 3189*b*.

[4] Cf. the detailed treatment of the Biblical system by Rothmüller, op. cit., pp. 79 ff.; Praetorius, *Über die Herkunft der hebräischen Accente*, Berlin, 1901; Elbogen, op. cit., p. 503; Kahle in Bauer–Leander's *Hist. Gramm. d. hebr. Sprache*, § 9.

the books of Lamentations and Esther have a system of their own.

Unfortunately, similar spade-work has not hitherto been undertaken for the notation of the *dəggwa*. We know, of course, that the musical signs consist of letters as well as dots and circles which are placed above the syllable to which they refer; they indicate the raising or lowering of the voice as well as other modes of voice production. We are in urgent need of a comprehensive examination of the Ethiopian system, and it would be well to bear in mind what we know of the Hebrew as well as other Oriental cantillation and notation methods. Marcel Cohen has recently given us a brief and valuable survey of existing knowledge on this subject,[1] including some important indications by Abba Jérôme.[2]

On a cursory examination I have been unable to detect any noticeable Greek traces, but this will need to be verified by someone more versed in these matters than I can claim to be. On the other hand, there appears to be a possibility of certain resemblances with the Hebrew Biblical system. This would seem to apply to the chanting rules as well as the meaning of some of the signs in common use, although I am unable to account for the way by which such connexions could have come about. I set out below, with some hesitation, the Ethiopian signs and their possible Hebrew equivalents in meaning as well as musical significance. It need scarcely be stressed that this is a very tentative outline:

አርፃ፡	אולא	'rapid'
አርኩርኽ፡	מירכא	'hold on, repeat'
አኅብር፡	מונח	'rest'
አንቀጥቃጤ፡	תביר	'break'
አቅና፡	קדמא	'forward'

As far as I know, the Ethiopian signs do not exhibit any of the syntactical or hermeneutical functions which the Biblical *ṭəʿāmīm* possess; their object seems to be exclusively concerned with the indication of the correct liturgical chant. Villoteau had already recognized the division of the *zema* into three modes or moods: *gəʿəz* pour les jours de férie; *ʿəzəl* pour les jours de jeûne et de

[1] 'Sur la notation musicale éthiopienne' (see p. 89, note 3). See also G. A. Villoteau in *Description de l'Égypte*, 2nd ed. xiv (1926), 270–98; Zotenberg, *Catalogue*, no. 67; photostats of a manuscript of the mass, with musical notation in part, in Mercer's *Ethiopic Liturgy*; Märsɔʿe Hazän, *yä-amarəñña säwasəw*, Addis Ababa, 1942/3, p. 211.

[2] For Abba Jérôme Gäbrä Muse see Cohen, *Pron. trad.*, p. 248.

carême, pour les veilles de fêtes et pour les cérémonies funèbres; *'araray* aux principales fêtes de l'année.' A similar division exists, of course, also in the case of the Hebrew *niggunīm* which vary in very much the same manner.

Liturgy

No attempt can here be made to investigate the Hebraic-Jewish background of the liturgy of the Ethiopian Church; such a study remains an important desideratum and naturally requires a monograph of its own. I shall here limit myself to a few hints in directions where further research is likely to be fruitful. The main difficulty in such an investigation derives from the pervasive influence which the liturgy of the Temple and, later on, the synagogue has exerted on services of the Christian Church in general and on the Oriental Christian Churches in particular.[1] It is, therefore, not always easy to disentangle strands peculiar to the Ethiopian Church that may reveal special dependence on Hebrew liturgical forms.

King Zar'a Ya'qob had decreed in his *Māṣḥafā Bərhan*[2] that religious instruction should be part of the divine worship. That tradition of 'learning' as an integral part of the service was undoubtedly inspired by the Second Temple and the early synagogue:[3] interpretation, discussion, exegesis of the Scriptures go back at least to the days of Ezra[4] and are reflected in the terminology. Both Midrash and Haggadah owe their origin to the didactic part of the service (cf. τοῖς σάββασιν εἰσελθὼν εἰς τὴν συναγωγὴν ἐδίδασκεν—Mark 1: 21). Ethiopic *dārāsā*, *mədras*, *dərsan* are used in virtually the same sense as their Hebrew or Jewish Aramaic equivalents.[5] *Māmhər* (root *mhr*[6] 'to teach'; reflex. 'to learn') is a 'teacher', 'doctor', or prior of a monastery, and this

---

[1] See W. O. E. Oesterley, *The Jewish Background of the Christian Liturgy*, Oxford, 1925; J. Schirmann, 'Hebrew Liturgical Poetry and Christian Hymnology', *JQR*, October 1953, pp. 123–61; Mercer, *The Ethiopic Liturgy* (see also below); Hammerschmidt, *Kultsymbolik*, pp. 222 ff.; idem, *Studies in the Ethiopic Anaphoras*, Berlin, 1961; Elbogen, *Gottesdienst, passim*.

[2] Edited by Conti Rossini and L. Ricci in *C.S.C.O.*, vols. Aeth. 47, 48, 51, 52. See esp. vol. 51, pp. 30 ff. Also Dillmann, *Kirchenordnung*, pp. 36 and 51 ff.

[3] I entirely agree with M. Rodinson (*Bi Or*, 1964, p. 241) that the object of Zar'a Ya'qob's prescriptions was 'à faire mieux pénétrer les bases du christianisme dans l'âme des fidèles'. I am not, of course, concerned here with motives but merely with the forms and the framework used to achieve those objects.

[4] Cf. Elbogen, op. cit., pp. 79, 194 ff.

[5] Cf. Nöldeke, *Neue Beiträge*, p. 38. Rodinson (loc. cit.) is not on firm ground when he argues that this terminology might just as well be derived from Syriac. Not only are the concepts Jewish, but the Ethiopic forms tally with their Hebrew rather than their Syriac counterparts (cf. Polotsky, *JSS* 1964, pp. 4 ff.). This is further confirmed by *tärgwamä* (see below).

[6] Hebrew and Arabic 'skilled', able'.

term is very largely coextensive with the Hebrew *ḥakam*. To the same category belongs *tärgwamä*[1] 'to interpret, expound, paraphrase' with a range of meaning similar to that in its Jewish connotation. The labio-velar sound in the Ethiopic form goes clearly back to an original *targum* which shows that this concept entered Abyssinia through Jewish influences from South Arabia rather than by way of the Syrian missionaries of the fourth and fifth centuries A.D.

The reading of the Scriptures and their exposition as an integral part of the church service had, of course, been taken over by early Christians from the practice of the synagogue.[2] But in the Ethiopic worship that reading occupies a rather more central place and is strongly reminiscent of synagogal arrangements. Zar'a Ya'qob had reaffirmed that the books of the Old and New Testaments were to be read in their entirety during church services and, in the manner of the *parašah* and the *hafṭarah*, he placed special emphasis on the reading from the Law and the Prophets.[3] The impression of a strong resemblance between the Hebrew *qəri'ah* and its Ethiopian counterpart is heightened by the not easily definable Hebraic atmosphere with which the Abyssinian service-ritual is imbued and, above all, by the musical rendering (cantillation) of the recitation.[4]

Antiphonal singing as part of the worship was an established form of the Hebrew liturgy since the earliest times (Exod. 15: 1 and 21)[5] and was taken over by the Christian Church, especially in the Eastern rites of the Jacobite Syrians and the Copts. It is unlikely, however, that Hebraic forms were anywhere more faithfully preserved than in the Ethiopian service with its emphasis on the *däbtära* 'cantor' and antiphony. In both the Jewish and the Abyssinian services the performance varies 'from simple recitation to elaborate cantillation with the character of the feast and in accordance with the liturgical prescription for the particular part of the service'.[6] It was Conti Rossini's authoritative verdict that 'nei riti, la chiesa abissina ha conservato non pochi tratti arcaici: così l'isolamento del *sanctum sanctorum*. Il

---

[1] Nöldeke, op. cit., p. 39. Examples of similar terminology will be dealt with in the excursus on linguistic factors below.

[2] Oesterley, op. cit., pp. 111 ff.   [3] Dillmann, *Kirchenordnung*, p. 65.

[4] Cf. above the section on music and especially chapter x on the 'lectio solemnis' of the Lessons in E. Wellesz's most valuable *History of Byzantine Music and Hymnography*.

M. Rodinson has rightly warned (op. cit., p. 242) that 'une impression non définissable se révèle souvent être une illusion', but in the present case the impression is one that has been widely reported by people of very different backgrounds. Besides there is a good deal of hard evidence to strengthen this impression.

[5] Later developments are described by Elbogen, op. cit., pp. 502 ff.

[6] Wellesz, op. cit., p. 27.

canto liturgico è accompagnato dal suono dei sistri e dal cadenzato battere dei piedi: i cantori o *debtera* intercalano il canto dei salmi con quello di brevi poesie (*qeniē*) da essi improvvisate.'[1]

The significance of hymns and psalms in the worship of the Ethiopians had already been noted with disapproval by Lobo. After having disposed of circumcision as an obviously Jewish custom he continues:

> The Jewish rites are in many other instances observed by the Abyssins; one brother takes the wife of another; the men do not enter a church the day after they have conversed with their wives; nor do the women come to the divine worship after childbirth, till the days of their purification are over. . . . Their manner of chaunting the Psalms has a great conformity with that of the Jews: And indeed in so many things do they agree, that it would not be easy to determine whether the Abyssins are more Jews or Christians.[2]

The attachment of Ethiopians to psalter and hymnary and the enormous number of Ethiopic manuscripts of this genre almost defy description. Most service books containing the complete psalter are followed by the ᾠδαί, a collection of usually nine odes which make up the basic text of the Morning office and which constitute a fairly close parallel to the Hebrew *Qəroba*,[3] i.e. the poetical passages inserted into the *Tefillah*. These odes consist generally of eight hymnal pieces from the Old Testament and one from the New Testament.

Details of the present Ethiopian liturgy may be studied in S. A. B. Mercer's *Ethiopic Liturgy* which contains facsimiles of the Ethiopic text. Despite many imperfections (some of which were pointed out by F. Praetorius in a review published in *ZDMG* 1916) this has remained a useful work which conveys to the student of liturgics an adequate idea of the Hebraic foundations of the Ethiopic service—overlaid as it is with Christian trappings which somehow seem to have failed to remove the unmistakable Jewish background.[4]

The *Trisagion*[5] in particular reveals its development from the *Qədušah* (cf. *qəddase*). We still know far too little of the original form and later development of the Ethiopic liturgy, though in recent years E. Hammerschmidt has applied his knowledge of

[1] *Etiopia e genti d'Etiopia*, p. 180.
[2] Lobo, *Voyage to Abyssinia*, p. 301. See also Rathjens, op. cit., p. 50.
[3] Cf. Elbogen, op. cit., pp. 212 ff.; Schirmann, op. cit., *passim* but esp. pp. 160–1; Wellesz, op. cit., pp. 168 ff.
[4] See also *Mäṣḥafä Qəddase*, published by the Vatican Library, Rome, 1945; and the Gəʿəz and Amharic *Mäṣḥafä Qəddase* published at Addis Ababa, 1949/50.
[5] Cf. Mercer, op. cit., pp. 325 ff.; Oesterley, op. cit., pp. 142 ff.; Hammerschmidt, *Ethiopic Anaphoras*, pp. 52, 86 ff., 105 ff.

liturgics to this neglected field. Future investigation of the evolution of the liturgy should offer a basis on which a detailed comparative study of the Hebrew and Ethiopian services will become possible. I see no reason to dissent from the substance of M. Rodinson's summing up:[1] 'origine juive de certains "traits culturels" chrétiens, spécialement chrétiens orientaux, que l'Église éthiopienne a adoptés en même temps que le christianisme ou par suite de ses rapports postérieurs avec les Églises d'Orient, en particulier l'Église syrienne et tout spécialement l'Église copte.' It is, however, essential to add to this the impact of the Old Testament and certain peculiarly Hebraic forms, for otherwise we should fail to discern some of the most characteristic Ethiopian developments which distinguish the Ethiopian Church from her sister churches in the Orient.

Dietary prescriptions

We must now briefly consider the relevant prescriptions governing the consumption of food. It is to be hoped that M. Rodinson[2] will soon publish the material he has collected in this field and give us a treatise comparable to his magisterial article *Ghidhā'* (غِذَاء) in the 2nd ed. of the *Encyclopaedia of Islam* (ii. 1057–72). It is important to appreciate here the discrepancy between the abstract doctrinal position of the Church, formulated centuries ago, and the actual state of affairs, both in the past and today. Failure to recognize that significant distinction has invalidated many of the conclusions at which Kromrei[3] arrived. We shall not be concerned, in the present context, with food preferences and taboos in general but only with such aspects as can be related directly to the dietary prescriptions in the Bible.

Zar'a Ya'qob's *Mäṣḥafä Bǝrhan* has very little to say on the subject of food taboos—except for the passage on p. 51 of the second part of the Conti Rossini–Ricci edition where, among the transgressions (ዐላውትት), certain foods are mentioned:

ቦእሰ ፡ ይትቃሙሱ ፡[4] በደሙ ፡ ከልብ ፡ መበሐሲበ ፡ ኤርግ ፡ በትእኀን ፡ መበቍናጽ ፡ በቍማለ ፡ መበዞሱበ ፡ . . .[5]

---

[1] *Bi Or*, 1964, p. 242.

[2] I am much indebted to M. Rodinson for his courtesy in sending me the typescript of a short paper, entitled 'Les Interdictions alimentaires éthiopiennes', which he read at the 3rd Int. Conf. of Eth. Stud. at Addis Ababa in April 1966. He has also been good enough to let me have his extensive notes on the gathering of material on this subject. See also the same author's 'Notes de vocabulaire alimentaire sudarabe et arabe' in *GLECS* ix (19 June 1963), 103–7.   [3] *Glaubenslehre und Gebräuche*, etc., pp. 42–43.

[4] This is the reading of the Berlin manuscript (Dillmann, *Kirchenordnung*, p. 39); the Vatican manuscript has ይትቃሙሱ, while the Paris manuscript (which the editors use as their

. . . and there are those who are tasting dogs' blood and asses' milk, bugs and fleas, lice and flies. . . .[1]

The *Fǝtḥa Nagast* (Guidi's ed., p. 147) decrees:

ወመብልዕስ፡ በውስተ፡ ሕግ፡ መሲሓዌት፡ አልቦ፡ ውስቴቱ፡ ሕርመት፡ ዘእንበለ፡ ዘከልኡ፡ ሐዋርያት፡ እምኔሁ፡ በመጽሐፈ፡ አብርክሲስ፡ ወበቀኖናቸሙ ፨

And as to food, there is no prohibition in the Christian Law— except what the Apostles have forbidden in the *Book of the Acts* and in their canons.

This is presumably a reference to Acts 15: 20 and 29 which maintain the Mosaic prohibition of the consumption of blood. In this general sense, this particular taboo is observed by all the Oriental Christian Churches. It is, however, important to recall that the *Fǝtḥa Nagast* is a thirteenth-century work of the Coptic Church in Egypt, made known under the title of مجموع قوانين and translated into Ethiopic, probably two centuries later. Its compiler, Ibn al-'Assāl, wrote for the benefit of Christians living in Egypt, and for this reason the *Fǝtḥa Nagast* has often—as Guidi (*Letteratura*, p. 79) remarked—'nessuna o ben poca utilità per gli Abissini'.

Similarly, we find in the *Confessio Claudii*:[2]

ወበእንት፡ በሲዐ፡ ሐራውያL፡ እኮ፡ ዘንትክላእ፡ በዐቂበ፡ ሕገጊ፡ እሪት፡ ከመ፡ አይሁድ ፨

And as to the consumption of pork,[3] we are not forbidden to eat it on account of the observance of the laws of the Pentateuch—like the Jews.

And Claudius goes on to cite in support the famous verses from Romans 14: 3, 17, 20, and Matthew 15: 11 and 17. It has to be realized, however, that the *Confessio Claudii* is part of the polemical literature of the sixteenth century and is thus a product of the monophysite–Catholic controversy. King Claudius' main purpose was to combat the Roman Catholic accusations that the Alexandrine Faith was full of Hebraic practices. It is,

base-text) has the metathetical reading ይትቀስሙ. Dillmann's 'genießen' is surely right, for Ricci's 'cercano auspici' does not produce a satisfactory sense in this context (p. 30 of translation).
  [5] The Vatican reading is ዝምብ፡ 'fly' which might give a better sense in this context.

---

  [1] Or 'hyenas'—see preceding note. Cf. the consumption of wolves' flesh in pre-Islamic and early Islamic Arabia, as well as other dietary oddities, as described by Wellhausen, *Reste*, pp. 168 ff.
  [2] See the text in Ludolf's *Commentarius*, pp. 237 ff.
  [3] Cf., however, the Amharic proverb at the end of this section.

therefore, not surprising that he was anxious to minimize the prevalence of Judaic elements in Ethiopian Christianity.

Ludolf mentions[1] that Abba Gregory had a great aversion to lobsters, crabs, hares, and the like, but it seems quite possible that they were to him not only, as Ludolf supposes, 'insueta animalia' (for there must have been a great deal of food in Italy and Germany to which he had been unaccustomed in his native Ethiopia) but animals prohibited in Leviticus chapter 11.[2]

In fact, the sentiments voiced on this subject in the *Fǝtḥa Nagast* and *Confessio Claudii* were not expressive of the true state of affairs in Ethiopia; they were merely ammunition in the fight against the Jesuits who had levelled such grave accusations against the Ethiopian Faith and its allegedly Jewish ingredients.[3] In reality, many of the Pentateuchal food laws have been, and are still being, observed with some strictness in Ethiopia.[4] Rathjens (*Juden in Abessinien*, pp. 51 ff.) has described in detail the division into clean and unclean animals as related to him by his informant from Ankober. This corresponds very closely to the food taboos which I experienced in traditional circles in Ethiopia. I recall many occasions in the past when at European dinner parties my Ethiopian neighbours would seek reassurance about the provenance of the meat course. The prescriptions regarding mammals and birds (Lev. 11) are generally scrupulously followed, and Conti Rossini testifies (*L'Abissinia*, p. 82) that 'dei pesci senza squame' are among forbidden items of food. Bruce also states:[5]

> The river Kelti has excellent fish, though the Abyssinians care not for food of this kind. The better sort of people eat some species in the time of Lent; but the generality of the common are *deterred by passages of scripture, and distinctions in the Mosaic law*, concerning such animals as are *clean and unclean*, ill understood [my italics].

Slaughtering and bleeding of the animal are performed according to Pentateuchal requirements (Gen. 9: 4; Lev. 3: 17,

---

[1] *Historia*, iii. 1, 50.

[2] It is unlikely, in the religious climate of the seventeenth century, that Abba Gregory was anxious to disclose the true reason of his abstention (i.e. the Old Testament prohibition), for Ludolf and his predecessors had aimed a great deal of criticism at the Jewish elements in Abyssinian Christianity (see next footnote).

[3] Cf. Littmann, *Gesch. d. aeth. Lit.*, p. 215. Thus also Ludolf (*Hist.* iii. 1, 69–70): 'Judaismi certe in Europa diu suspecti fuerunt Habessini et adhuc multis sunt. Id animadvertens Rex Claudius. . . . Confessionem edidit . . . illius praecipuus scopus fuit, suspicionem illam a se suisque dimovendi. . . .'

[4] Cf. Leslau, *Coutumes et Croyances des Falachas*, p. 55, note 5; Aešcoly, *Sefer ha-Falashim*, p. 50: גם החבשים הנוצרים שומרים על האסורים האלה; Harris, *Highlands of Aethiopia*, iii. 150; Rodinson, *E. of I.* ii. 1062: 'it [this abstention] was also adopted by the Christians of Ethiopia in imitation of the Old Testament.'   [5] *Travels*[3], v. 221.

4: 6, etc.). When Bruce describes, in somewhat gruesome detail, the slaughter of a cow, he remarks:[1] 'Having satisfied the Mosaical law,[2] according to his conception, by pouring the six or seven drops [of blood] upon the ground. . . .' Mansfield Parkyns reports[3] that 'no nation is more scrupulous' in its choice of food than the Abyssinians. 'Besides refusing all animals which have teeth in their upper jaw—as the hare; and all such as have not cloven feet—as the camel, whose foot is only cloven above; and many others, from religious prejudice. . . .'[4] Parkyns further declares:[5] 'Following to the letter the commands of Moses, they [the Ethiopians] refuse to eat animals which do not chew the cud, and those which have not cloven hoofs. Thus the hare is considered as disgusting. The generality of the people, however, do not know whence these rules are derived, but merely believe that such food is not proper. . . .'[6]

There is no ban on the simultaneous consumption of milk and meat, but since this Jewish prohibition is post-Biblical (Mishnah *Ḥullin* 8—deriving from the law against seething a kid in its mother's milk: Exodus 23: 19, 34: 26; Deuteronomy 14: 21), it is scarcely surprising that Ethiopians are unaware of it. The same applies, incidentally, to the Falashas who are equally innocent of any knowledge of this taboo.[7] The prohibition on eating the sinew of the thigh (גיד הנשה—Gen. 32: 33) is widely observed in Ethiopia, 'more especially by members of the royal blood' (W. C. Harris, *Highlands of Aethiopia*, iii. 150). This sinew, *šulləda* or *šəlluda* in Amharic, is called in Gəʿəz ሥጋ፡ ክፉም፡ 'the forbidden muscle'—as had already been recognized by Ludolf (*Historia*, iii. 1, 66). The most rigorous prohibition is, naturally, that directed against pork[8] which is observed through-out Ethiopia with great strictness. Abstention from pork is, of course, a facet also of Islam (*E. of I.* ii. 1061) and of Judaeo-Christians (ibid., p. 1062), but in Ethiopia it is practised with quite remarkable single-mindedness:

ሥጋ፡ ያሰግ፡ እንኳን፡ በበላው፡ በሰማው፡ ገግ ::[9]

Pork taints not only him who eats it but also him who hears about it.

---

[1] Op. cit. iv. 487.   [2] Cf. *Lev.* 4: 6, 17.

[3] *Life in Abyssinia*², new impression 1966, pp. 207–8.

[4] Cf. also Strelcyn in *Africana*, i (1964), 81.

[5] Op. cit., pp. 291–4.   [6] Cf. also Littmann, *Princeton Expedition*, ii. 236–40.

[7] Cf. Faitlovitch, *The Falashas*, p. 8; see also Leslau, *Coutumes et Croyances des Falachas*, p. 55, note 6.

[8] Lev. 11: 7; Deut. 14: 8.   [9] Baeteman, *Dictionnaire*, col. 575.

Ritual cleanness

A few brief words must here be added on the subject of ritual cleanness. Again, this is not—as M. Rodinson has rightly said[1]— 'spéciale à l'Éthiopie', although it is admittedly due to influence 'incontestablement juive'. However, even if some of the principles, on which the Ethiopian Church bases its adherence to these Old Testament laws, are applicable to the Coptic Church as a whole, the Abyssinian observance is both more detailed and strict in its imitation of Hebraic practice.

Fitness for contact with the consecrated included abstinence from sexual relations. This is expressly stated in Exodus 19: 15; Leviticus 12: 2, 15: 19 ff.; 1 Samuel 21: 4–6, etc. And, similarly, in the *Fətḥa Nagast* (Guidi ed., p. 114) we find:

ወኢ.ይኢግም ፡ ብእሲ ፡ ምስለ ፡ ብእሲቱ ፡ በመዋዕለ ፡ ጾም ፡፡

And a man may not sleep with his wife during the days of fasting.

The *Fətḥa Nagast* (p. 169) also enumerates all the other occasions on which sexual intercourse between husband and wife is forbidden, i.e. during the days of menstruation or any other impurity.[2] That this is not here a general Semitic ban, but the result of Hebraic law, is expressly stated (loc. cit.): ተዘከር ፡ ዘአዘዘከ ፡ እግዚአብሔር ፡ በአፈ ፡ ሙሴ ፡ 'remember what God has commanded thee by the mouth of Moses'; and then follows a quotation from (or paraphrase of) Leviticus 20: 18.

M. Rodinson (loc. cit.) finds it 'remarquable' that I should cite the *Fətḥa Nagast*, originally a document addressed to the Copts in general, in support of my contentions. But, in the first place, there are a number of significant additions in the Ethiopic text[3] which are absent from the Arabic original (e.g. Guidi, transl., p. 249). And, secondly, many of these regulations have long passed into desuetude in the Coptic Church of Egypt (if they were ever observed at all), while in Ethiopia they were, and are, strictly adhered to. That this was so, long before the *Fətḥa Nagast* was translated into Gə'əz, may be gathered from Zar'a Ya'qob's *Mäṣḥafä Bərhan*—and there seems little doubt that the prescriptions in the latter go back to a long-standing attachment and fidelity to the Old Testament position.

The regulations in the *Mäṣḥafä Bərhan* will be found in part ii, pp. 7–13, of the Conti Rossini–Ricci edition.[4] Anyone who has been rendered unclean by intercourse, seminal flow, or menstruation must not enter a church—be he priest or layman. These

---

[1] *Bi Or*, 1964, p. 244.   [2] Cf. also Mishnah *Ṭohoroth, Miqwa'oth, Niddah, passim.*
[3] Cf. *The Ethiopians*, p. 138.   [4] Cf. also Dillmann, *Kirchenordnung*, pp. 51–52.

prohibitions are set out in considerable detail, and in their attention to particulars and in their casuistry fall little short of the minutiae of Talmudic disquisitions. They are based on— and indeed cite *in extenso*—the passages in Exodus 19: 15 ff. and 1 Samuel 21: 4–6. Study of the Old Testament regulations relating to ritual cleanness[1] makes one strongly aware of the milieu in which the Ethiopian practice has developed. Here again the specifically Biblical character can be recognized, for similar customs among the early Arabs[2] differed in several significant aspects, notably the exclusion of men from defilement.

Observers of the Ethiopian scene who approached things with an innocent eye, such as Mansfield Parkyns,[3] have always come away with the impression that this emphasis laid on the distinction between 'cleanness or uncleanness is purely Mosaic':

A man who is, for certain reasons, unclean cannot enter the church till he is purified. Among other causes of uncleanness, to have entered a room where a child has been recently born is . . . sufficient to render one unclean; to have touched polluted garments is another cause; and many more might be named,[4] but that they are mostly to be found in the book of Jewish law.

The situation as regards ritual purity differs very little among the Falashas,[5] and both they and their Christian compatriots derive their ideas from their loyalty to the laws of the Old Testament.

Circumcision

Herodotus (ii. 104) thought that 'the Colchians, Egyptians, and Ethiopians are the only nations of the world who, from the first, have practised circumcision. . . . Of the Egyptians and Ethiopians I am unable to say which learnt it from the other, for it is evidently a very ancient custom.'[6] We now know that this custom was not confined to Egyptians, Ethiopians, and Semites, but was—and indeed is—widely practised in Africa, Australia, and America. The significance of the rite and the age at which it is performed vary: in some cases it appears to be a tribal badge, in others an initiation rite or a preliminary to marriage. There are, of course, other explanations as well, and

[1] Cf. Benzinger, *Hebr. Arch.*, § 80; W. Robertson Smith, *Religion of the Semites*[2], pp. 446 ff.
[2] Wellhausen, *Reste*, p. 170.
[3] *Life in Abyssinia*, p. 291.
[4] Cf. Rathjens, op. cit., p. 58.
[5] Cf. Leslau, *Falasha Anthology*, p. xix; idem, *Coutumes et Croyances*, pp. 28–29.
[6] Herodotus, translated from Baehr's text by Henry Cary, London, 1891.

these have been discussed in detail in the ample literature concerned with this subject.[1]

As circumcision has always been specially associated with the
Jews, it is scarcely surprising that early accounts of Ethiopia
see in circumcision yet one more custom borrowed by the
Ethiopians from the Jews. Lobo's *Voyage to Abyssinia* contains a
special excursus on circumcision among the Abyssinians (pp. 289–
301), and the author finds it proven beyond doubt that they
received this practice from the Jews.[2] Ludolf (*Historia*, iii. 1,
17 ff.), on the other hand, draws attention to the existence of
this custom among many other peoples and denies that any
special Jewish connexion can be established.[3] He quotes, in
support of his position, from Claudius' *Confessio*:[4]

ወበእንተ፡ ሥርዐት፡ ግዘረትኒ፡ እኩ፡ ዘንተገዘር፡ ከመ፡ አይሁድ፡፡ እስመ፡ ንሄ፡
ናአምር፡ ቃለ፡ ጳውሎስ፡ ለጸውሎስ፡ . . . ዘይቤ፡ ተገዝሮ፡ ኢይበቍዕ፡ ወኢተገዝሮ፡
ኢይሁልጥ፡ . . . ወባሕቱ፡ ግዘረትስ፡ ዘኊ፡ በኅቤነ፡ በልማደ፡ ሀገር፡ ከመ፡ ብጥነተ፡
ገጽ፡ ዘኢትዮጵያ፡ ወኑባ፡፡

And as to the institution of circumcision, we are not circumcised
like the Jews. For we understand the teaching of St. Paul who says:[5]
'to be circumcised does not profit and not to be circumcised does not
avail . . .'. Indeed, circumcision among us is in accordance with the
custom of the country—just like the incisions of the face practised in
Ethiopia and Nubia. . . .

However, the limited value of the *Confessio Claudii* as evidence
for or against the emulation of Hebraic practices has already
been explained.[6]

The *Fətḥa Nagast* (chapter 51) clearly reflects the conflict
between the Christian doctrinal position and the actual custom
as practised in Ethiopia and among the Copts in Egypt. After
recounting the Old Testament prescription and its significance,
the *Fətḥa Nagast* decrees that according to the 'New Law'
(ሕግ፡ ሐዲስ፡) circumcision is merely a 'custom' (ልማድ፡) and does
not possess the sanction of a 'legal precept' (ቀኖና፡ ሕጋዊ፡). The
Pentateuchal command required it to be carried out on the

---

[1] See, *inter alia*, Hastings's *Dictionary of the Bible*; *Encyclopaedia Britannica*[11]; Hastings's
Encyclop. of Religion and Ethics, iii. 659–80; *Jewish Encyclopaedia*; Wellhausen, *Reste*, pp. 174 ff.;
de Vaux, *Ancient Israel*, pp. 46 ff.
[2] See also the Lobo quotation on p. 99, above.
[3] Cf. also *Commentarius*, pp. 268 ff.
[4] As printed in Ludolf's *Comm.*, p. 240.
[5] Gal. 5: 6; cf. also 1 Cor. 7: 18–19.
[6] See p. 101, above.

THE IMPACT OF THE OLD TESTAMENT

eighth day, but under the New Law that date was not binding.
It is, however, clear from the wording of these passages in the
Confessio Claudii and the *Fǝtḥa Nagast* that, in fact, circumcision
was practised fairly strictly in accordance with Old Testament
prescriptions.

The same picture emerges from the *Mäṣḥafä Bǝrhan*.[1] King
Zar'a Ya'qob justifies not only male circumcision but also female
excision.[2] He does so by having recourse to the inclusive terms
'house', 'seed', כל אנשי ביתו[3] (ኰሉ፡ ሰብአ፡ ቤቱ፡[4]), in Genesis 17,
which are interpreted to comprise women (thus completely
neglecting the repeated Pentateuchal emphasis on *zakar*).

The doctrinal position of the Ethiopian national Church was
always unenviable, caught as it was between the deeply rooted
Judaic customs of the country and the necessity to maintain
its theological prestige as a truly Christian body. Fortunately,
these stresses became acute only in times of foreign pressure or
religious controversy (the ridicule of the Jesuits or the intervention of other Christian missionaries). At other times the Abyssinian monophysite Church and the Ethiopian nation have been
at peace with their syncretistic Judaeo-Christian civilization.
In the case of circumcision, the Church neither demands nor
rejects it—yet it is practised with devotion.[5] Alvares, in his early
sixteenth-century narrative of Ethiopia,[6] finds that, though
circumcision is done by everybody without special ceremony,
people hold that it is written in the Book and that 'God commanded circumcision'. Guidi observes that 'la circoncisione è
generalmente praticata e da molti ritenuta come *un dovere re-
ligioso*[7] [my italics], ma dalla Chiesa non è riguardata ufficial-
mente tale'.[8]

Since circumcision was, and is, so widespread a practice in
many parts of the world, it would not be possible to establish
any special Old Testament connexion for its existence in Ethiopia,

---

[1] Conti Rossini–Ricci ed., pp. 151 ff. See also Dillmann, *Kirchenordnung*, pp. 41 ff.

[2] This custom is still widespread in Ethiopia and elsewhere and has been observed, with
astonishment and often disgust, by writers from Alvares, Ludolf, and Bruce (*Travels*[3], v. 26)
to the present day. It is also practised by the Falashas and the Cushitic inhabitants of Ethiopia.
Female 'circumcision' is probably a type of clitoridectomy, and it has been suggested by one
scholar that female excision was at one time also practised by Jews and other Semites (cf.
Louis Marcus in *Nouveau Journal Asiatique*, iii, 409–31; iv, 51–73 [1829] , though I am not
aware of any positive evidence to support this opinion.

[3] Gen. 17: 27.

[4] Conti Rossini–Ricci ed., p. 154, 14.

[5] Cf. K. G. Roden, *Fǝtǝḥ Maḥari* (in his *Le tribù dei Mensa*), section 17; Littmann, *Princeton
Expedition*, ii. 147–8.

[6] Translated by Beckingham and Huntingford (1961), i. 109; ii. 349.

[7] Conti Rossini (*Etiopia e genti d'Etiopia*, p. 178) uses exactly the same words.

[8] *OM* 1922, p. 253.

unless we were able to detect something of the two principal characteristics which distinguish Hebraic circumcision as decreed in Genesis 17, i.e. its special function as a visible sign of the covenant (*brīṯ*) between God and His people; and its performance on the eighth day after birth. Now, we have seen in the foregoing that, while the Church takes no official cognizance of circumcision (though it does celebrate the circumcision of Christ (*Gəzrät*) on the 6th day of Ṭər),[1] it is yet regarded by Ethiopians as a 'religious duty'. In fact, such a duty can only originate from a time prior to the introduction of Christianity[2] and from the continued veneration accorded to the Old Testament.[3] With the strong consciousness among Ethiopians of being the heirs of Israel[4] as the chosen people, circumcision has become to Ethiopians a religious as well as a national duty, the symbol of their status as the new Zion.

The date of circumcision on the eighth day is shared, to my knowledge, by Jews and Ethiopians only. This is expressly attested by Täsämma Habtä Mika'el[5] (የብልት ፡ ጫፍን ፡ ወሸላን ፡ በስምንት ፡ ቀን ፡ መቁረጥ ፡ መግHC ።[6]), by Conti Rossini,[7] Hyatt,[8] Rathjens,[9] and others. Falasha circumcision takes place on the eighth day,[10] and since the Falashas also practise female excision it is virtually certain that their circumcision rites are part of the general Ethiopian heritage and not the result of any separate Jewish inspiration. The Ethiopian adherence to the Pentateuchal eighth day is the more remarkable because members of the Coptic Church in Egypt are circumcised at an age of between six and eight years; and Gallas, Muslims, and other influences in Ethiopia, with widely varying dates for circumcision, would all combine to shake the Ethiopian confidence in the eighth day.

---

[1] Cf. Baeteman, *Dictionnaire*, col. 1004.

[2] So also Nöldeke (*Neue Beiträge*, p. 36) on linguistic grounds in discussing the Ethiopic and Aramaic root *gzr* 'to circumcise': 'Die Beschneidung wird nach Abessinien durch Juden gekommen sein.'

[3] Cf. the express reference to the Pentateuchal origin of circumcision in Täsämma Habtä Mika'el's *Käsate Bərhan Täsämma: yä'amarəñña mäzgäbä qalat* (Addis Ababa, 1958/9), p. 1190: መግHƐ ። በኦሪት ፡ ሥርዐት ፡ በስምንተኛ ፡ ቀን ።

[4] Faitlovitch (*Quer durch Abessinien*, p. 133) reports that when the Emperor Menelik saw some Hebrew writing he inquired what language it was. Upon being informed that it was Hebrew, Menelik exclaimed: 'Ich möchte die Sprache meiner Vorfahren hören.' It is a pity that Faitlovitch did not give us the original Amharic words used by the emperor.

[5] Op. cit., cols. 1189–90. See also note 3, above.

[6] 'To cut the extremity of the penis, the prepuce, on the eighth day.'

[7] *Etiopia e genti d'Etiopia*, p. 178.   [8] *Church of Abyssinia*, p. 179.

[9] *Juden in Abessinien*, p. 56.

[10] Leslau, *Falasha Anthology*, pp. xvi–xvii; idem, *Coutumes*, pp. 44 and 93.

See also Walker, *Abyssinian at Home*, p. 2; Aešcoly, *Sefer Ha-Falashim*, pp. 39–40. The occasional discrepancies in our sources as regards the seventh or eighth day after birth do not relate to different practices but merely to different methods of reckoning.

Yet this date has been steadfastly maintained, no doubt under the influence of the Biblical injunction.

Sabbath observance

One of the principal accusations levelled by the Portuguese against the monophysite Ethiopians was the latter's adherence to the 'Jewish' Sabbath. Yet the history of Sabbath observance in Ethiopia is rather chequered; the sources, though fairly ample, are occasionally ambiguous. In the following it will not be possible to do more than offer some summary observations and a brief outline of a subject which is both central in its importance and vast in its ramifications and implications. My 'Hebraic-Jewish Elements in Abyssinian (Monophysite) Christianity'[1] deals with some of the broader implications in slightly more detail. That study has also been taken as a point of departure for Hammerschmidt's monograph on *Stellung und Bedeutung des Sabbats in Äthiopien* which contains a collection of much important material bearing upon this question.

The ambiguity to which I have referred is reflected in the terminology:[2] in Gə'əz the usual word for 'Saturday' is *qädam* and for 'Sunday' *'əhud* (the etymology shows that this nomenclature is in itself indicative of some confusion). Often 'Sunday' is called *sänbätä*[3] *krəstiyan* and 'Saturday' *sänbätä 'ayhud* (Ludolf, *Historia*, iii. 6, 86); in the *Confessio Claudii* 'Saturday' appears as *qädamit sänbät* (Ludolf, *Comm.*, p. 239). In present usage in the modern Ethiopian languages *sänbät* on its own is ambiguous, though it usually refers to 'Sunday'; more often in Amharic and elsewhere *qədame* is employed for 'Saturday' and *əhud* for 'Sunday'. The latter is also called *'abiy sänbät* and the former *nə'us sänbät*, i.e. 'big' or 'small Sabbath', respectively (cf. Guidi, *Suppl.*, col. 60).

The Portuguese charge directed against the Jewish-inspired observance of the Sabbath was, of course, rejected by Claudius in his *Confessio*.[4] After describing the Jewish celebration of the Sabbath in its most restrictive terms, he sketches a sharply contrasting picture of the Ethiopian Sabbath:

ወባሕቱ ፡ ንሕነ ፡ ናከብራ ፡ እንዘ ፡ ናቐርብ ፡ ባቲ ፡ ቁርባነ ፡ ወንገብር ፡ ባቲ ፡ ምሳሐ ፡ በከመ ፡ አዘዘነ ፡ አበዊነ ፡ ሐዋርያት ፡ በዲድስቅልያ ።

We, on the other hand, honour it [the Sabbath] by celebrating eucharist

---

[1] *JSS* 1956, pp. 216–56.
[2] See now also Leslau's 'The Names of the Weekdays in Ethiopic', *JSS*, Spring 1961.
[3] Cf. Nöldeke, *Neue Beiträge*, p. 37. [4] Ludolf, *Comm.*, p. 239.

and agape as our fathers, the Apostles, have commanded us in the Didascalia.

Yet, even Claudius cannot deny the observance of the Sabbath as such, though in his contrasting description of the Jewish and Ethiopian celebrations he comes close to what Hammerschmidt[1] has aptly characterized as an 'apologetischen Kunstgriff'. The distinction had to be made mainly on doctrinal grounds,[2] for no one could seriously dispute the existence of these Hebraic practices. The Emperor Susenyos who, in the early seventeenth century, embraced the Roman Faith even resorted to outright banning of the Sabbath celebration: 'Sabbati observationem, tanquam Judaicam et Christianis moribus adversam, edicto publico prohibuit.'[3] But he encountered heavy opposition, and even penalties did not avail.

The conception and observance in Ethiopia of the Old Testament Sabbath drew support from a number of unimpeachable sources:[4] chapter xxxviii of the *Ethiopic Didascalia*[5] enjoins the keeping of both the Sabbath and the Sunday. Gregory of Nyssa —whose authority among Ethiopians stands high—had argued: 'quibus oculis diem Dominicam intueris, qui Sabbatum dede-corasti? au nescis, hos dies germanos esse, ac si in alterum injurius sis, te in alterum impingere?'[6] And, perhaps, most significantly: is not the continued validity of the Decalogue and the Law expressly prescribed in Matthew 5: 18 that 'one jot or one tittle shall in no wise pass from the Law?'[7]

M. Rodinson maintains, rightly, that 'la pratique [of observing both Saturday and Sunday] était courante aux origines du christianisme',[8] but only in some of the Oriental Christian Churches has it survived.[9] In the Coptic Church of Egypt as

[1] *Sabbat*, p. 53.

[2] The same reservation applies to the discussion in chapter xix of the *Fətḥa Nagast* (which, in its basic tenets, reflects the position of the Coptic Church in Egypt) where anxiety to distinguish Christian from Jewish observance of the Sabbath goes hand in hand with the injunction that servants are to work on five days of the week only and to attend for religious instruction on Saturday and Sunday. See now also Hammerschmidt, *Sabbat*, pp. 58–61.

[3] Ludolf, *Historia*, iii. 10, 64.

[4] Among these the Old Testament has naturally pride of place: 'Et sabbata custodite, ut in lege Moysis praeceptum est, et in libris omnium prophetarum, et in canonibus sanctorum apostolorum patrum nostrorum' (Turaiev, *Acta S. Eustathii*, p. 18).

[5] Cf. J. M. Harden's translation: *The Ethiopic Didascalia*; T. P. Platt's edition (*The Ethiopic Didascalia*) was, unfortunately, based on an incomplete manuscript.

[6] Cf. Ludolf, *Historia*, iii. 1, 55. See also Hammerschmidt, op. cit., note 382 (though I cannot accept H.'s strictures, since Ludolf does quote the source and Ludolf's work is one to which all *ēthiopisants* have ready access).

[7] This had also been the argument used by Abba Gregory, Ludolf's friend (*Comm.*, p. 276).

[8] *Bi Or*, 1964, p. 240.

[9] In the case of the Seventh Day Adventists it is, of course, likewise an aspect of the emulation of the Old Testament.

well as the monophysite Church of Ethiopia it was the influence and veneration of the Old Testament which had brought about this state of affairs. Yet the closer approximation to Old Testament practice and its enduring importance in Ethiopia represent a singular phenomenon which has to be evaluated in association with the Judaic elements from South Arabia which had crossed the Red Sea in the early centuries of the first millennium A.D.[1]

The observance of the Sabbath constitutes the major concern of Zar'a Ya'qob's *Mäṣḥafä Bərhan*. The doctrinal and historical background[2] has been authoritatively sketched by Dillmann in his *Kirchenordnung* (esp. pp. 47 ff.), but we now also possess the complete text edited by Conti Rossini and Ricci. In his preface (vol. i, transl., pp. ii and iii) Ricci says: 'ma sugli altri argomenti hanno la preminenza l'imposizione dell'osservanza del sabato, di cui si dimostra e si sancisce la canonicità con l'autorità dei libri sacri . . .' and again he finds that Sabbath observance constitutes 'l'argomento su cui insiste lo scritto per tutta la sua estensione, ripetutamente tornandovi sopra'.[3] A cursory glance at the text suffices to establish the centrality of the Sabbath theme in this famous medieval treatise: 'As the creation of darkness preceded that of light, thus the observance of the Sabbath preceded that of the Sunday. Hence it was called the 'first Sabbath' because Sunday was given after it, but the Apostles established Sabbath and Sunday as one day . . .'.[4] Detailed regulations are issued as regards work that is not permitted on the Sabbath,[5] and the entire book exhibits an almost passionate preoccupation with the importance of the Sabbath.

This anxious concern of the *Mäṣḥafä Bərhan* arises, of course, from the doubts and acute theological struggles which characterized the era of Zar'a Ya'qob's predecessors, and it was not until the middle of the fifteenth century that the firm grip of that great king and reformer resolved those difficulties. It has sometimes been argued[6] that the celebration and sanctity of the

---

[1] It is in this sense that I would wish to reinterpret the passages in Doresse, *L'Empire du Prêtre Jean*, ii. 115, note 1; pp. 152–3. Cf. also K. Wendt in *Atti del Convegno*, p. 140.

[2] See also Cerulli, *Storia*, pp. 133 ff.; idem, *Miracoli di Maria*, pp. 94 ff.

[3] Cf. also Hammerschmidt, *Sabbat*, pp. 19–35, which contains a helpful summary of the contents of the *Mäṣḥafä Bərhan* (written before the publication of the Conti Rossini–Ricci edition).
See also Wendt in *Atti del Convegno*, p. 146; idem, *Maṣḥafa Milad*, i (transl.), 87 ff. (= text, pp. 99 ff.).

[4] *Mäṣḥafä Bərhan*, ii (text), 60.

[5] Op. cit., pp. 6–7; Dillmann, *Kirchenordnung*, pp. 49–50.
Zar'a Ya'qob's list of what is allowed or prohibited on the two Sabbaths makes interesting reading in the light of Jewish practice and reveals, incidentally, an astonishing mixture of knowledge as well as misconception of the latter. See now also Hammerschmidt, *Sabbat*, pp. 25–30.   [6] e.g. by Conti Rossini, *Etiopia e genti d'Etiopia*, p. 181.

Sabbath were, in fact, introduced by Zar'a Ya'qob. This I find hard to accept, for what the latter did was, above all, the successful removal of the threatening schism between the two great monastic orders. The main point at issue in this theological controversy was the strict observance of the two Sabbaths (Saturday and Sunday) by the northern Eustathian monks,[1] mainly based on Debra Bizen. By deciding the dispute in favour of the followers of Eustathius, Zar'a Ya'qob did not introduce a new conception of the equality of the two Sabbaths, but merely gave preference to the long-established northern tradition which, in the original home of the Semitized Aksumites, had always preserved Judaic ingredients more faithfully than the somewhat 'diluted' southern tradition.[2] There can thus be little doubt, to my mind, that the status of the Sabbath in Ethiopian Christianity derives from the veneration of the Old Testament and from the imitation of the Hebraic lore contained in it.[3] This tendency was buttressed by the leaven of Judaic practice introduced into Ethiopia from South Arabia in the early centuries of the Christian era.

Moving towards recent times, we note that in the 1840s W. C. Harris[4] found that

the Jewish Sabbath is strictly observed throughout the kingdom. The ox and the ass are at rest. Agricultural pursuits are suspended. Household avocations must be laid aside, and the spirit of idleness reigns throughout the day . . . and when, a few years ago, one daring spirit presumed, in advance of the age, to burst the fetters of superstition, His Majesty the King of Shoa,[5] stimulated by the advice of besotted monks, issued a proclamation[6] that whoso violated the Jewish Sabbath should forfeit his property to the royal treasury, and be consigned to the state dungeon.

For the present time, Conti Rossini states:[7] 'si considera obbligatoria l'osservanza del sabato, al pari di quella della domenica.' Similar verdicts may be found in many other contemporary

---

[1] On Eustathius (fourteenth century) and the Eustathian order see Ludolf, *Historia*, iii. 3, 29 ff.; *Commentarius*, pp. 286, 434; Dillmann, *Kirchenordnung*, pp. 45 ff.; Littmann, *Gesch. d. aeth. Lit.*, pp. 204, 212, 232, 244; Guidi, *Storia d. lett. et.*, p. 59; idem in *OM* 1922, pp. 127–8, 187; Turaiev, *Acta S. Eustathii* (*C.S.C.O.*, 32/Aeth. 15); Conti Rossini-Ricci, *Mäṣḥafä Bərhan*, ii. 145 ff. (= transl. p. 82).   [2] Cf. my *Sem. Langg. of Ethiopia*, p. 226.

[3] Thus also Rodinson, despite reservations of various kinds, in *Bi Or*, 1964, p. 241: 'cela implique une imitation de l'Ancien Testament.'

[4] *Highlands of Aethiopia*, iii. 150–1.

[5] i.e. King Sahla Sellassie, ancestor of the Emperor Haile Sellassie I.

[6] The Amharic text of this proclamation is not known to me, but it is interesting and relevant to compare the text of the Sabbath observance proclamation issued in 1928 and printed on p. 545 of Balambaras Mahtämä Səllase's *Zəkrä nägär* (Addis Ababa, 1949/50). See also Eadie, *Amharic Reader*, p. 183.

[7] *L'Abissinia*, p. 82.

works, among them Hyatt's *Church of Abyssinia* (p. 224), Rathjens's *Juden in Abessinien* (p. 53), Pollera's *L'Abissinia di ieri* (p. 153), etc.[1] Finally, it is instructive to look at the entry *snbt* in the various dictionaries of the modern Ethiopian languages, both for the terminology and the substance of Sabbath observance: Baeteman (*Dictionnaire*, col. 212) maintains that 'les Éthiopiens conservent une partie de la loi mosaïque conjointement avec la loi chrétienne. Ils ont gardé les deux *sänbät*.' Coulbeaux–Schreiber (*Dictionnaire de la langue Tigrai*, p. 243) also find that 'les Éthiopiens, conservant les deux lois, ont gardé les deux *sänbät*'.

Concluding observations

It would not be difficult to extend the list of parallels and influences demonstrating the abiding impact of the Bible in general, and the Old Testament in particular, on Abyssinian Christianity and on the fabric of Ethiopian society. This impact goes far beyond anything experienced in the other Oriental Christian Churches and cannot be accounted for by general references to the Judaizing character of the early Church in the East. A case in point is the feasts and fasts observed by the Church in Ethiopia. Of course, the relationship between Christian forms and their Old Testament substratum is generally one of great complexity.

The Ethiopian New Year (1 Mäskäräm = 11 September) is almost certainly related to *roš haš-šana*; its date, as well as that of *Mäsqäl* ('feast of the cross'), corresponds closely to the Hebrew season of the *yamim nora'im*.[2] With the introduction of Christianity into Ethiopia it became necessary to transform the celebration of the New Year into a Christian feast—without undue interference with the deep-rooted religious practices and customs traditionally observed. In this way the Christian feast of *Qəddus Yohannes*, St. John the Baptist, was superimposed on the ancient Hebraic structure; and though no great violence was done to the date (29 August) on which the Church commemorates the execution of St. John, it is clear that the ceremonies associated with this day in Ethiopia reveal a distinctly pre-Christian character.

The same applies to *Mäsqäl* (17 Mäskäräm = 27 September) which is tied to New Year in much the same way as *roš haš-šana*

---

[1] See also Cheesman, *Lake Tana*, pp. 54–55.

[2] That is also Pollera's view (*L'Abissinia di ieri*, p. 156). Other Old Testament and Jewish elements have been pointed out by Ludolf, *Commentarius*, pp. 368 ff.

and *yom hak-kippurim* are connected by the period of expiation and atonement. There is, of course, no clear consciousness in Ethiopia of the original functions of each of these days, but the idea of purification and atonement is prominently present.[1]

Mäsqäl, the feast of the finding of the True Cross, appears to have received its Christian sanction at the end of the fourteenth century, but the pagan and Hebraic rites associated with it point to a more ancient and more complex origin. On the morning of Mäsqäl the celebration of the *Dämära* takes place. The *dämära* is a large heap of dry wood around which the people assemble and which is eventually set ablaze to the accompaniment of shouts, songs, dances, and ululations. Some say that it marks the ultimate act in the cancellation of sins, while others hold that the direction of the smoke and the final collapse of the heap indicate the course of future events—just as the cloud of smoke of the Lord over the Tabernacle offered guidance to the children of Israel (*Exod.* 40: 34–38).

Of particular interest in this connexion is a somewhat neglected treatise on the calendar whose redaction goes back to the reign of the Emperor ʿAmda Ṣəyon (fourteenth century). Its editor, P. Mauro da Leonessa,[2] has drawn attention to what he terms the 'ricorrenze giudaiche del calendario abissino' (pp. 304, 306). He shows that the feast of *mäṭqəʿ*[3] is 'propriamente il novilunio del settimo mese degli Ebrei' (*tišri*), that the *bädr*[4] is 'precisamente il *yom kippur* ossia il digiuno della espiazione dei Giudei'. Other connexions relate to *mäṣällät* 'Tabernacles', *fəsḥa ʾorit* 'Passover', etc.

The most ancient meaning of these feasts—as was also the case in Israel—was no doubt seasonal: the month of Mäskäräm marked the end of the rains, the resumption of work, and the reopening of communications.

The Ethiopian Church has an enormous number of days of fasting,[5] but Ludolf (*Historia*, iii. 6, 90 ff.) had already observed—correctly, I believe—that the two regular weekly Abyssinian fasts are a remnant of the two days of fasting each week observed by Jews. The change from Monday and Thursday to Wednesday and Friday was no doubt meant to invalidate accusations of imitating the Jews.

If the Judaization of the Ethiopian Church and its veneration of the Old Testament were simply an aspect of the nature of all

---

[1] For Hebraic parallels cf. *JSS* 1956, p. 246.   [2] *RSE* 1943, iii, pp. 302–26.
[3] Cf. Dillmann, *Lexicon*, col. 1225.   [4] Op. cit., col. 541.
[5] Details in Rathjens, op. cit., p. 54; *Fətḥa Nagast*, chapter xv; Guidi *OM* 1922, p. 254.

the Christian Oriental Churches (as M. Rodinson has at times argued),[1] it would be hard to explain the wellnigh universally reported impression of the Hebrew or Biblical character of the Ethiopian ambience (see esp. above, pp. 26–30, 99, 102, note 3, etc.) and the absence of such virtually unanimous judgement in relation to the Jacobite, Coptic, and other Oriental Churches. It seems to me that this argument by itself is strong enough to uphold the general view that the Old Testament character of Ethiopian Christianity is a phenomenon *sui generis*.

I have no doubt that the parallels that have been drawn and the influences which have been sketched in this necessarily superficial examination may well be tentative and may require correction at various points, but in their cumulative effect they cannot fail to reveal a truly remarkable sediment of Hebraic lore settled in this remote outpost of the Semitic world. I have endeavoured to indicate no more than a few lines along which research might profitably be undertaken; and I have said nothing of many important facets, such as customary law, marriage, and divorce (in particular levirate marriage[2]—so obvious an Old Testament institution) or of the theological structure. Could it be that *täwaḥdo*, the monophysite doctrine, has been so stubbornly and passionately defended in Ethiopia over the centuries because it was felt to accord more closely with the strict concepts of Old Testament monotheism? The all-pervading effect of Ethiopian Christianity on Ethiopian life will be clear to anyone who has grasped the identity of religious and secular life in a Semitic civilization.

EXCURSUS ON THE FALASHAS

The present examination cannot conclude without a few summary remarks on the Falashas who have for long been dubbed, with questionable justification, the 'Jews of Ethiopia'. In the present context we shall have to determine whether they can, in fact, be considered the carriers of those Old Testament and Hebraic elements discussed in the foregoing or if they are merely one sector of the population peculiarly exposed to the general impact.[3]

---

[1] I find myself, however, in substantial agreement with most of the conclusions (p. 245) at which M. Rodinson has arrived in his exceptionally valuable and learned review-article in *Bi Or*, 1964. Here he states that he does not deny 'la possibilité d'influences juives sur le christianisme éthiopien *spécifiquement*', speaks of 'l'imitation systématique de l'Ancien Testament', and affirms that 'l'expérience historique . . . nous apprend qu'une judaïsation de ce genre peut se faire sans aucune intervention des Juifs réels, par simple lecture des textes et raisonnement sur ceux-ci'.

[2] Deut. 25: 5–10.

[3] For a brief bibliographical orientation on the Falashas see Aeścoly, 'The Falashas

A good deal of legendary information about the Falashas appears
already in such medieval writings as *Sefer Eldad* and in an account
given by Benjamin of Tudela who gathered some news on the Falashas
while on his way from the Yemen to Egypt.[1] Ludolf included some notes
and questions in his monumental work on Ethiopian history—based, to
a large extent, on information supplied by Abba Gregory who thought
that the Falashas 'dialecto Talmudica corrupta inter se utuntur'[2] (no
doubt a reference to their Agaw vernacular which Gregory did not
understand). Thus misled, Ludolf is understandably curious to know
'quando vel qua occasione Judaei isti primum in Aethiopiam venerint?
Karraeorumne vel aliorum Judaeorum sectae sint addicti?'[2]

James Bruce of Kinnaird[3] provides a fairly detailed, though not
necessarily accurate, picture of Falasha life which became the stimulus
of subsequent interest in this peculiar form of 'Judaism'. With the
exception of such noted scholars as Guidi, Conti Rossini, Rathjens,
Leslau, and a few others, nineteenth- and twentieth-century preoccupation with the Falashas has been marked by either Christian or Jewish
missionary zeal[4] which has vitiated most attempts at a scholarly approach and has plunged Falasha 'studies' into an atmosphere charged
with a surfeit of *ira et studium*. Earlier works, such as those by the
Christian missionaries H. A. Stern,[5] J. M. Flad,[6] and others nevertheless possessed considerable intrinsic value, while the Alliance Israélite
Universelle was uncommonly fortunate in the choice of J. Halévy, the
famous Semitist, as its first emissary to the Falashas. Such good fortune
cannot be said to have attended more recent excursions into Falasha
country.

The Falashas, who live to the north of Lake Tana in Begamedr,
Semien, and Dembiya, are Ethiopians of Agaw stock. They have survived in small nuclei representing a total number that has been variously
estimated at between 15,000 and 60,000 (but which is almost certainly
nearer the lower figure). Their cult embodies a curious mixture of
pagan-Judaic-Christian beliefs and ceremonies, but the Falashas are
neither the only non-Christian and unconverted tribe nor the only
sector of the Ethiopian population that has clung to so strange a religious amalgam. The Falashas do not know of any religious prescriptions outside the Pentateuch; Mishnah and Talmud are unknown to

(bibliography)' in *Kiryath Sepher*, xii, xiii (1935–7); Leslau in *Studies in Bibliography and Booklore*, June 1957; Aešcoly, *Sefer ha-Falashim*; idem, *Recueil de Textes Falachas*; Leslau, *Falasha
Anthology*; idem, *Coutumes et Croyances des Falachas*; Ullendorff in *BSOAS* 1953, pp. 174–7; 1961,
pp. 419–43.
  [1] Cf. Conti Rossini, 'Leggende Geogr. Giudaiche del IX secolo (il Sefer Eldad)'; idem,
'L'itinerario di Beniamino da Tudela e l'Etiopia'; Cerulli, *Etiopi in Palestina*, i. 234, 320.
  [2] *Historia*, i. 14, 42 ff.   [3] *Travels*[3], ii. 396 ff.
  [4] 'Most of the reports that have so far been made about the Falashas have been incomplete
and characterized by a Christian or Jewish missionary tendency which appreciably diminishes
their usefulness and objectivity' (Leslau, *Falasha Anthology*, p. x). See also Aešcoly's strictures
on the subject of Falasha 'research' in *Sefer ha-Falashim*, 176 ff.
  [5] *Wanderings among the Falashas in Abyssinia*, London, 1862.
  [6] *The Falashas of Abyssinia*, London, 1869; *60 Jahre in der Mission unter den Falaschas*, Gießen,
1922.

them. They have no knowledge of Hebrew, and the language of their prayers is Gə'əz—as is the case with their Christian compatriots. The feasts mentioned in the Pentateuch are observed by the Falashas in a manner often materially different from that of Jews elsewhere. Post-exilic feasts are not celebrated by them. The Sabbath is observed with considerable strictness, and the prescriptions regarding ritual cleanness are practised with great zeal—both features which exist among very many other Ethiopians. In common with their monophysite neigh-bours the Falashas carry out circumcision on boys and excision on girls. Monasticism plays an important part in their community—and here, surely, is a fundamental distinction from Judaism. Their place of worship is significantly called *masgid*!

A dispassionate appraisal of the ethnic and religious position of the Falashas places them squarely into the main-stream of Ethiopian life, yet outside the doctrinal tradition of monophysitism. Study of the historical background makes it clear beyond reasonable doubt that the occasionally canvassed origin of the Falashas from the Jewish garrison of Elephantine[1] or the conjecture that Jewish influences in Abyssinia had penetrated by way of Egypt are devoid of any reliable historical basis. In the section dealing with the historical background (Introduc-tion) I have endeavoured to muster some of the evidence in rebuttal of such views and in support of the now widely accepted proposition that such Judaized elements must have entered Ethiopia via South Arabia. There is no need to cover the same ground once more, for all the evidence available points to the conclusion that the Falashas are descendants of those elements in the Aksumite kingdom who resisted conversion to Christianity. Their so-called Judaism is merely the reflexion of those Hebraic and Judaic practices and beliefs which were implanted on parts of south-west Arabia in the first post-Christian centuries and subsequently brought into Abyssinia. The general Ethiopian tendency towards the emulation of the world of the Old Testament had the effect of strengthening their adherence to these elements and of pro-viding a quasi-doctrinal underpinning of this structure.

If this opinion is correct, then the religious pattern of the Falashas—even though it will have undergone some change in the past 1,600 years—may well mirror to a considerable extent the religious syncretism of the pre-Christian Aksumite kingdom. It is in their living testimony to the Judaized civilization of the South Arabian immigrants and their wellnigh complete cultural ascendancy over the Cushitic and other strata of the original African population of Ethiopia that we must seek the value and great interest of the Falashas today—and not in their rehabilitation as a long lost tribe of Israel (which is historically quite

---

[1] This view was resuscitated by so exalted an authority as the late President of Israel (Mr. Y. Ben-Zvi) in an important article on the early settlement of Jewish tribes in Arabia (*Erets Israel* (Jerusalem), vi (1960), 146) where this opinion is parenthetically expressed with-out any proof being adduced in its support—nor does Mr. Ben-Zvi appear to have seen the full documentation concerned with this question.

unwarranted). Like their Christian fellow Ethiopians, the Falashas are stubborn adherents to fossilized Hebraic-Jewish beliefs, practices, and customs which were transplanted from South Arabia into the Horn of Africa and which may here be studied in the authentic surroundings and atmosphere of a semitized country.

Falasha literature forms an integral part of the literary tradition of Ethiopia, both in its themes and in the manner of their treatment. There exist, however, a few works which are peculiar to the Falashas, but, despite the valiant spadework by Halévy, Conti Rossini, Aeščoly, Leslau, Wurmbrand,[1] and a few others, this literature has not yet received the detailed scholarly examination it deserves, both for its own sake and for the detection of historical and literary ramifications. Among original Falasha works appear to be the 'Commandments of the Sabbath', the 'Book of Abba Elijah', and some of their prayers. Books which have received at least a measure of specific elaboration by the Falashas include the Apocalypses of Gorgorios and Ezra, the 'Book of Disciples', the 'Testament of Abraham',[2] the 'Book of the Angels', and one or two others of less certain provenance. All this literature is, of course, in Gəʿəz; the Falashas are, it is worth reiterating, entirely innocent of Hebrew, and their Agaw vernacular is not employed for literary purposes.

A small Falasha work of some interest is the *Mota Muse* ('Death of Moses') or *Zena Muse* ('Story of Moses'), though one should not be too dogmatic about its exclusive connexion with the Falashas.[3] There exist Arabic, Hebrew, and other opuscula on this subject, and the literary filiation of this work is capable of shedding some light on the cultural and historical provenance of the Falashas. Close examination of this document has shown that the Falasha *Mota Muse* does not originate from a Jewish source nor does it contain anything of specifically Jewish character. On the contrary, its contents reveal that it is directly derived from Muslim sources which, in a remote past, may themselves have drawn on a Jewish legend that was subsequently reshaped in accordance with Arabic literary and national trends.

It would be hazardous to see in this more than just one facet of Falasha dependence on non-Jewish elements. On the other hand, it is both unscholarly and impolitic to stretch the evidence beyond permissible limits and place the Falashas against a background which is far removed from their genuine native ambience. Falashas and Ethiopians in general are the heirs of a civilization in which the veneration and imitation of the Old Testament occupy a central and enduring position.

[1] See Bibliography.
[2] Cf. *The Falasha Version of the Testaments of Abraham, Isaac and Jacob*, Manchester Ph.D. thesis submitted by M. Gaguine (1965).
[3] Cf. Faitlovitch, *Mota Muse*, Paris, 1906; Ullendorff, 'Death of Moses' in *BSOAS* 1961, pp. 419–43.

THE LINGUISTIC FACTORS

Introductory

THE linguistic elements involved in our subject can be approached in a number of different ways. The most obvious group is, perhaps, represented by Hebrew words which have simply been transliterated or transcribed (generally the latter, but this remains to be established in detail) into Gǝʿǝz. In MS. 5 in Zotenberg's *Catalogue*, p. 8 (Éth. 94) we find a list of Hebrew words with their explanation in Ethiopic:

ኤሎሃ፡ ብዜል፡ አግሞላክ። አይናይ፡ ብዜል፡
እግዚእ። ፀአኦት፡ ብዜል፡ ዘጎይሳጎት። . . ., etc.

If I am not in error, the full list has never yet been subjected to systematic scrutiny. Words like መና፡ 'Manna' (Exod. 16: 33, 35), ሴሙፅታን፡ or ሴፅያታን፡ 'Leviathan', etc., are, of course, merely transcriptions. Other examples have been mentioned on p. 42, above.[1] In a sense —as Nöldeke[2] had already observed—even words like ሲኦል፡, ገሀነም፡ are originally transcriptions, but that applies to many loanwords until they are adapted to the phonetic system of the recipient language.

I shall not be concerned here with passages which deliberately employ such Ethiopic roots as correspond with their equivalents in the Hebrew original,[3] nor with Ethiopic expressions which are clearly intended as approximations to the Hebrew text.[4] Instead, I shall have two main objects in mind: (1) The Hebrew and particularly Aramaic loanwords in Gǝʿǝz which reflect either the Judaic leaven in Abyssinian civilization or which are expressive of specifically Christian ideas; and (2) the value for the exegesis of the Hebrew Bible of the Ethiopian languages, ancient or modern. In this latter context I shall not be collecting etymological equivalents as such,[5] but shall only adduce those words which can be held to contribute to an elucidation of the text.

While my principal concern in this study will be with loanwords which have found a home in Ethiopic, there exists, of course, an export, by no means negligible, of Gǝʿǝz words into other languages, notably Arabic. One need only think of

[1] See also Heider, *Aeth. Bibelübersetzung*, p. 9.
[2] *Neue Beiträge*, p. 33.
[3] Cf. p. 42, above, and Zotenberg, *Catalogue*, p. 9.
[4] Zotenberg, op. cit., p. 11; see also p. 43, above.
[5] That has already been done by W. Leslau, *Ethiopic and South Arabic Contributions to the Hebrew Lexicon*, University of California Press, 1958.

مائدة — ማእድ:	منبر — መንበር:	جهنم — ገሃነም:
برهان — ብርሃን:	شيطان — ሠይጣን:	رجيم — ርጉም:

etc. Wellhausen[1] and especially Nöldeke[2] have collected the Ethiopic
vocabulary in Arabic; also relevant is S. Fraenkel's *Die Aramäischen
Fremdwörter im Arabischen*, p. 323.

In view of the relatively close relationship between the Semitic
languages, it is not always easy to be certain either about the direction
of the loan-movement or about the process of borrowing as such. For in
many cases it is not at all clear whether the phenomenon goes back to
proto-Semitic agreement or to subsequent import from an alien source.
In such instances it is often possible to reach acceptable conclusions by
investigating the historical ramifications and the phonetic circumstances. 'Like loanwords elsewhere, these Aramaic words, if correctly
interpreted, are evidence of cultural contacts and influences. Such
evidence is especially welcome if it can shed some light on so obscure
a subject as the rise of Christianity in ancient Ethiopia and the circumstances in which the Bible was translated into Gǝʿǝz. The potential
significance of the Aramaic loanwords in this connexion has, of course,
long been realized. The question is whether certain conclusions which
seem to be widely accepted at present rest on sound foundations'.[3] It
would be well to take these programmatic words by Polotsky as our
guide-post.

Hebrew and Aramaic loanwords in Gǝʿǝz

H. J. Polotsky (loc. cit.) has rightly insisted that the correct evaluation
of the linguistic evidence hinges very largely on matters of Aramaic dialectology. The accurate attribution of a word to a given Aramaic dialect
is clearly of paramount importance, for, while Syriac is Aramaic, the
converse is not necessarily true. Polotsky has incontrovertibly shown
(op. cit.) that 'some of the most important words [in Ethiopic] are
manifestly not Syriac'; yet to classify all of them as 'Aramaic' *simpliciter*
is not only lacking in precision but falls short of that refinement which
alone will allow us to draw the appropriate cultural and historical
inferences.

Unhappily such dialectal distinctiveness is not always attainable, as
the majority of words exhibit a regrettable measure of indeterminate-
ness in this respect. There would, of course, be no problem if we could
be sure that all those Aramaic loanwords form a homogeneous group.
Polotsky has stated his 'personal belief' that this is, in fact, the case;
he thinks that it is a sound working hypothesis 'to start from the assumption that Aramaic words fulfilling the conditions of antiquity and of
general use throughout the Ethiopic Bible are homogeneous'. These are,
indeed, pretty stringent conditions and do not leave a great deal of
leeway for dialectal deviation. We shall have to see in the following

---

[1] *Reste*[3], p. 232, note.   [2] *Neue Beiträge*, pp. 46–64.   [3] Polotsky in *JSS* 1964, p. 1.

whether closer study of this material will corroborate Polotsky's 'assumption' which is probably a good deal more than a mere hunch.[1]

The first to refer to 'Chaldaean' (i.e. Jewish-Aramaic) and Syriac words in Ethiopic was Ludolf (*Commentarius*, pp. 201–2). Polotsky has recently dealt[2] with Ludolf's views on this topic, and there is no need to traverse the same ground once more. We now possess three studies on this subject, written by such masters of Semitic philology as Dillmann,[3] Nöldeke,[4] and Polotsky.[5] All three have shown, in one way or another, that the Aramaic words were borrowed at the time when the Abyssinians ruled over parts of South Arabia and had commercial contacts with the Jews of Arabia.[6] This linguistic evidence is thus of profound . significance in establishing the fact that Abyssinian–Jewish contacts existed during the Aksum era before the Ethiopians evolved any tendency towards the emulation of the Old Testament.

Dillmann has enumerated the relevant *verba peregrina* and divided them into distinct categories, such as 'res sacrae et literariae', 'res Christianae', 'res mundanae', etc.,[7] while Nöldeke[8] allocated them to such subjects as 'religion', 'dress', 'utensils', 'plants', etc. I should prefer to rehearse them here in a completely haphazard manner, so as not to prejudge the issue. We shall eventually try to find out whether their cultural distribution corresponds to any recognizable dialectal pattern.

It is, perhaps, well to begin with the most unequivocal term, i.e. *məṣwat* 'alms' of which Nöldeke (op. cit., p. 36) has long ago said, in a much-quoted remark, that this word alone would suffice 'jüdischen religiösen Einfluß bei den alten Abessiniern zu konstatieren'. The specific semantic range of this word, in its Jewish connotation, had, of course, been recognized by Dillmann (*Lexicon*, col. xxii) who also established that this 'nomen a Judaeis petitum' (col. 228) represents the Aramaic plural of the Hebrew מצוה 'commandment'. מִצְוָתָא in Rabbinic literature is 'charity'—exactly as in Ethiopic. That this term is in no way connected with the translation of the Hebrew Bible, but derives from a different setting altogether, has been abundantly proved by Polotsky[9] who checked all the relevant passages—some 180—'in order to be able to state positively that not in a single case does *məṣwat* correspond to מצוה in Hebrew'. The noun *məṣwat* has also produced some quaint verbal derivatives: Gə'əz *māṣwätä* 'to give alms', Amh. *mäṣäwwdtä*;[10] Nöldeke's statement (loc. cit.) that Tña has formed a new verb ጸወተ፡ from *məṣwat* has not been confirmed by my inquiries in Eritrea

---

[1] I am not clear, though, why Polotsky thinks (op. cit., p. 2) that 'the burden of proof must rest upon those who may wish to maintain the contrary', i.e. that these words are dialectally heterogeneous.

[2] Op. cit., p. 3.

[3] *Lexicon*, cols. xxi–xxii, dealing with 'verba, maxime nomina, peregrina'.

[4] *Neue Beiträge*, pp. 31 ff.   [5] 'Aramaic, Syriac, and Gə'əz' in *JSS* 1964, pp. 1–10.

[6] See the relevant Dillmann quotation on p. 24, above.

[7] *Lexicon*, col. xxii.   [8] Op. cit., *passim*.   [9] *JSS* 1964, p. 6.

[10] Cf. *māṣwäl* 'charitable, giving alms'; *məṣwatäñña* 'living on alms, beggar'.

where, in fact, the Gəʿəz *maṣwätä* is used (thus also Coulbeaux–Schreiber's and da Bassano's dictionaries).

Ethiopic *ṭaʿot* 'idol' clearly shows its specifically Jewish connexion[1] (the post-Biblical טעות). The Syriac form is *ṭāʿyūṭā* and means 'error'; the specialized significance 'idol' is not attested in Syriac and appears to be peculiar to Jewish Aramaic—and hence to Gəʿəz.

Similar considerations apply to *tabot*[2] which has been discussed in general terms in the main part of this chapter. Nöldeke (op. cit., 37) had already found that this word is 'nur jüdisch bezeugt'; and Polotsky has drawn attention (loc. cit.) to the fact that it 'exhibits characteristically different forms in Jewish Aramaic and Syriac, respectively': *tēḇūṭā* (*tēḇōṭā*) as compared with Syriac *qēḇūṭā*;[3] the latter is thus 'ruled out as the source of *tabot*'.

Nöldeke[4] and Guidi,[5] in particular, have argued that *haymanot* 'faith' is specifically Christian and Syriac.[6] Linguistically, the term is neutral and represents both Jewish Aramaic and Syriac *haymānūṭā*; semantically, it is indeed more exclusively religious than is the case in Jewish Aramaic. Polotsky's detailed study of the scriptural occurrences of this word has shown that the argument in favour of a Christian-Syriac origin falls short of being conclusive.[7] Jewish Aramaic derivation has also been claimed by Dillmann[8] and Rahlfs.[9] Polotsky's verdict that *haymanot* 'belongs to the same group' as *maṣwat*, *ṭaʿot*, *tabot*, etc., and that its use in the Ethiopic Bible is 'actually easier to understand, if it was in the first instance borrowed as a Jewish word' carries conviction. The qualification *in the first instance* is, however, of crucial importance, for *haymanot* is one of several examples where the original borrowing from Jewish Aramaic sources was subsequently developed by Syriac and conducted into specifically Christian channels.

Ethiopic *ʾarami*[10] 'pagan' reflects, in form, Hebrew *ʾarammi* rather than Syriac *ʾarmāyā*.[11] *ʾOrit* 'law, Torah' represents, of course, Jewish Aram. and Syriac *ʾorayṭā*; it is thus linguistically indeterminate. Nöldeke was undecided as to whether Jews or Christians introduced this term into Ethiopic,[12] but it seems to me that the considerations which have been put forward in the case of *haymanot* would apply *a fortiori* to *ʾorit*.[13]

---

[1] So also Dillmann, *Lex.* xxii; Nöldeke, op. cit., p. 35; Polotsky, op. cit., p. 6.

[2] Cf. Dillmann, *Lex.* xxii and 560; Nöldeke, op. cit., pp. 37, 49; Polotsky, loc. cit.; and above, p. 82, where further references are cited in footnote 5.—I find it difficult to accept Rabin's verdict (*West-Arabian*, pp. 109–10) that Ethiopic must have received this word via West Arabian.

[3] Cf. Mand. *qabuta, qubita* (Drower and Macuch, *Mand. Dict.*, pp. 398, 405); Greek κιβωτός; see Brockelmann, *Lex. Syr.*, p. 645. I am uncertain whether the resemblance between *tēḇūṭā* and *qēḇūṭā* is fortuitous or is the result of a process of palatalization of the type described in *Sem. Langg. of Ethiopia*, p. 68, note 71.

[4] Op. cit., pp. 23 and 35.   [5] *Storia della lett. et.*, p. 14.   [6] See above, p. 40.

[7] Op. cit., pp. 6–7.   [8] *Lexicon*, col. xxii.   [9] *Äth. Bibelübersetzung*, p. 675.

[10] Cf. Dillmann, *Lexicon*, col. xxii; Nöldeke, op. cit., p. 35; Rahlfs, op. cit., p. 675.

[11] Cf. Nöldeke, *Syr. Gramm.*[2], p. 80, note 1. I cannot agree here with Conti Rossini, *Storia*, p. 155, who postulates Syriac origin. I am not sure, however, if his use of 'Syriac' is intended to be precise and is not simply a (mistaken) blanket term for Aramaic in general.

[12] *Neue Beiträge*, p. 35.   [13] Rahlfs, op. cit., p. 675.

si'ol 'nether world' has not only its well-known Hebrew and Syriac counterparts but also Jewish Aram. שיאל;[1] it is thus linguistically neutral and semantically indifferent. To the same range of meaning belongs *gähannäm* 'Gehenna', but here the retention of the final *m*—in contrast to Syriac ܓܗܢܐ and Greek γεεννα—points to Jewish provenance.[2] The Arabic جَهَنَّم is, of course, derived from Gə'əz.[3]

I have already referred (p. 98, above) to *tärgwamä* 'to interpret'; here the semantic area as well as the labio-velar sound (indicative of an original *targum*) testify to the Hebraic-Jewish origin of this concept. Gə'əz *'aṭharä*, too, derives from the same ambience;[4] it is specifically applied 'de lustrationibus Judaeorum sacris'[5] and does not occur in Syriac. In Gə'əz *fəsḥ* 'Passover' the sibilant shows that the word came from Hebrew or Jewish Aramaic,[6] since in Syriac we encounter *ṣ* instead of *s*.

'arb 'eve of Sabbath, Friday' is probably taken from Hebrew rather than from Aramaic or Syriac *'arubtä*.[7] In *ḥanafi* (*ḥonafi*), on the other hand, the semantic development to 'pagan' in both Gə'əz and Syriac (in contrast to Hebrew *ḥanef* 'hypocrite') makes borrowing from a Syriac source the more likely course. The term possesses, however, theological complexities and wide ramifications.[8]

In *mäsiḥ* 'anointed' and *näbiy* 'prophet' it is impossible to assert that absence of the Aramaic ending necessarily suggests Hebrew provenance, for the Aramaic ending disappears not infrequently when rendered into another language.[9] Similarly inconclusive is *sänbät* whose nasal sound is not attested either in Hebrew or any Aramaic dialect. Dillmann (*Lex.* xxii) includes *sayṭan* among the words of Jewish provenance, and Nöldeke (op. cit., p. 34) lists it among the Hebrew and Aramaic words accepted into Ethiopic. While this view is probably correct, it is not at all easy to account for the phonetic development which has occurred in this case.

qäsis 'priest' seems, one would agree with Nöldeke (op. cit., p. 37), 'specifically Christian', both semantically and in form (despite the existence of קשיש it is almost certainly derived from Syriac). *fərqan* 'salvation', on the other hand, may have its source in either the Jewish Aramaic or Syriac equivalent.

Dillmann (*Lexicon*, xxii) is unduly restrictive in mentioning among *res Christianae* Greek borrowings only (e.g. *məsṭir*, *'askema*, *sinodos*, etc.). We have already noted some Syriac words falling within this category and some others will follow presently. Among his *res mundanae* (ibid.)

---

[1] Rahlfs, ibid.   [2] Cf. Nöldeke, op. cit., p. 34; Conti Rossini, *Storia*, p. 143.
[3] Nöldeke, op. cit., p. 47.
[4] Nöldeke, op. cit., p. 36; Dillmann, *Lex.* xxii; Conti Rossini, *Storia*, p. 143.
[5] Dillmann, *Lex.*, p. 1213.   [6] Nöldeke, op. cit., p. 37; Conti Rossini, loc. cit.
[7] Against Conti Rossini, *Storia*, p. 155.
[8] Nöldeke, op. cit., pp. 30, 35; Conti Rossini, *Storia*, p. 155; Dillmann, *Lex.* xxii, 605; *Encyclopaedia of Islam*², iii. 165–6.
[9] Nöldeke, op. cit., p. 34.

Dillmann fails to include *ḥanot* 'tavern, shop' which, rather oddly, is listed among *res sacrae*; dialectally, the word can be either Syriac or Jewish Aramaic.[1]

Gə'əz *ḥaṭ'a* does not usually have the meaning 'to sin' but rather 'to fail' in the widest sense. It would appear that the religious significance of *ḥaṭ'a* and the noun *ḥaṭi'at* is an Aramaic, but dialectally indistinct, *calque*.[2] *täkänsä* 'to congregate (in church)' is as likely to derive from a Hebrew source (on account of the sibilant *s*) as from a Syriac one (*š*).

mäläkot 'divine rule' as well as 'divinity'[3] is, again, not explicit as to its origin which may be either Hebrew (or Jewish Aramaic) or Syriac. *mäl'ak* 'angel' reflects the Hebrew rather than the Syriac pronunciation, but the verb *l'k* 'to send' has remained active in Ethiopic. *täsäqlä* is the usual word for 'to crucify' in Gə'əz, but Aramaic *täṣälbä* is attested as well. This is, of course, a specifically Christian term. Nöldeke had already shown[4] that this word is unlikely to have reached Ethiopic by way of Arabic (in view of ስቅ-ለ፡ = صليب).

ṣälläyä 'to pray' and *ṣälot* 'prayer' are neutral in terms of Aramaic dialectology. The same is true of *ṣom* 'fasting', *gäzärä* 'to circumcise',[5] *sägädä* 'to prostrate oneself'.

In *qʷərban* 'sacrifice, eucharist' the labio-velar might suggest Syriac (*qurbānā*) rather than Hebrew or Jewish Aramaic provenance. While *qʷərban* has acquired specifically Christian overtones, it was also used to render the Old Testament notion of sacrifice (*qorban*). *qobə'* 'priestly headgear' may go back to either a Hebrew or a Syriac source. *däräsä*, *mədras*, etc., have already been discussed on p. 97, note 5, above. *zämän* 'time' in Gə'əz betrays its Jewish Aramaic origin, for the noun is *zbn* in Syriac (though the verb appears as *zmn*). Similar certainty can be postulated for Gə'əz *'asot* 'healing' which corresponds to Jewish Aram. *'asūṭā*,[6] while the Syriac form is *'asyūṭā*. *täbsil* (or *təbsil*) reflects Jewish Aramaic *taḫšil* (Syriac *būšālā*); one need only compare Genesis 25: 29. Forms like *täbsil* and *tälmid* in Gə'əz had already been recognized by Brockelmann[7] as Aramaic and alien to Ethiopic.

This list could, of course, be expanded, but I do not think that further documentation would add anything either in substance or in statistical terms. Of the thirty-five words here considered fifteen are clearly of Jewish Aramaic origin, while sixteen are dialectally neutral. Only four are characteristically Syriac and distinctively Christian in meaning. This confirms Polotsky's view (*JSS* 1964) that the overwhelming number of such words are derived from Jewish Aramaic and belong to the pre-Christian Jewish leaven in Ethiopia. The Syriac-mediated loan-words must be ascribed to a later linguistic layer. The historical and

---

[1] See the interesting observations by Polotsky, *JSS* 1964, p. 3.
[2] Cf. Nöldeke, op. cit., p. 36; Praetorius, 'Beiträge zur äth. Gramm. und Etymologie' in *Beiträge zur Assyriologie*, i (1890), 29.
[3] Nöldeke, op. cit., p. 33.   [4] Op. cit., p. 35.   [5] Cf. p. 108, note 2, above.
[6] See also S. Fraenkel, *Die Aramäischen Fremdwörter im Arabischen*, p. 261.
[7] *Grundriß*, i. 386; Nöldeke, op. cit., p. 45.

linguistic pieces of evidence thus combine to favour the assumption of two independent strands of Aramaic loanwords originating from different Aramaic dialects and different periods. It is likely that the later linguistic layer facilitated the absorption of the earlier Jewish Aramaic stock and afforded home rights to a Hebrew Aramaic tradition which became intimately blended with the Syriac and Christian superstratum.

The great majority of Aramaic loanwords thus belongs to the homogeneous group of Jewish notions introduced into Ethiopia by Judaized immigrants from south-west Arabia. The dialectal pattern conforms closely to cultural distribution: The Jewish Aramaic words, while predominantly of a religious type, also include some notions of a more general kind. The small Syriac minority, on the other hand, is confined to narrowly Christian religious terminology.

The contribution of Ethiopic to Old Testament lexicography

The object of this section is to illustrate, with the aid of a few representative examples, the contribution which the Ethiopian languages, and Gə'əz in particular, have to offer to the elucidation of the Hebrew vocabulary of the Bible.[1] The close connexion between Ethiopic and Hebrew had already been recognized in the seventeenth century by that remarkable linguist and Orientalist, Job Ludolf,[2] whose writings remain a mine of valuable information to this day. Thereafter, we only find the occasional reference to Ethiopic in Hebrew grammars and dictionaries. In 1825 the theologian, Hebraist, and Orientalist, H. Hupfeld, published his *Exercitationes Aethiopicae*, and other distinguished grammarians of Hebrew, among them Gesenius,[3] Ewald,[4] and König,[5] began to give attention to the claims of Ethiopic. The great August Dillmann also came to this discipline from theology and the Old Testament.[6]

The major dictionaries of Old Testament Hebrew have, of course, long included at least some Ethiopic and South Arabian material. And Dillmann's monumental *Lexicon Linguae Aethiopicae* contains a very large number of comparative Hebrew etymologies, many of which will not, however, withstand critical examination in the light of modern linguistic knowledge. Gesenius's *Handwörterbuch* to the Old Testament and Brown, Driver, Briggs's dictionary include ample and generally sound references to the South Semitic languages, but Koehler's *Lexicon* represents, in this and other respects, a retrograde step; incidentally,

---

[1] The substance of many of the following observations first appeared in my article in *Vet. Test.*, 1956, pp. 190–8.

[2] Cf. J. Flemming in *Beiträge zur Assyriologie*, i (1890), ii (1894).

[3] *Hebräisches Elementarbuch*, later *Hebräische Grammatik*.

[4] *Ausführliches Lehrbuch der hebräischen Sprache*.

[5] *Neue Studien über Schrift, Aussprache, und allgemeine Formenlehre des Aethiopischen*.

[6] Cf. the valuable biographical sketch of Dillmann by Enno Littmann, reprinted in the latter's *Ein Jahrhundert der Orientalistik*, Wiesbaden, 1955.

a large proportion of the Ethiopic words listed in it appear in oddly misspelt forms (a criticism which does not apply to Baumgartner's Aramaic part).[1]

Here are a few examples of the value that will accrue to Hebrew lexicography through closer examination of the Ethiopian languages:

The root '*dm* connotes in Hebrew, Arabic, Ugaritic, etc., 'to be red' or 'brown' or generally the colour of the human skin (so also in some of the Cushitic languages[2]). In Ethiopic this root appears in this particular meaning only as an Arabic loanword '*adīm* 'of red skin'; the usual word for 'red' is *qyḥ* in the Abyssinian languages. The meaning of the word '*dm* (and its derivatives) in Ethiopic is 'to be pleasant', 'to enjoy', 'voluptate afficere' (Dillmann, *Lexicon*, col. 800). There can be little doubt, in my view, of the semantic connexion between the colour 'red' and the notion 'pleasant, enjoyable, delightful'. Esau asks Jacob to give him מן האדם (Gen. 25: 30), the 'sweet' or 'pleasant smelling', the 'delicious', the 'red stuff'. In *Song of Songs* 5: 10 we find: דודי צח ואדום 'my beloved is white and ruddy'; and since *ṣaḥ* is 'milk-white', 'pure-white',[3] '*adom* might well be 'pleasant', 'desirable' in this particular context. That 'red' was considered 'beautiful', 'pleasant', becomes also clear from the description of David in 1 Samuel 16: 12 as אדמוני עם יפה עינים וטוב ראי 'reddish with fine eyes and good looks'.

There exist quite a few well-attested instances of 'irregular' laryngal and sibilant correspondences between Hebrew and South Semitic, but we cannot go into the details and causes of this phenomenon in the present context.[4] May it suffice here to mention such well-known roots as *zrʻ* 'to sow' in Hebrew, Arabic, Syriac (Ugaritic *drʻ*),[5] but *zrʼ* in Ethiopic and *ḏrʼ* in South Arabian; Hebrew '*egel* 'young bull', 'young animal', but Ethiopic '*əgʷəl*, etc. I mention this matter because I have not hitherto seen it pointed out that Hebrew *leḥem* 'bread', Arabic *laḥm* 'meat', etc., should be placed together with Ethiopic *laḥm* 'cow'. Thus the root *lḥm* expressed in Semitic simply the staple-diet and would, therefore, vary in the different regions. In Ugaritic the verb *lḥm* is 'to eat', and the noun may possibly signify nothing more definite than 'food' in general. In the South Arabian language of the island of Soqoṭra *leḥem* means 'fish'[6] (shark).

Somewhat similar considerations apply to Hebrew '*aryeh* 'lion', for Akkadian *arū* is 'eagle', Arabic أَرْوَى 'mountain-goat'. In Gəʻəz '*arwe* is a 'wild beast' or 'serpent'; in Tigre it is the usual word for 'snake'. Tňa '*arä* signifies any wild beast, but a 'leopard' in particular. There is

---

[1] I find myself in very reluctant, but almost complete, agreement with the general tenor of J. Reider's review of this dictionary in *JQR*, July 1955. See also Y. Blau in *TARBIZ*, April 1956, and A. M. Honeyman in *Vet. Test.*, April 1955.

[2] Cf. M. Cohen, *Essai comparatif sur le vocabulaire et la phonétique du chamito-sémitique*, nos. 15 and 74.   [3] See Gordis, *Song of Songs*, p. 89.

[4] See, however, the present writer's *Sem. Langg. of Ethiopia*, pp. 29 et seqq.

[5] Cf. Gordon, *Ugaritic Textbook*, §§ 5: 3 and 4.

[6] Leslau, *Lexique Soqoṭri*, p. 232. Incidentally, I feel sure Leslau would now wish to reconsider what he said in *Eth. . . . Contr. to Heb. Lex.*, p. 29.

no reason to think, as Koehler does, that 'aryeh is an African loanword: the Ethiopic word for 'lion' is 'anbäsa. Since the animal which we now call 'lion' was not indigenous in Palestine, we may, in fact, doubt whether 'aryeh always and necessarily describes that particular animal; it might, perhaps, be the generic term for the principal wild and strong beast of the Palestinian fauna.

Already on a previous occasion[1] I had briefly invited attention to the connexion between Hebrew *pittah* 'to seduce' and Ethiopic *fätäwä* 'to desire, love'. In Ugaritic, *pty* is attested in the probable meaning of 'to copulate'.[2] In Arabic *fty* is 'to be youthful'. We may thus suppose that the general Ethiopic idea of 'desire, love'[3] is at the source of the semasiological development of this word.

Failure to distinguish between two different roots has led Koehler (and some of his predecessors) to describe Hebrew *hamor* 'ass' as the 'red animal'. But in post-Biblical Hebrew and in Aramaic *ḥmr* is 'to load, to carry'; *heḥmīr* is 'to render heavy, difficult'; *ḥomer* is the dry measure which is equivalent to the 'load of an ass'. In Ethiopic the word is not 'wanting', as Koehler asserts, but appears, as a variant of the basic connotation of 'loading', 'carrying', in the meaning of 'ship' (*hamär*).[4] Thus *hamor* is undoubtedly the beast of burden *par excellence* and derived from the root *ḥmr* which is connected with *ḥml* (by an exchange of final liquids) possessing a similar range of meaning in Arabic. In this way we can clearly see the connexion between the Hebrew *hamor* 'ass' and the Ethiopic *hamär* 'ship' which resides in the general Semitic *ḥmr* 'to carry, to load'; and we also get rid of the fanciful explanation of the donkey as the 'red animal'.

Ludolf, in the seventeenth century, had already collected a number of Hebrew words which, in his opinion, could best be explained by having recourse to Ethiopic.[5] From this list I shall now choose one or two examples and offer certain amplifications.

Hebrew and Aramaic '*mr* 'to say'; Arabic and ESA 'to command'; Akkadian *amāru* 'to see' (thus also in Ugaritic); Gə'əz 'to show'; Tigre 'to know, to be clear'. Original meaning: 'to be clear, bright'; hence 'to make clear', etc. The passage in Deuteronomy 26: 17, 18 has not been properly understood (cf. dictionaries and commentaries): האמיר corresponds here precisely to Gə'əz አእመረ: 'to recognize': 'Thou hast *recognized* (האמרת) the Lord this day to be thy God . . .' and 'the Lord hath recognized thee this day to be his peculiar people . . .'.

It is interesting to note that Hebrew *bəhēmāh* 'animal' is related, semantically, to Ethiopic *bəhəmä* 'to be mute' in much the same way as 'brute' (beast) is to *brutus*.

---

[1] In a paper read to the 23rd International Congress of Orientalists, Cambridge, 1954, and published in *Africa*, 1955, p. 158.   [2] Gordon, op. cit., text 52: 39.

[3] Cf. also Tigre *fatyät* (Munzinger, *Vocabulaire*, col. 52; Littmann–Höfner, *Tigre-Wörterbuch*, p. 666) 'prostitute'.

[4] For the meanings of 'donkey' and 'part of a ship' in Akkadian see Delitzsch, *Assyrisches Handwörterbuch*, pp. 91–92; Bezold, *Glossar*, p. 43.

[5] *Commentarius*, pp. 203–7.

The *hapax legomenon* in Amos 7: 14 בּוֹלֵס שִׁקְמִים (Amos explaining that he was not a prophet, nor a prophet's son—but a herdman and . . .) is best elucidated by recourse to Ethiopic *bäläs* 'fig', i.e. a 'cultivator of figs'. The Hebrew expression would thus be parallel—as Ludolf (loc. cit.) has pointed out—to *korem* vis-à-vis *kerem*.

גֶּבֶא is a word which occurs only twice in the Old Testament. Its meaning, in for instance Isaiah 30: 14, is usually guessed from the context: וְלַחְשֹׂף מַיִם מִגֶּבֶא 'to drain water out of the pit', 'out of the cistern'. In the Ethiopian languages and in South Arabian the root *gb'* is frequent and well known; it means 'to collect'. It corresponds, in fact, exactly to the Hebrew *qwh* which is used for the 'gathering' of the water in Genesis 1: 9; thus גֶּבֶא closely resembles מִקְוֶה.

Or Hebrew כִּלְאַיִם 'of two kinds', which is attested also in other North Semitic languages, appears in the form *kəl'e* as the numeral 'two' in Ethiopic.

Professor D. Winton Thomas has shown[1] that Hebrew *mkr* does not always mean 'to sell'. A particularly instructive instance of the uses of this root was discovered by Ludolf in the famous crux in Genesis 49: 5: שִׁמְעוֹן וְלֵוִי אַחִים כְּלֵי חָמָס מְכֵרֹתֵיהֶם, though commentators do not seem to have paid attention to his interpretation, and Koehler still lists this word (מְכֵרֹתֵיהֶם) as 'unexplained'. In Ethiopic *mkr* is 'to counsel'— a word of frequent occurrence—and our verse can thus be rendered: 'Simeon and Levi are brothers; strong weapons are their counsels'.

In 1 Samuel 19: 20 we hear that Saul sent messengers to take David and that they saw לַהֲקַת הַנְּבִיאִים which is commonly rendered as 'the company of the prophets'. לַהֲקָה is a *hapax legomenon* and is usually explained as a metathesis of קְהָלָה, but the root *lhq* is well attested in Ethiopic where it means 'to be old, senior'.[2] The noun *liq* (contracted from *ləhiq*) connotes 'senior, princeps' and occurs principally in such expressions as *liqä mäla'əkt* 'archangel', *liqä kahnat* 'high priest', etc. There seems to me little doubt, therefore, that לַהֲקָה is not a metathesis of קְהָלָה and does not refer to an 'assembly of prophets', but rather to the 'senior ones among the prophets'.[3]

Hebrew *rkb* generally means 'to ride', and that meaning is, of course, also found in Akkadian, Ugaritic, and elsewhere. In Ethiopic *rkb* is 'to find, come upon, get hold of'. Now, in post-Biblical Hebrew and also in Aramaic, *rkb* (especially in the *hif'il* as *hirkīḇ*) means 'to graft upon, to join, to connect'. The link between the meaning variants in these two phases of Hebrew may well be seen in the South Semitic connotation of 'to come upon, gather, collect'. In the Ugaritic hymns *rkb 'rpt* (parallel to the expression רֹכֵב בָּעֲרָבוֹת in Psalm 68: 5) should probably be

---

[1] *JTS* 1936 and 1952.
[2] Cf. Arabic *lhq* 'to be snow-white'.
[3] So already well explained by Ludolf (*Lexicon*², 1699, col. 635) as 'senatus prophetarum'.

It was only after these observations had been committed to paper that I noticed that the same suggestion had already been made by Professor G. R. Driver in the *JTS* xxix (1927), 394, in an article which contains also other important remarks on the value of the South Semitic vocabulary for Hebrew lexicography.

compared to the Homeric νεφεληγερέτης, 'the cloud-*gatherer*'.[1] The connexion between 'to gather, to join' and 'to ride' is, of course, to be found in the action of harnessing (best expressed in the Greek ζεύγνυμι); and Dillmann was probably right when he voiced the opinion that 'potestas radicis prima in . . . componendo esse videtur' (*Lexicon*, col. 302).

The root *mhr* in Hebrew appears to connote 'haste, hurry', while the verb *mhr* in Ethiopic means 'to teach' and in the reflexive stem 'to learn'. It is probable that the basic meaning of this Semitic word is 'to be skilled' which, of course, implies both an element of speed (Hebrew) as well as of knowledge (Ethiopic). It is, indeed, well known that the Hebrew adjective *mahīr* (which occurs four times in the Old Testament) means 'practised, expert, skilled', and it is time the dictionaries dispensed with the rendering 'quick'. איש מהיר במלאכתו (Prov. 22: 29) is, of course, a 'man skilled in his work', 'trained' but not necessarily 'quick'. And when Ezra is described as ספר מהיר בתורת משה it is his 'knowledge' that is stressed and not his 'speed'. Arabic *mhr* and Syriac *məhīrā*, too, convey 'skill' and 'knowledge'. In South Arabian the element *mhr* occurs in some proper names which again would suggest, in that context, 'skill' and 'expertness' rather than 'haste'. It is interesting to compare the curiously parallel development in the root *lmd* which in Hebrew means 'to learn' and in Ethiopic 'to be accustomed', almost exactly the opposite semantic distribution. Of course, in expressions such as לְמֻדֵי הָרֵעַ (Jer. 13: 23) 'accustomed to do evil' the basic root meaning appears also in Hebrew.

In Joel 1: 20 and especially in the well-known verse 2 in Psalm 42 we hear that the soul 'yearns' for God as the deer 'yearns' for the water brooks. The Hebrew verb used here is *'rg* for which Arabic and particularly Ethiopic *'rg* should be compared. In the latter two the well-attested meaning is 'to ascend', while Hebrew 'to yearn' is presumably a contextual, though fairly ancient, guess. It seems to me very likely that Psalm 42: 2 should be rendered: 'As the deer goes up to the water brooks, so my soul rises to thee, O God.'

Dillmann[2] had already drawn attention to the fact that Hebrew and Ethiopic share a fairly large number of important words which either do not appear in Arabic at all or in very different meanings. Among these may be mentioned:

እሳት፡	אֵשׁ	ትማልም፡	תמול
ዕፅ፡	עֵץ	እስኪት፡	אֲשֶׁךְ
እብን፡	אֶבֶן	ክህል፡	יכול
ወርኅ፡	יֶרַח	ወፅአ፡	יצא

I have considered the possibility that the contribution of Ethiopic to Hebrew lexicography may conceivably affect some areas of the

---

[1] Cf. my note in *Orientalia*, 1951, p. 272, note 2.
[2] *Ethiopic Grammar*[2] (Crichton transl.), pp. 6–7.

vocabulary more than others, but I have been unable to identify any such special spheres.

At first sight it might, perhaps, appear odd that the South Semitic languages[1] should be in a position to make a notable contribution to the elucidation of the Hebrew vocabulary. But such doubts are scarcely well founded, for we frequently encounter astonishing resemblances between geographically widely separated language groups. C. Rabin has collected a list of some twenty-eight instances of words common to the Yemenite or 'Himyaritic' dialect and to North-west Semitic, especially Hebrew.[2] The habitat of the Semitic peoples as it appears in historical times may well effectively disguise true genetic connexions, and later geographical distribution offers scant indication of special affinities and relationships which may originally have existed. Moreover, it frequently happens that one language has preserved a word or a meaning-variant which was accidentally lost from another.

To the language of the Old Testament the tongues of Abyssinia can, perhaps, contribute some matters of detail only, but to an understanding of the life and spirit of the Old Testament the country and people of Ethiopia can offer much of their own life and spirit.

[1] Cf. the list of South Arabian correspondences in *Vet. Test.*, 1956, pp. 196 ff.
[2] *Ancient West-Arabian*, pp. 26–28.

III

THE QUEEN OF SHEBA[1]

THE notion of sacral kingship in Ethiopia can only be briefly referred to in the present context, for its detailed treatment would go beyond the framework of this treatise and would also lie outside the competence of the present writer. Moreover, we possess at least three recent studies of exceptional value, based on differing areas of evidence and reaching partially conflicting conclusions: Conti Rossini's 'la regalità sacra in Abissinia' and Caquot's 'la royauté sacrale en Éthiopie' both proceed from similar premises, i.e. the Semitic civilizations of the ancient orient, while Haberland's important *Untersuchungen zum äthiopischen Königtum* are essentially the work of an ethnographer who sees in Ethiopian kingship an aspect of the general African 'Königskultur' (op. cit., p. 9), though not denying the importance of its Christian and Old Testament roots.

In this context it is important that any future study of Ethiopian kingship should examine not only the literary documents, such as the *Kebra Nagast* and *Fǝtḥa Nagast*, the royal chronicles, the Aksum inscriptions, the *bǝ'ǝlä nägäst*[2] or *sǝr'atä mängǝst*,[3] etc., as well as the original *Sitz im Leben* of this central institution of kingship,[4] but it is also essential to undertake a meticulous investigation of the terminology. This must involve such basic concepts as *nǝgusä nägäst* or *janhoy*[5] or the nomenclature of the Ethiopian Constitution of 1955.[6] Here one might compare, for instance, the ቀባ፡ መንግሥት፡ in Article 4 with the

---

[1] The substance of this chapter was first published in the *Bulletin of the John Rylands Library*, vol. xlv, March 1963. I am grateful to Mr. Ronald Hall, the Librarian of that magnificent storehouse of Oriental treasures, for permission to reprint that paper with some minor changes. I should like to take this opportunity of expressing my appreciation to Mr. Hall and Dr. Taylor of the John Rylands Library for their unfailing courtesy and helpfulness. I hope soon to be able to resume cataloguing the library's fine collection of Ethiopic manuscripts.

[2] Cf. I. Guidi 'Il Be'la Nagast' in *Festschrift Paul Haupt*, Leipzig, 1926; C. Conti Rossini in *RRAL* 1922.

[3] Cf. I. Guidi in *RRAL* 1922; Varenbergh, *ZA* 1915.

[4] Reference should also be made to A. R. Johnson's *Sacral Kingship in Ancient Israel*[2] and J. Ryckmans's *L'Institution monarchique en Arabie méridionale*. I am greatly indebted to Professor Johnson for his kindness in sending me an early copy of the second edition of his work which traverses an area of which I am woefully ignorant.

[5] Cf. Mittwoch, 'Dschanhoi — die amh. Bezeichnung für "Majestät" ', *ZA* 1911.

[6] *Revised Constitution of Ethiopia*, Addis Ababa, 1955.

anointing in 1 Samuel 10: 1 and 16: 13. The English version in this article speaks of the person of the emperor as 'sacred', while the Amharic text (presumably, though not necessarily, the original) has ክብሩ ፡ የማይቀነስ ፡ i.e. his honour must not be diminished. There is here a pregnant distinction—as has already been pointed out by E. Hammerschmidt.[1]

But we must now turn to the source from which most notions of Ethiopian kingship spring: The story of the Queen of Sheba, based on the Biblical account of the queen's visit to King Solomon, has undergone extensive Arabian, Ethiopian, Jewish, and other elaborations and has become the subject of one of the most ubiquitous and fertile cycles of legends in the Middle East. Its mythopoeic power persists up to the present time[2] and remains in some areas a favourite formula for literary and artistic inventiveness. In European painting and music the Queen of Sheba legend represents a theme with countless variations (including a Hollywood spectacular of rather lurid propensities). On one hand, she is Lilith the seductress and, on the other, the virtuous ancestress of the Ethiopian people. Several places of origin and many different names are ascribed to her, yet from this vast and confused skein of traditions and tales it is possible to disentangle some basic features which are common to all the stories about that famous encounter between the Queen of the South and the greatest of the kings of Israel.

The earliest extant form of the Queen of Sheba narrative is the version preserved in 1 Kings 10: 1–13 and 2 Chronicles 9: 1–12. There are some small, but not insignificant, differences between these two Old Testament accounts[3] which are of little relevance to the development of the Solomon–Sheba legend but of considerable interest to the methods of text-transmission. Moreover, the dependence of the Ethiopic Bible translation on the Septuagint (at least in this passage) and the reliance of the *Kebra Nagast* on this Ethiopic text can here be studied in the most favourable circumstances.[4] The Old Testament story represents, at the same time, the briefest and most concise version, and it is, perhaps, this terseness which has encouraged later elaborations and embellishments. There are two Hebrew expressions in particular which appear to have invited the widespread tale of the union of king and queen in either marriage or at least concubinage: the queen '*came* to Solomon and communed

---

[1] *Oriens Christianus*, 1964, p. 129.
[2] See Bertrand Russell's 'The Queen of Sheba's Nightmare', Penguin, 1962.
[3] Summarized in I.C.C. on Chronicles (Curtis), pp. 357–8.
[4] Hubbard, op. cit., pp. 279–81.

with him of all that was in her heart' (1 Kings 10: 2). The
Hebrew verb בוא 'to come, to enter' is also used as the technical
term for coitus.[1] In verse 13 we are told that 'Solomon gave unto
the queen of Sheba all her desire . . .'. Rashi, in his commentary
to this verse, emphasizes that this refers exclusively to לימוד
חכמה, the teaching of wisdom; but the very fact that Rashi felt
impelled to stress this aspect demonstrates quite clearly that he
was aware of less innocent embellishments to this verse.[2]

The salient features of the Old Testament narrative[3] are as
follows: the Queen of Sheba had heard of Solomon's fame and
decided to come to Jerusalem to test the king's wisdom. She
brought with her spices, gold, and precious stones. Solomon
answered all her questions, while the queen inspected the house
he had built and all the manifold details of the administration of
Solomon's realm. Finally, the queen was convinced that reality
exceeded by far the reports which had reached her. She blessed
Solomon and his God, rejoiced in the good fortune of the king's
subjects, and delivered the rich presents which she had brought.
She then returned to her own country together with her retinue.

This narrative appears to be interrupted, in both its versions
in 1 Kings and 2 Chronicles, by two verses relating to the
Ophir fleet which fetched gold, precious stones, and wood
which was particularly suitable for the manufacture of musical
instruments. This might be either a glossator's interpolation[4]
apropos of the queen's gifts which reminded him of similar
imports by Solomon assisted by Hiram's sailors or it might well
be part of the story referring to additional gifts which the queen
had delivered by the Red Sea fleet. In any event, the mention of
these commercial and seafaring activities in the area of the
southern Red Sea corroborates the historicity of the Queen of
Sheba's visit to King Solomon[5]—shorn, of course, of its more
extravagant features. It scarcely matters very greatly whether

---

[1] Cf. Gen. 16: 2.

[2] In fact, there is a bracketed interpolation printed in Rashi's commentary which is
attributed to the sixteenth-century Kabbalist, R. Isaac Luria:

כל חפצה (בא אליה ונולד ממנה נבוכדנצר והחריב הבית שעמד ת"י שנים בחלק כל
י"ב שבטים בהאר"י ז"ל).

[3] N. H. Tur-Sinai has expressed the opinion (10, הלשון והספר, כרך הספר) that it is
impossible to understand this story except on the assumption that the sources from which the
books of Kings derived their material did, in fact, contain the riddles and their solutions
mentioned in verse 1. Some riddles appear in the *Targum Sheni* to Esther (see below).

[4] Thus Benzinger in Marti's *Kurzer Hand-Commentar zum Alten Testament* (Books of Kings,
1899, p. 72; vv. 11 and 12).

[5] See C. H. Gordon, *Introduction to Old Testament Times*, pp. 174–5; de Vaux, *Ancient Israel*,
p. 78; W. F. Albright in Peake's *Commentary on the Bible* (ed. Black and Rowley), 1962, 50c; cf.
also ibid. 94j, 295e.

we have to seek the queen's home in South-west Arabia or in the horn of Africa (the reference to rich forests [vv. 11 and 12] might possibly favour the latter assumption), for the connexions between the two shores of the southern Red Sea have at all times been close.[1]

Again, queens have been attested among the ancient Arabs, and we have therefore no reason to suspect the genuineness of the Biblical tradition. Cuneiform records enumerate many North Arabian queens,[2] but to assert that there was none in the south would merely be an *argumentum e silentio*. No South Arabian inscriptions have hitherto been discovered which either refer to this queen or indeed to any Sabaean ruler earlier than about 800 B.C. By the time our records begin to flow, a century and a half after King Solomon's meeting with the Queen of Sheba, the Sabaeans have Mukarribs, i.e. priest-kings. Meanwhile, however, we have no reason to doubt the historical reality of the Queen of Sheba, and the day may come when archaeological or epigraphic finds confirm her existence—as has indeed happened to many other Biblical stories. At Marib in South Arabia the remains of the splendid circular *Maḥram Bilqīs*, the Sanctuary of Bilqīs (the Arabic name of the Queen of Sheba), bear witness to the popularity of the queen, even though she herself has no historical connexion with this ancient temple.

References, real or alleged, to the Queen of Sheba in the New Testament and in the Apocryphal Acts of the Apostles have already been discussed above (pp. 9–13), where we saw some aspects of the network of conflation. The confusion of the Queen of Sheba legend with the New Testament story of Candace was not, however, a deliberate forgery on the part of the Abyssinians but was part of the ancient blending of Candace-Sheba and Solomon-Alexander stories. The Syriac and Ethiopic versions of the Alexander romance[3] contain an account of the meeting of Alexander and Queen Candace which is, in some of its features, reminiscent of the encounter between Solomon and the Queen of Sheba.

Alvares reports[4] how Ethiopians believe that 'in this town of

---

[1] E. Ullendorff, *The Ethiopians*, pp. 47–57.

[2] Cf. Pritchard, *ANET*, p. 283. It'amra, the Sabaean, is mentioned by Sargon (*ANET*, pp. 285–6).

[3] See especially p. 117 of Budge's edition of the Ethiopic version of the *Life and Exploits of Alexander the Great*, vol. i.

[4] Cf. Beckingham and Huntingford, *The Prester John of the Indies*, i. 148 ff. Ludolf (*Historia Aethiopica*, book ii, chap. 4, and book iii, chap. 2) was the first scholar, if I am not mistaken, to attack in vigorous terms the fact that '. . . Aethiopum nonnulli [Reginam Candacem] pro sua agnoscunt'.

Aksum was the principal residence of Queen Candace'. The ancient Abyssinian capital Aksum became the repository of the Hebraic traditions and the seat of the Ark of the Covenant (which Menelik I, the son of King Solomon and the Queen of Sheba—according to the Ethiopian legend—is said to have removed from Jerusalem); but Aksum was also the capital of the Christian Queen Candace. Ethiopians are not conscious of any dichotomy here, for the complete blending of Jewish and Christian traditions into one indissoluble whole is one of the most remarkable features of the syncretistic Abyssinian civilization.

Josephus[1] gives us a slightly expanded and somewhat 'smartened up' version of the Old Testament story; yet he remains essentially faithful to the Biblical narrative and is entirely innocent of those accretions which later on attached themselves to the queen and her meeting with Solomon. The way in which he tells the story no doubt reflected the state of contemporary interpretation, and it is in this light that we shall have to see his interesting reference to Sheba as 'the Queen of Egypt and Ethiopia'. Even though this is probably intended to cover Nubia-Meroe rather than Abyssinia proper, it does show a concentration on an African, instead of Arabian, origin.

The Talmud contains, strangely enough, only one solitary reference to the Queen of Sheba, but one which is of some significance. The subject of discussion is the date of Job, and Rabbi Nathan declares, on the basis of Job 1: 15, that Job lived in the days of Sheba.[2] This causes Rabbi Jonathan to assert that Sheba was not a woman but a kingdom.[3] The difference can only be understood by reference to the defective spelling of Hebrew. It is virtually certain that this strange dictum is meant to apply not only to the one verse in Job 1 but is intended to reveal a general truth.[4] If we look at the Targum's rendering of

---

[1] *Antiquities*, viii. 6, 5–6. [2] *Baba Batra* 15, *b*.
[3] Ibid.:

א״ר שמואל בר נחמני א״ר יונתן כל האומר מלכת שבא אשה היתה אינו אלא טועה מי מלכת שבא מלכותא דשבא.

[4] So also G. Salzberger, *Die Salomo-Sage in der semitischen Literatur* (Berlin, 1907), p. 14. I cannot in this case agree with the arguments adduced by Hubbard, op. cit., p. 287. It seems to me obvious that the Rabbis were aware (as the Targum to Job 1: 15 proves) of the strange tales about the relationship between Solomon and Sheba and set out to discredit them (cf. also Rösch, *Jahrbücher f. Protest. Theol.* 1880, pp. 547–8). The *Midrash Hagadol* (ed. Schechter, p. 379) states:

אל תקרא מלכת שבא אלא מלכות שבא, שבאה כל מלכות שבא בימי שלמה לשמש את ישראל.

For some further details see my article 'The Biblical sources of the Ethiopian national saga' [in Hebrew] in *Sefer Ṭur-Sinai*, Jerusalem, 1960.

Job 1: 15, we find that the seemingly innocuous שבא 'Sheba' of the Hebrew original is translated 'and suddenly Lilith, the Queen of Smaragd, fell upon . . .'. Here then we possess two early indications of the Queen of Sheba's role as temptress, although detailed literary reflections of this legend appear only somewhat later. While there can thus be little doubt that the visit of the Queen of Sheba excited imagination and experienced early Jewish Midrashic exposition, the first attested full-blown version of the Sheba legend is embodied in Islamic sources. When Jews migrated to Arabia, in the early years of the Christian era, they brought with them stories and Midrashim which formed part of their oral tradition and which subsequently penetrated Islam in Arabia and monophysite Christianity in Abyssinia, where these legends received specific Arabian and Ethiopian elaborations and embellishments. It is difficult to decide, however, whether later Midrashic accounts (such as the *Targum sheni* to Esther or the *Alphabet of Ben Sira*—to which I shall return presently) are derived from Arabic sources or are, in fact, remnants from early Midrashic collections which have been lost.

Before I deal with these later aspects of Jewish literature, I must trace the fate of the Queen of Sheba in Islamic documents which chronologically precede those late Midrashic developments.

The Sheba story in the Qur'an (Sūrah xxvii. 15–45) reflects some of the principal elements of the fully developed legend.[1] It describes the sun-worship of the queen, how a hoopoe (*hudhud*) carries a letter to her from Solomon, the queen's consultation with her nobles, and the dispatch of presents to Solomon. When these are not well received by the king, the Queen of Sheba comes herself and, by a ruse (mistaking the polished floor for a pool of water), is made to uncover her legs. Eventually she surrenders (together with Solomon) to Allah, i.e. she becomes a Muslim.

This Qur'anic account closely resembles the fuller version in the later *Targum Sheni* to Esther—except that the Qur'an makes no mention of the reason for the polished floor which is meant to discover whether the queen has hairy legs. Neither the Qur'an nor the *Targum Sheni* refers to the queen's marriage to Solomon or even to any tender relations between them. Also the queen's Arabic name Bilqis does not yet appear in the Qur'an.

[1] Cf. the entry *Bilḳis* in the *Encyclopaedia of Islam* (new ed.). See also G. Weil, *Biblische Legenden der Muselmänner*, Frankfort, 1845, pp. 225–79.

Muslim commentators and writers[1] supplement the story at various points: the queen's name is given as Bilqis; the demons at Solomon's Court, afraid that the king may marry Bilqis, spread the rumour that the queen has hairy legs and the foot of an ass. Hence Solomon's stratagem of constructing a glass floor which the queen mistakes for water, thus causing her to lift her skirts. Solomon then commands his demons to prepare a special depilatory to remove the disfiguring hair. According to some, he then married the queen, while other traditions assert that he gave her in marriage to one of the Tubba's of the tribe of Hamdān.

This picture represents a conglomerate from various Arabic accounts.[2] One of the most convenient versions, comprehensive in its coverage of the more important motifs of the Arabic legend, is that by the early eleventh-century Arabic author aṯ-Ṯa'labī and contained in his qiṣaṣ al-'anbiyā' 'stories of the Prophets'.[3] Although Islamic sources have preserved the earliest literary reflexion of the complete Bilqis legend, we still maintain that the principal elements of the narrative are derived from Jewish traditions. This judgement is based not only on intrinsic probability and our knowledge of the general influence of the Midrashic genre on early Islam, but it is also supported by the following considerations: (1) the story in the Qur'ān represents a curiously abrupt version which clearly presupposes prior development; (2) the Talmudic insistence[4] that it was not a woman but a kingdom of Sheba (based on varying interpretations of Hebrew mlkt) that came to Jerusalem makes sense only on the assumption that a highly discreditable version of the Solomon–Sheba story was known to the Rabbis; (3) the Ethiopic loan-word ṣarḥ[5] in Sūrah xxvii. 44 suggests that the Arabic legend was most probably drawn from some foreign prototype; (4) Bilqis, the Arabic name of the Queen of Sheba, is almost certainly connected with the Hebrew (though non-Semitic) פילגש (cf. Greek παλλακίς) which would point to the area from which the basic features of the tale originated. I shall return later on to the subject of the queen's names.

---

[1] Especially Ṭabarī, Zamaḫšarī, Bayḍāwī.

[2] Cf. Hamdāni, Iklil, 8th book, ed. N. A. Faris, Princeton, 1940, p. 24; Rosenthal's translation of Ibn Khaldun's Muqaddimah, ii. 259; for more detailed references to Mas'ūdi, Ṭabarī, Ibn al-Aṯīr, Ibn Khaldun, etc., see Rösch, op. cit., pp. 526–7. Bayḍāwī's commentary to the relevant portions of Sūrah xxvii is concise but embodies most of the important elements of the Sheba cycle.

[3] Printed in A. Socin's Arabic Grammar, pp. 49–71. See also M. Grünbaum, Neue Beiträge zur semitischen Sagenkunde, pp. 216–20.

[4] Baba Batra, 15, b.

[5] Cf. Nöldeke, Neue Beiträge zur Sem. Sprachwissenschaft, p. 51.

Arab authors deal also with other features of the Sheba cycle: there is considerable speculation as well as a fair measure of conflicting evidence as to the identity of the queen's father;[1] her mother's person is equally shrouded in mystery (was she some spirit [*jinn*], demon, serpent, or other animal?).[2] After her father's death, Bilqis is said to have succeeded him as queen. Her reign was, however, challenged by one of her subjects whom she removed by a ruse.[3] The description of Bilqis as Solomon's wife[4] is fairly widespread among Arab writers, and so is the motif of the birth of a son to the queen.

Chronology now takes us back to Jewish sources, and here it is Midrashic material to which we have to turn. The early Midrashim refer to the Queen of Sheba only in the most conventional terms, and if they were aware of any scandal attaching to her relations with King Solomon, they were certainly most assiduous in suppressing all mention of it. The most important Jewish source is the *Targum Sheni* ('the second Targum') to the book of Esther.[5] Its date is uncertain and is variously thought to range between A.D. 500 and 1000. The gist of this version is as follows:

Solomon was in the habit of summoning all the beasts, birds, reptiles, and spirits[6] to perform in front of him and his fellow kings from neighbouring countries. They all came of their own accord. On one occasion the hoopoe[7] was missing; when finally it was found, it reported to the king that it had been in search of a country anywhere in the world that might not be subject to the authority of Solomon. Eventually the hoopoe had found the city of Qiṭor in the East, full of gold and silver, and trees watered from the Garden of Eden; its ruler was the Queen of Sheba. Solomon then commanded his scribes to tie a letter to the hoopoe's wing which it delivered to the queen. This missive contained a somewhat peremptory invitation to present herself before the king. The queen thought it prudent to comply and arrived accompanied by vast quantities of precious gifts. Meanwhile, Solomon sat in a house of glass[8] to receive her; Sheba thought the king was sitting in water and, as she crossed the floor, she lifted her cloak[9] and thus revealed her hairy legs.

---

[1] Rösch, op. cit., pp. 528–34.   [2] Ibid., pp. 534–9.

[3] Ta'labī (ed. Socin), pp. 54–55.   [4] بلقيس زوجة سليمان ibid., p. 71.

[5] Cf. מקראות גדולות; and for part-translations see Ginzberg, *Legends of the Jews*, iv. 142 ff. Cf. also Grünbaum, op. cit., pp. 209 ff.

[6] שידין ורוחין ולילין.   [7] תרנגלא ברא.   [8] בית זוגיתא.

[9] חליית חילוזה.

Whereupon the king remarked, somewhat unchivalrously: 'Thy beauty is the beauty of women, but thy hair is the hair of man; while hair is an ornament to a man, it is a disfigurement to a woman.'[1] The queen, as befits a lady, seems to have pretended not to have heard and, instead, proceeded to recite her riddles and questions.

Here, then, we have most of the essential ingredients of the non-Ethiopian Sheba legend. Two important elements are, however, still missing: (1) a mention of the queen's name; and (2) a reference to either marriage or concubinage between Solomon and Sheba. The first Jewish document in which the nature of these relations is expressly, rather than covertly, stated appears to be the eleventh-century *Alphabet of Ben Sira* in which Nebuchadnezzar is described as a son of King Solomon and the Queen of Sheba.[2] The union of king and queen occurred as soon as the depilatory had removed the disfiguring hair.

We have now pieced together most of the principal elements which make up the Sheba legend as it appears outside Abyssinia.

In turning to the Ethiopian version, we become at once conscious of a fundamental change of atmosphere: the emphasis is no longer on Solomon and his wisdom but on the Queen of Sheba and her nobility; no longer is Solomon exposed to the wiles of the seductress, Lilith, the earthy demon, but he himself assumes the role of seducer and, by a ruse, takes the virgin queen who—and this is the culmination and purpose of the entire Ethiopian saga—gives birth to a son, Menelik,[3] the founder of the Ethiopian dynasty. From him are descended all the kings of Ethiopia down to the present day, to Haile Sellassie—as is embodied in Article 2 of the 1955 Ethiopian Constitution ('the Imperial dignity shall remain perpetually attached to the line . . . [which] descends without interruption from the dynasty of Menelik I, son of the Queen of Ethiopia, the Queen of Sheba, and King Solomon of Jerusalem'). Here, in the cold terms of legal phraseology, we find the continued insistence on the

---

[1] ‏שופרך שופרא דנשי וסערך סער דגברא וסער לגברא שפר ולאתתא גנאי‎.

[2] See also n. 2, p. 133. *Alphabet of Ben Sira*, ed. M. Steinschneider, Berlin, 1858, fol. 21*b*:
‏כשבאה . . . מלכת שבא אל שלמה והביאה לו דורון לראות חכמתו ישרה בעיניו‎
‏ובקש לשכב עמה ומצאה כולה שער והביא סיד וזרניך . . . ובא עליה באותה שעה‎.

[3] Possibly corrupted from الحكيم ابن (cf. Praetorius, *Fabula de regina Sabaea apud Aethiopes*, Halle, 1870, p. viii) or الملك ابن. Cf. also Strelcyn's attractive Polish book which embodies fragments from the *Kebra Nagast* (*Kebra Nagast czyli Chwała Królów Abisynii*, Warsaw, 1956).

mystique of a direct descent from King Solomon and the Queen
of Sheba, a powerful reminder of the enduring efficacy of the
Old Testament story and its wide ramifications.

Apart from this totally different atmosphere, the Ethiopian
Kebra Nagast (which contains the Sheba cycle in chapters 21 ff.)
exhibits other significant changes of detail: nothing is said about
the queen's hairy limbs, nothing about the glass floor, or Sheba's
descent from demons. The tale of the hoopoe is replaced by the
realistic story of Tamrin, the head of Sheba's caravans, who is
engaged in large-scale trading operations with Solomon and is
impressed with the king's wisdom and might. On his return to
his own country he reports to the queen in such enthusiastic
terms that she decides to go and see for herself. The following
chapters in the *Kebra Nagast* do not deviate substantially from
the Biblical account but simply supply many details on which
the concise story in the Old Testament is silent. One of the more
important embellishments is the queen's decision to abandon
the worship of the sun and to worship, instead, the Creator of
the sun, the God of Israel (chapter 28).

The centre-piece and, at the same time, the original contribution of the Ethiopian version lie in the events leading up to the
birth of Menelik: when Solomon gave a banquet in the queen's
honour he had the meat specially seasoned. At the end of the
evening the king invited the queen to spend the night in his
chambers. The queen agreed on condition that Solomon swore
to her that he would not take her by force. The king complied
with this request—provided Sheba promised not to take anything in the king's house. Solomon then mounted his bed on
one side of the chamber and had the queen's bed prepared at the
other end. Near her bed he placed a bowl of water. Sheba soon
awoke, for the seasoned food had made her very thirsty. She
rose and drank of the water, but Solomon seized her hand and
accused her of having broken her oath. He then worked his will
with her. The king dreamt that a great light of brilliance, the
shekhina, the divine presence, had left Israel and moved to
Ethiopia. The queen departed and returned to her country
where, nine months and five days later, she gave birth to a son.
When the boy had grown up he went to visit his father who
received him with great honour and splendour. After some time
at Solomon's Court he determined to return to his mother's
realm. Thereupon the king assembled the elders of Israel and
commanded them to send their first-born sons with Menelik, in
order to found a kind of Israelite colony. Before the young men

departed they abducted the Ark of the Covenant and took it
with them to Ethiopia which now became the second Zion.

The veneration of the Queen of Sheba and her appropriation
as the national ancestress of the Ethiopian people are of considerable antiquity and certainly precede the medieval *Kebra
Nagast*. An interesting piece of evidence is furnished by the
Ethiopian Bible translation which usually adheres fairly closely
to the text of the Septuagint, but in 1 Kings 10:1 ותבא
לנסותו בחידות 'she came to prove him with hard questions' the
Ethiopic version interprets the Greek ἐν αἰνίγμασιν as 'with
wisdom'.¹ This deliberate alteration is, perhaps, the earliest
indication of the Ethiopian attitude towards the Queen of
Sheba, for in this reading the quality of wisdom is related not to
King Solomon but to the queen.²

The main components of the story must have had a very long
period of gestation in Ethiopia and elsewhere and have possessed all the elements of a gigantic conflation of legendary
cycles. When it was committed to writing, early in the fourteenth century, its principal aim was to support and buttress
the Solomonic dynasty in Ethiopia. The *nǝburä ǝd* Yeshaq of
Aksum, the compiler of the work, thus performed not only
a literary task but carried out a political and national duty of
far-reaching consequences.

There also exist a Christian Arabic³ and a Coptic⁴ version of
our legend. The former is almost certainly dependent on the
Ethiopian type of the story and thus constitutes a process of
borrowing in a direction opposite to the usual flow.⁵ This
Arabic legend is of a composite nature: it omits all mention of
an intermediary (hoopoe or merchant) between king and queen,
restores the tale of the polished floor, and, to heal the queen's
affliction, it introduces a piece of wood which was later used for
the Cross.⁶ The details of Sheba's seduction by Solomon tally
very largely with the Ethiopic prototype. The Coptic version
offers little of special interest, but it seems to have been current
throughout the Christian Church in Africa.

A modern form of the legend, which yet embraces many
archaic elements as well as comparatively recent folkloristic

---

¹ ግብለ፡ ፕበብ፡፡
² Oddly enough, in the parallel verse in 2 Chron. 9: 1 the Ethiopic version does follow the
reading of the Septuagint.
³ Published by Bezold (*Abh. d. Königl. Bayer. Akad. d. Wissensch.* xxiii, Munich, 1909),
pp. xliv–li.
⁴ Published by A. Erman (*Abh. d. Königl. Preuss. Akad. d. Wissensch.*, 1897). See also Bezold,
op. cit., p. xli.   ⁵ Cf. Cerulli, *Storia della lett. et.*, p. 47.
⁶ Cf. A. Caquot in *Annales d'Éthiopie*, i. 137 ff.

accretions, has been preserved among the Tigre in the north.[1]
A Tigre girl by the name of *Eteye Azeb* (i.e. 'Queen of the South')
seeks a cure for her deformed foot which had turned into an
ass's heel. When she hears of King Solomon's powers she de-
parts for Jerusalem together with a companion. They appear
disguised as men, but the king's suspicions are aroused. At night
he has a skin with honey suspended in the room, and when the
two girls believe him to be asleep they get up and start licking
the honey. Solomon then finds his suspicions confirmed and he
takes the two women by force. The remainder of the story
follows the *Kebra Nagast* version fairly closely: the birth of the
son, his visit to his father, and the removal of the Ark from
Jerusalem to Aksum.

The ass's heel is, of course, the counterpart of the deformed or
hairy foot, but it is remarkable that this feature, so carefully
avoided in the classic account of the *Kebra Nagast*, was allowed
to survive in this north-Ethiopian tale. Otherwise there is—
mutatis mutandis—broad agreement, and the bed-chamber scene
reveals a close connexion in all essential matters.

Finally, a word about the queen's names: in the Old Testament she is, of course, the 'Queen of Sheba',[2] while in the New
Testament she appears as the 'Queen of the South'.[3] This latter
idiom goes back to a Semitic *mlkt ymyn* or *mlkt tymn*[4] (for south
is on the right-hand side when you stand facing the rising sun).
I have already mentioned that the Arabic Bilqis is almost certainly related to Hebrew *pilegesh* and Greek παλλακίς. In the
Kebra Nagast the queen's name is given as Makeda which has no
obvious explanation: some have thought it might be connected
with (Alexander) the 'Macedonian', while I would not exclude
the possibility that Makeda might reveal a popular identification with Candace.[5]

---

[1] Edited by E. Littmann, *The Legend of the Queen of Sheba in the Tradition of Axum*, Leyden, 1904.

[2] מלכת שבא.   [3] βασίλισσα νότου.

[4] Thus in the Arabic version ملكة التيمن (Bezold, op. cit., p. xlv). In the Ethiopic ንግሥተ፡ አዜብ፡ the possibility cannot be excluded that አዜብ፡ might be a metathetical approximation to שבא (*sbʾ*). The Arabic أزيب is, of course, a loanword from Ethiopic (Nöldeke, *Neue Beiträge*, pp. 62–63).

[5] So already Socin, privately, as reported by Rösch, op. cit., p. 557. Candace is almost certainly the Meroitic *Katake* (cf. Budge, *History of Ethiopia*, i. 112), while the Syriac form is ܩܢܕܩ and the Ethiopic forms ቀንደቄ (Budge, *Life and Exploits of Alexander*, i. 106, line 19) as well as ሐንደቄ and ህንደቄ. The name of the Queen of Sheba in the Ethiopian tradition is ማክዳ or ማክዶ. This name has hitherto defied all attempts at an explanation (see Conti Rossini, *Storia*, p. 254), but I do not consider it impossible that Makeda is, in fact, a corruption of Candace (Kandake). One must not try to discover any phonetic reasons behind this corruption. If my conjecture is correct, then we have in the mixture of the names a complete parallel to the conflation of the stories. The fact that the name Hendake continues to coexist

Echoes of the Sheba legend can be heard in European literature and art, though in the former they are not as plentiful as
I was at first inclined to suppose. Cranmer in Shakespeare's
Henry VIII[1] speaks of the queen in these terms: 'Saba was never
more covetous of wisdom and fair virtue than this pure soul
shall be.' George Wither (1588–1667) in a love sonnet:

> I loved a lass, a fair one
> As fair as e'er was seen;
> She was indeed a rare one,
> Another Sheba queen.

Lascelles Abercrombie, in a poem on Judith,[2] includes a long
love song ascribed to Bilqis from which I quote a few lines from
the beginning and the end:

> Balkis was in her marble town,
> And shadow over the world came down. . . .
> 'Is there no man, is there none,
> In whom my beauty will but move
> The lust of a delighted love;
> In whom some spirit of God so thrives
> That we may wed our lonely lives?
> Is there no man, is there none?'—
> She said, 'I will go to Solomon.'

And Kipling:

> There was never a Queen like Balkis,
> From here to the wide world's end;
> But Balkis talked to a butterfly
> As you would talk to a friend.

> There was never a King like Solomon,
> Not since the world began;
> But Solomon talked to a butterfly
> As a man would talk to a man.

> *She* was Queen of Sabaea—
> And *he* was Asia's Lord—
> But they both of 'em talked to butterflies
> When they took their walks abroad!

Professor J. F. Kermode[3] has very kindly drawn my attention
to two Yeats poems 'Solomon to Sheba' and 'Solomon and the

---

does not invalidate this assumption, as we possess respectable parallels for the coexistence of
original and corrupt forms. The popular etymology, adduced by the *Kebra Nagast* (chap. 91),
explaining Makeda as derived from لَاكَ لا must, of course, be rejected.

[1] Act v, scene 4.
[2] *Emblems of Love*, London, 1912.
[3] I am greatly indebted to him for his very helpful observations.

Witch' which reflect several facets of the oriental legend. Professor Kermode says that 'the second poem is loaded with doctrine. It stems partly from Arthur Symons's "The Lover of the Queen of Sheba" (published in 1900) and partly from Mme Blavatsky's *The Key of Solomon the King*.'

In Symons the Queen of Sheba is a learned occultist. Yeats seems to interpret the lovemaking as imitating the action of the Divine Parents (Creator and 'celestial matrix'). The Cock is Hermetic, also perhaps Cabbalistic like so much else. The point is that the sexual act figures the perfect renewal which will undo the work of the 'brigand apple', I think. They are platonic in hoping to find themselves replaced by their platonic forms. I suppose we are to believe that when they achieve perfect sexual union Choice and Chance will be one and the world will end.

See also the detailed discussion in F. A. C. Wilson, *Yeats's Iconography* (1960), pp. 276 ff.

Handel deals with the Sheba theme in his Oratorio *Solomon*, and especially in Act III whose introductory 'symphony' is generally referred to as 'The Arrival of the Queen of Sheba'.[1] Karl Goldmark (1830–1915) has written an opera *Die Königin von Saba* which I have, unfortunately, never seen performed. Professor D. Winton Thomas has very kindly drawn my attention to Gounod's opera *La Reine de Saba* (1862).

The Queen of Sheba has experienced her greatest and most far-flung development in the area of painting. In Persian art she may often be seen standing in water before King Solomon. In Ethiopian traditional art this theme has had an enduring influence to the present day: its conventional tableau form divides the story into forty-four pictures, arranged in four rows of eleven. It tells the legend as embodied in the *Kebra Nagast* and includes most realistic representations of the royal bedchamber scenes (the removal men who recently handled my large Sheba canvas described the picture as a strip-cartoon).

There is a window in King's College Chapel, Cambridge, which depicts the visit of the Queen of Sheba to King Solomon: the king is seated on his throne and between him and the queen is an area of blue glass representing the pool of the Muslim legend.[2] In European art the queen has often become web-footed and can thus be seen in the company of apostles, prophets, patriarchs, and kings in groups of symbolic statuary over church doors, at Chartres or Dijon or Le Mans. On the other hand, she

---

[1] Cf. Winton Dean, *Handel's Dramatic Oratorios and Masques*, O.U.P., 1959, p. 523.
[2] An exceptionally learned article on this subject appeared in *The Times* of 28 June 1954.

has become *La reine pédauque* ('Queen Goose-foot') to adorn the signboards of restaurants and taverns. Lorenzo Ghiberti, Piero della Francesca, Tintoretto, and many others have painted magnificent pictures of the Queen of Sheba arriving at King Solomon's Court, and some young Ethiopian artists have recently endeavoured to represent an amalgam of the Byzantine and Western traditions.[1]

Many features and details of the Sheba legend remain elusive, and the Queen's provenance, person, and character will be shrouded in the twilight of mystery. 'Behold, the half was not told me', she said in taking leave of Solomon. Had his answer been recorded, he might well have said: 'Nor to me, Madam, about you.' But most probably he said nothing. 'As the wisest of men and the husband of 700 wives he must surely have known where the last word belongs.'[2]

[1] A charming cartoon of King Solomon in an aeroplane and the Queen of Sheba with a transistor radio set (by Sprod) appears in Sir Leonard Woolley's *As I Seem to Remember*. This is accompanied by a somewhat modernized version of the story (pp. 64–67).

[2] *The Times*, 28 June 1954.

BIBLIOGRAPHY

D'ABBADIE, A., *Catalogue raisonné de manuscrits éthiopiens*, Paris, 1859.

ABRAHAM, M., *Légendes juives apocryphes sur la vie de Moïse*, Paris, 1925.

ABU ṢĀLIḤ, *Churches and monasteries of Egypt and some neighbouring countries* (transl. and ed. by B. T. A. Evetts, with notes by A. J. Butler), Oxford, 1895.

ABUL-HAGGAG, Y., *A contribution to the physiography of Northern Ethiopia*, London, 1961.

Accademia Nazionale dei Lincei, *Atti del Convegno Internazionale di Studi Etiopici*, Rome, 1960.

AEŠCOLY, A. Z., 'The Falashas (bibliography)' in *Kiryath Sepher*, xii, xiii (1935–7).

—— *Sefer Ha-Falashim* (in Hebrew), Jerusalem, 1943.

—— *Recueil de textes falachas*, Paris, 1951.

ALBRIGHT, W. F., 'Dedan' in *Albrecht Alt Festschrift* (*Geschichte und Altes Testament*), Tübingen, 1953.

—— 'The archaeology of the ancient Near East' in Peake's *Commentary on the Bible* (ed. by M. Black and H. H. Rowley), 1962.

ARMBRUSTER, C. H., *Initia Amharica*, Part I, Grammar, Cambridge, 1908.

—— *Initia Amharica*, Part II, English–Amharic vocabulary, Cambridge, 1910.

BAARS, W., and ZUURMOND, R., 'The project for a new edition of the Ethiopic Book of Jubilees', in *JSS* ix. 1, Spring 1964.

BACHMANN, J., *Der Prophet Jesaia nach der aethiopischen Bibeluebersetzung*, (I. Teil: Der aethiopische Text; II. Teil: Der aethiopische Text in seinem Verhältnis zur Septuaginta), Berlin, 1893.

BAETEMAN, J., *Dictionnaire amarigna-français*, Dire Daoua, 1929.

BARTH, J., *Die Nominalbildung in den semitischen Sprachen*, Leipzig, 1889.

BASSANO, F. DA, *Vocabolario tigray-italiano e repertorio italiano-tigray*, Rome, 1918.

—— *Old Testament* in Ge'ez, 4 vols., Asmara, 1922–6.

BASSET, R., *Histoire de la conquête de l'Abyssinie* (*XVIᵉ siècle*) (Arabic text and French transl. of Shihāb ad-Dīn's *Futuḥ al-Ḥabaša*), Paris, 1897–1901.

BECKINGHAM, C. F., and HUNTINGFORD, G. W. B. (translators), *Some records of Ethiopia, 1593–1646* (Manoel de Almeida and Bahrey), Hakluyt Society, London, 1954.

—— *The Prester John of the Indies*, 2 vols., Hakluyt Society, London, 1961.

BECKINGHAM, C. F., 'The "Itinerario" of Jeronimo Lobo' in *JSS* x. 2, Autumn 1965.

—— *The achievements of Prester John* (Inaugural Lecture), School of Oriental and African Studies, London, 1966.

BEESTON, A. F. L., 'ABRAHA' in *Encyclopaedia of Islam*, new edition.

—— *A descriptive grammar of Epigraphic South Arabian*, London, 1962.

BEN YEHUDA, ELIEZER, *Thesaurus totius Hebraitatis et veteris et recentioris*, American ed., 8 vols., New York, 1960.

BENT, T., *The Sacred City of the Ethiopians* (with a chapter by D. H. Müller on the Yeha and Aksum inscriptions), London, 1893.

BENZINGER, I., 'Die Bücher der Könige' in Marti's *Kurzer Hand-Commentar zum Alten Testament*, Tübingen, 1899.

—— *Hebräische Archäologie*, 3rd ed., Leipzig, 1927.

BEVAN, A. A., *The hymn of the Soul* (Syriac text and English transl.), Cambridge University Press, 1897.

BEZOLD, C., *Kebra Nagast*, Munich, 1905.

—— 'Das arabisch-aethiopische Testamentum Adami' in *Nöldeke Festschrift*, Gießen, 1906.

BLACK, M., *An Aramaic approach to the Gospels and Acts*, 2nd ed., Oxford, 1954.

BOYD, O., *The Octadeuch in Ethiopic, according to the text of the Paris Codex, with the variants of five other MSS.* in *Bibliotheca Abessinica*, Part I: Genesis, Leiden and Princeton, 1909; Part II: Exodus and Leviticus, 1911.

BREASTED, J. H., *History of Egypt*, 2nd ed., London, 1948.

BROCKELMANN, C., *Grundriß der vergleichenden Grammatik der semitischen Sprachen*, 2 vols., Berlin, 1908–13.

—— *Lexicon Syriacum*, 2nd ed., Halle, 1928.

BRUCE, J., *Travels to discover the source of the Nile*, 1st ed., 5 vols., Edinburgh, 1790; 3rd ed., 8 vols., Edinburgh, 1813.

BUDGE, SIR E. A. WALLIS, *The life and exploits of Alexander the Great*, 2 vols., London, 1896.

—— *Life of Hanna* (Lady Meux MSS. 2–5; text and transl.), London, 1900.

—— *A history of Ethiopia*, 2 vols., London, 1928.

—— *Book of the saints of the Ethiopian Church*, 4 vols., Cambridge, 1928.

—— *The Queen of Sheba and her only son Menyelek*, London, 1932.

—— *Amulets and talismans*, New York, 1961.

BURKITT, F. C., 'Text and versions' in *Encyclopaedia Biblica*, iv, London, 1903.

BUTLER, A. J., see ABU ṢĀLIḤ.

BUXTON, D. R., *Travels in Ethiopia*, London, 1949.

CAQUOT, A., 'La Reine de Saba et le bois de la croix' in *Annales d'Éthiopie*, i, 1955.

—— 'La royauté sacrale en Éthiopie' in *Annales d'Éthiopie*, ii, 1957.

CASTANHOSO, *The Portuguese expedition to Abyssinia* (transl. and ed. by R. S. Whiteway), Hakluyt Society, London, 1902.

CERULLI, E., 'Canti popolari amarici' in *RRAL* 1916.

—— 'Di alcune varietà di inni della chiesa etiopica' in *Orientalia*, 1934.

—— *Studi etiopici:*

    I. *La lingua e la storia di Harar*, Rome, 1936.

    II. *La lingua e la storia dei Sidamo*, Rome, 1938.

CERULLI, E. *Studi etiopici* (cont.):

    III. *Il linguaggio dei Giangero*, etc., Rome, 1938.

    IV. *La lingua caffina*, Rome, 1951.

—— *Il libro etiopico dei miracoli di Maria e le sue fonti nella letteratura del Medio Evo latino*, Rome, 1943.

—— *Etiopi in Palestina*, 2 vols., Rome, 1943–7.

—— *Storia della letteratura etiopica*, Rome, 1956.

—— *Scritti teologici etiopici dei secoli XVI–XVII*, 2 vols., Città del Vaticano, 1958–60.

CHAÎNE, M., *Catalogue des manuscrits éthiopiens de la Collection Antoine d'Abbadie*, Paris, 1912.

—— *Catalogue des manuscrits éthiopiens de la Collection Mondon-Vidailhet*, Paris, 1913.

Chamber of Commerce, *Guide book of Ethiopia*, Addis Ababa, 1954.

CHARLES, R. H., *The Ethiopic version of the Hebrew Book of Jubilees*, Oxford, 1895.

—— *The Book of Jubilees or The Little Genesis* (transl. from Ethiopic text, introduction, notes), London, 1902.

—— *The Ethiopic version of the Book of Enoch* (Anecdota Oxoniensia), Oxford, 1906.

—— *The Book of Enoch* (English transl.), 2nd ed., Oxford, 1912.

—— *The Apocrypha and Pseudepigrapha of the Old Testament*, 2 vols., Oxford, 1913.

CHEESMAN, R. E., *Lake Tana and the Blue Nile*, London, 1936.

COHEN, M., 'La prononciation traditionnelle du guèze', *JA*, Paris, 1921.

—— 'Couplets Amhariques du Choa' in *JA* 1924.

—— *Études d'éthiopien méridional*, Paris, 1931.

—— *Traité de langue amharique*, Paris, 1936.

—— *Nouvelles Études d'éthiopien méridional*, Paris, 1939.

—— *Essai comparatif sur le vocabulaire et la phonétique du chamito-sémitique*, Paris, 1947.

—— 'Sur la notation musicale éthiopienne' in *Levi Della Vida Festschrift*, Rome, 1956.

CONTI ROSSINI, C., 'Sulla versione e sulla revisione delle sacre scritture in Etiopico' in *ZA* x, Leipzig, 1895.

—— 'Note per la storia letteraria abissina' in *RRAL* 1899.

—— *Vitae Sanctorum Indigenarum: Acta Marqorewos* (text and transl.), *C.S.C.O.*, vols. 33 and 34 (= Aeth. 16 and 17), 1904.

—— *Vitae Sanctorum Indigenarum: Acta S. Baṣalota Mika'el et S. Anorewos*, 2 vols. (Eth. text 28/11; transl. 29/12), *C.S.C.O.* 1905.

—— 'Sugli Habašat' in *RRAL* 1906.

—— *Liber Axumae*, *C.S.C.O.* 1909.

—— 'Un documento sul cristianesimo nello Iemen ai tempi del re Šaraḥbil Yakkuf' in *RRAL* 1910.

—— 'L'itinerario di Beniamino da Tudela e l'Etiopia' in *ZA* xxvii, Leipzig, 1911–12.

—— 'Sul Metropolita Salama d'Etiopia' in *ZA* xxvii, Leipzig, 1911–12.

—— 'Notice sur les manuscrits éthiopiens de la Collection d'Abbadie', *JA* 1912–15.

—— 'Appunti di storia e letteratura falascià' in *RSO* viii, 1920.

—— 'Expéditions et possessions des Ḥabašat en Arabie' in *JA* 1921.

—— Review of Rathjens: *Die Juden in Abessinien* in *OM* 1921.

—— 'Le lingue e le letterature semitiche d'Abissinia' in *OM* 1921–2 (pp. 38–48, 169–76).

—— 'Nuovi appunti sui giudei d'Abissinia' in *RRAL* 1922.

—— 'La caduta della dinastia Zague e la versione amarica del Be'ela Nagast' in *RRAL* 1922.

—— 'Leggende geografiche giudaiche del IX Secolo (Il Sefer Eldad)' in *Bollettino della R. Società Geografica Italiana*, 1925.

—— *Storia d'Etiopia*, Bergamo, 1928.

—— *L'Abissinia*, Rome, 1929.

—— *Etiopia e genti d'Etiopia*, Florence, 1937.

—— *Lingua tigrina*, Milan, 1940.

—— *Proverbi, tradizioni e canzoni tigrine*, Verbania, 1942.

—— 'La regalità sacra in Abissinia e nei regni dell'Africa centrale ed occidentale' in *Studi e materiali di storia delle religioni*, xxi, Bologna, 1948.

—— and RICCI, L. (ed.), *Maṣḥafa Berhan: Il Libro della luce del Negus Zar'a Ya'qob* (text and transl.; 4 parts), *C.S.C.O.* 1964/5.

Cosmas Indicopleustes, *see* McCRINDLE, J. W.

COULBEAUX, P. S., and SCHREIBER, J., *Dictionnaire de la langue tigrai*, Vienna, 1915.

COWLEY, A., *Aramaic Papyri of the fifth century B.C.*, Oxford, 1923.

CURTIS, E. L., *The Books of the Chronicles*, I.C.C., Edinburgh, 1910.

DEAN, WINTON, *Handel's dramatic oratorios and masques*, Oxford University Press, 1959.

DILLMANN, A., *Catalogus Codicum MSS. Aethiopicorum qui in Museo Britannico asservantur*, London, 1847.

—— *Catalogus Codicum Manuscriptorum Bibliothecae Bodleianae Oxoniensis*, pars VII, Oxford, 1848.

—— *Liber Henoch Aethiopice*, Leipzig, 1851.

—— *Liber Jubilaeorum*, Kiel, 1859.

—— *Chrestomathia Aethiopica Edita et Glossario Explanata*, Lipsiae, 1866.

—— *Lexicon Linguae Aethiopicae*, Lipsiae, 1865.

—— *Ascensio Isaiae*, Leipzig, 1877.

—— *Verzeichniss der abessinischen Handschriften*, Königliche Bibliothek, Berlin, 1878.

—— 'Zur Geschichte des Axumitischen Reichs im vierten bis sechsten Jahrhundert' in *Abh. d. Königl. Akad. d. Wissensch. zu Berlin*, 1880.

—— *Über die Regierung, insbesondere die Kirchenordnung des Königs Zar'a-Jacob*, Berlin, 1884.

—— 'Die Kriegsthaten des Königs 'Amda-Sion gegen die Muslim' in *Sitzungsberichte d. K. Preuss. Akad. d. Wissensch.*, Berlin, 1884.

DILLMANN, A., *Biblia Veteris Testamenti Aethiopica*, Bd. I (1853): Oct.;
Bd. II, Fasc. 1 (1861): Reg. I, II; Fasc. 2 (1871): Reg. III, IV; Bd. V
(1894): Libri Apocr., Leipzig, 1853–94.
—— *Ethiopic grammar* (transl. by J. A. Crichton), London, 1907.
DORESSE, J., *Au pays de la Reine de Saba; l'Éthiopie antique et moderne*,
Paris, 1956.
—— *L'Empire du Prêtre Jean*, 2 vols., Paris, 1957.
DREWES, A. J., *Inscriptions de l'Éthiopie antique*, Leiden, 1962.
DROWER, LADY, and MACUCH, R., *A Mandaic dictionary*, Oxford,
Clarendon Press, 1963.
DUHM, B., *Die Psalmen* in Marti's *Handkommentar*, 2nd ed., Tübingen,
1922.
EADIE, J. I., *An Amharic reader*, Cambridge University Press, 1924.
ELBOGEN, I., *Der jüdische Gottesdienst in seiner geschichtlichen Entwicklung*,
2nd ed., Frankfurt, 1924.
EPSTEIN, ABRAHAM, *Eldad Hadani*, Pressburg, 1891.
Ethiopia Observer, Journal published in Ethiopia and Britain from
December 1956– .
*Ethiopian Studies: Proceedings of the International Conference of Ethiopian
Studies at Manchester University, 1963*, edited by E. Ullendorff and
C. F. Beckingham, *JSS*, Spring 1964.
'Ethiopia' and 'Eritrea' in *Enciclopedia Italiana*, vol. xiv (pp. 220–34,
459–92).
EVETTS, B. T. A. (transl. and ed.), *see* ABU ṢĀLIḤ.
FAITLOVICH, J., *Mota Muse* (texte éthiopien traduit en hébreu et en
français — annoté et accompagné d'extraits arabes), Paris, 1906.
—— *The Falashas*, Philadelphia, 1920.
FARIS, N. A. (ed.), Hamdāni, *Iklīl*, 8th book, Princeton, 1940.
FARMER, H. G., *A history of Arabian music*, London, 1929.
FINDLAY, L., *The monolithic churches at Lalibela in Ethiopia*, Cairo, 1944.
FISHER, W. B., *The Middle East*, London, 1950.
FLAD, J. M., *The Falashas of Abyssinia*, London, 1869.
—— *60 Jahre in der Mission unter den Falaschas*, Gießen, 1922.
FLEMMING, J., 'Hiob Ludolf — Ein Beitrag zur Geschichte der orienta-
lischen Philologie' in *Beiträge zur Assyriologie*, i and ii, 1890, 1894.
—— *Das Buch Henoch* (aeth. Text), Leipzig, 1902.
FRAENCKEL, S., *Die aramäischen Fremdwörter im Arabischen*, Leiden, 1868
(reprint Hildesheim 1962).
FUMAGALLI, G., *Bibliografia etiopica*, Milan, 1893.
GAGUINE, M., *The Falasha Version of the Testaments of Abraham, Isaac and
Jacob*, Manchester University Ph.D. thesis, 1965.
GEIGER, A., *Was hat Mohammed aus dem Judenthum aufgenommen*, Bonn,
1833.
GESENIUS, W., *Hebräisches und aramäisches Handwörterbuch über das Alte
Testament* (bearbeitet von Frants Buhl), 15th ed., Leipzig, 1910.
GILDEMEISTER, J., 'Brief an C. R. Gregory vom 20. April 1882' in
Gregory's *Prolegomena zu Tischendorf's N.T. graece*, vol. 3, 1894.

GINZBERG, L., *The legends of the Jews*, 7 vols., Philadelphia, 1947.

GLASER, E., *Die Abessinier in Arabien und Africa*, Munich, 1895.

GLEAVE, H. C., *The Ethiopic version of Song of Songs*, London, 1951.

GOLDENBERG, G., *The Amharic tense-system*, Ph.D. thesis, in Hebrew, Jerusalem University, 1966.

GOLDSCHMIDT, L., *Das Buch Henoch* (transl. from Ethiopic into Hebrew), Berlin, 1892.

—— *Die abessinischen Handschriften der Stadtbibliothek zu Frankfurt a/M* (Rüppelsche Sammlung), Berlin, 1897.

GOLDZIHER, I., *Muhammedanische Studien*, i and ii (reprint), Hildesheim, 1961.

GORDIS, R., *The Song of Songs* (study, translation, commentary), New York, 1954.

GORDON, C. H., *Introduction to Old Testament times*, Ventnor, N.J., 1953.

—— *Ugaritic textbook*, Rome, 1965.

GRAF, G., *Geschichte der christlichen arabischen Literatur*, 5 vols., Città del Vaticano, 1944–53.

GRÉBAUT, S., and TISSERANT, E., *Codices Aethiopici Vaticani et Borgiani Barberinianus Rossianus 865*, 2 vols., 1935–6.

GRÉBAUT, S., *Catalogue des manuscrits éthiopiens de la Collection Griaule*, 3 vols., Paris, 1938, 1941, 1944.

GREGORY, C. R., *Prolegomena zu Tischendorf's N.T. Graece, editio octava*, vol. iii, 1894.

GRÜNBAUM, M., *Neue Beiträge zur semitischen Sagenkunde*, Leiden, 1893.

Guida dell'Africa Orientale Italiana, Milan, 1938.

GUIDI, I., 'Le traduzioni degli Evangelii in arabo e in etiopico' in *MRAL* 1888.

—— *Il Fetha Nagast* (Eth. text, Italian transl.), 2 vols., Rome, 1897 and 1899.

—— 'Qene o inni abissini' in *RRAL* 1900.

—— *Vocabolario amarico-italiano*, Rome, 1901.

—— *L'Arabie antéislamique*, Paris, 1921.

—— 'La Chiesa abissina' in *Oriente moderno*, Rome, 1922.

—— 'Contributi alla storia letteraria di Abissinia' (I. I. Ser'ata Mangest) in *RRAL* 1922.

—— 'Il Be'la Nagast' in *Festschrift Paul Haupt*, Leipzig, 1926.

—— (*Breve*) *Storia della letteratura etiopica*, Rome, 1932.

—— *Grammatica elementare della lingua amarica*, Rome, 1936.

—— 'Le synaxaire éthiopien' (Sane, Hamle, Nahase, Paguemen) in *Patrologia Orientalis*, ix. 4, Paris.

—— and others, *Supplemento al Vocabolario amarico-italiano*, Rome, 1940.

—— *Storia e cultura degli arabi fino alla morte di Maometto*, Firenze, 1951.

GUILLAUME, A., 'The influence of Judaism on Islam' in *The legacy of Israel*, Oxford, 1927.

HABERLAND, E., *Galla Süd-Äthiopiens*, Stuttgart, 1963.

—— *Untersuchungen zum äthiopischen Königtum*, Wiesbaden, 1965.

HACKSPILL, L., 'Die äthiopische Evangelienübersetzung' in *ZA* xi, 1896.

HALÉVY, J., *Prières des Falashas*, Paris, 1877.
—— *Te'ezaza Sanbat*, Paris, 1902.
—— 'La légende de la Reine de Saba' in *Annuaire de l'École des Hautes Études* (Section des sciences historiques), 1905.
HAMMERSCHMIDT, E., *Studies in the Ethiopic Anaphoras*, Berlin, 1961.
—— 'Kultsymbolik der koptischen und äthiopischen Kirche' in *Orthodox. und orient. Christentum*, 1962.
—— *Stellung und Bedeutung des Sabbats in Äthiopien*, Stuttgart, 1963.
—— *Symbolik des orientalischen Christentums, Tafelband*, Stuttgart, 1966.
HARDEN, J. M., *The Ethiopic Didascalia*, Soc. for Promoting Christ. Knowledge, London, 1920.
HARPER, W. R., *Amos and Hosea* (I.C.C.), Edinburgh, 1936.
HARRIS, W. CORNWALLIS, *The highlands of Æthiopia*, 3 vols., London, 1844.
HARTOM, A. S. (U. Cassuto, General Editor), *Psalms* (in Hebrew), Tel Aviv, 1957.
HASTINGS, JAMES (ed.), *A dictionary of the Bible*, 5 vols., Edinburgh, 1906.
HEIDER, A., *Die äthiopische Bibelübersetzung* (Ihre Herkunft, Art, Geschichte, und ihr Wert für alt- und neutestamentliche Wissenschaft), Leipzig, 1902.
Herodotus (transl. into English by Henry Cary), London, 1891.
HERZOG, J. J., *Realencyklopädie für protestantische Theologie und Kirche*, 3rd ed., 22 vols., 1896–1913.
HIRSCHBERG, H. Z., *Yisra'el ba'Arab*, Tel Aviv, 1946.
HITTI, P. K., *History of the Arabs*, 4th ed., London, 1949.
HÖFNER, M., 'Über sprachliche und kulturelle Beziehungen zwischen Südarabien und Äthiopien im Altertum' in *Atti del Conv. Internaz. di Studi Etiopici*, 1960.
HOMMEL, F., *Ethnologie und Geographie des Alten Orients*, Munich, 1926.
HUBBARD, D. A., *The literary sources of the Kebra Nagast*, as yet unpublished Ph.D. thesis, St. Andrews University, 1956.
HUNTINGFORD, G. W. B., *The glorious victories of Amda Seyon*, Oxford, 1965.
HYATT, H. M., *The Church of Abyssinia*, London, 1928.
Illustrated London News, 'The Abyssinian expedition and the life and reign of King Theodore', history by R. Acton, London, 1868.
IRVINE, A. K., 'ḤABASHAT' in *Encyclopaedia of Islam*, 2nd ed., 1965.
—— 'On the identity of Ḥabashat in the South Arabian inscriptions' in *JSS* x. 2, Autumn 1965.
Isaiah in Tigre (ed. and transl. by G. R. Sundström), Asmara, 1925.
ISENBERG, C. W., *Dictionary of the Amharic language*, London, 1841.
—— *Grammar of the Amharic language*, London, 1842.
JAMME, A., *Sabaean and Ḥasaean inscriptions from Saudi Arabia* (Studi semitici, 23) Rome, 1966.
JOHNSON, A. R., *Sacral kingship in Ancient Israel*², Cardiff, 1967.
JOSEPHUS, *see* WHISTON, W.
JOWETT, W., *Christian researches in the Mediterranean*, London, 1822.

KAMMERER, A., *Essai sur l'histoire antique d'Abyssinie*, Paris, 1926.

KATSH, A. I., *Judaism in Islam*, 1954.

KOEHLER, L., and BAUMGARTNER, W., *Lexicon in Veteris Testamenti Libros*, Leiden, 1948–53; *Supplementum*, Leiden, 1958.

KOLMODIN, J. A., 'Meine Studienreise in Abessinien, 1908–10' in *MO*, Uppsala, 1910.

KÖNIG, E., *Neue Studien über Schrift, Aussprache und allgemeine Formenlehre des Aethiopischen*, Leipzig, 1877.

KRAPF, J. L., *Evangelia sacra . . . in linguam tigricam vertit Debtera Matheos Habessinus*, Adoae; Tigriae oppido, natus, nunc primum in lucem edita per J. L. Krapf . . . Basileae . . . in officina typographica Chrischonae. MDCCCLXVI.

—— *The Books of the Old Testament*, translated into the Amharic language by Abba Rukh, an Abyssinian Learned. For the first time corrected and edited in England by the Revd. Thomas Platt. Now improved after the Hebrew original by the Revd. Dr. Krapf in Germany. Printed at the expense and by the request of the B. & F.B.S. in London at the Mission-Press of St. Chrishona, near Basle, Switzerland, 3 vols., 1871–3.

KRAUSS, S., 'Talmudische Nachrichten über Arabien' in *ZDMG* 1916.

KROMREI, E., *Glaubenslehre und Gebräuche der älteren abessinischen Kirche*, Leipzig, 1895.

LANTSCHOOT, A. VAN, 'Abbā Salāmā, métropolite d'Éthiopie (1348–1388) et son rôle de traducteur' in *Atti del Conv. Internaz. di Studi Etiopici*, 1960.

LEONESSA, MAURO DA, 'Un trattato sul calendario redatto al tempo di re 'Amda-Ṣyon I' in *RSE* iii. 3, 1943.

LESLAU, W., *Lexique Soqoṭri (sudarabique moderne)*, Paris, 1938.

—— *Documents ṭigrigna*, Paris, 1941.

—— *Falasha Anthology*, New Haven, 1951.

—— *Coutumes et Croyances des Falachas*, Paris, 1957.

—— 'A supplementary Falasha bibliography' in *Studies in bibliography and booklore*, iii. 1, June, 1957.

—— *Ethiopic and South Arabic contributions to the Hebrew lexicon*, Univ. of California Press, 1958.

—— 'The names of the weekdays in Ethiopic' in *JSS*, Spring 1961.

—— *An annotated bibliography of the Semitic languages of Ethiopia*, The Hague, 1965.

LEVINE, D. N., *Wax and Gold*, University of Chicago Press, 1965.

LIFCHITZ, D., *Textes éthiopiens magico-religieux*, Paris, 1940.

LIPSKY, GEORGE A., *Ethiopia (its people, its society, its culture)*, New Haven, Conn., 1962.

LITTMANN, E., *The legend of the Queen of Sheba in the tradition of Axum*, Leiden, 1904.

—— 'Geschichte der äthiopischen Litteratur' in *Geschichte d. christlichen Litteraturen des Orients*, 2nd ed., Leipzig, 1909.

LITTMANN, E., *Publications of the Princeton expedition to Abyssinia; tales, customs, names and dirges of the Tigre tribes*, Leiden, 1910–15.
—— *Deutsche Aksum Expedition*, Berlin, 1913.
—— Review of S. A. B. Mercer's *The Ethiopic text of the book of Ecclesiastes* (London 1931) in *OLZ* 1933/6.
—— *Abessinische Klagelieder*, Tübingen, 1949.
—— 'Richard Sundström— 1869–1919' in *Ein Jahrhundert Orientalistik*, Wiesbaden, 1955.
—— and HÖFNER, M., *Wörterbuch der Tigre-Sprache*, Wiesbaden, 1956–1962.
LOBO, J., *A voyage to Abyssinia* (transl. into French by Le Grand and into English by Dr. Samuel Johnson), London, 1735.
LÖFGREN, O., *Die äthiopische Übersetzung des Propheten Daniel*, Paris, 1927.
—— 'Die äthiopische Bibelausgabe der Katholischen Mission' (mit einer Kollation des Danieltextes) in *MO* xxiii, 1929.
—— *Jona, Nahum, Habakuk, Zephanja, Haggai, Sacharja und Maleachi äthiopisch unter Zugrundelegung des Oxforder M.S. Huntington 625 nach meheren Handschriften herausgegeben*, Uppsala, 1930.
—— Review of S. A. B. Mercer's *The Ethiopic text of the book of Ecclesiastes* (London 1931) in *MO* xxvii, 1933.
—— 'The necessity of a critical edition of the Ethiopian Bible', paper submitted to 3rd Int. Conf. of Eth. Stud., Addis Ababa, 1966 (still unpublished at the time of writing, Spring 1967).
LONGRIGG, S. H., *A short history of Eritrea*, Oxford, 1945.
LUDOLF, H., *Grammatica Aethiopica*, Frankfort, 1661.
—— *Historia Aethiopica*, Frankfort, 1681.
—— *Commentarius ad suam Historiam Aethiopicam*, Frankfort, 1691.
—— *Grammatica Linguae Amharicae*, Frankfort, 1698.
—— *Lexicon Aethiopico-Latinum²*, Frankfort, 1699.
—— *Psalterium Davidis aethiopice et latine cum duobus impressis et tribus MSStis codicibus diligenter collatum et emendatum*, Frankfort, 1701.
MCCRINDLE, J. W. (transl. and ed.), Cosmas, *Christian Topography*, Hakluyt Society, London, 1897.
MAREIN, N., *The Ethiopian empire, federation and laws*, Rotterdam, 1954.
MARIANUS VICTORIUS, *Chaldeae seu Aethiopicae linguae institutiones*, Rome, 1552.
MARKHAM, C. R., *A history of the Abyssinian expedition*, London, 1869.
Mäṣhafä Qeddase (Missale Aethiopicum), published by the Vatican Library, Rome, 1945.
—— Ge'ez and Amharic, Addis Ababa 1949/50.
MATHEW, D., *Ethiopia. Study of a polity 1540–1935*, London, 1947.
MERCER, S. A. B., *The Ethiopic Liturgy*, London, 1915.
—— *The Ethiopic text of the Book of Ecclesiastes*, London, 1931.
MESFIN WOLDE MARIAM, 'An estimate of the population of Ethiopia' in *Ethiopia Observer*, v. 2, 1961.
—— *A preliminary atlas of Ethiopia*, Addis Ababa, 1962.

Missione Cattolica dell'Eritrea, *Grammatica della lingua tigre*, Asmara, 1919.

MITTWOCH, E., 'Dschanhoi — die amharische Bezeichnung für "Majestät"' in *ZA* 1911.

—— *Die traditionelle Aussprache des Aethiopischen*, Berlin, 1926.

MONDON-VIDAILHET, F. M. C., 'La musique éthiopienne' in *Encyclopédie de la musique et dictionnaire du Conservatoire*, 1re partie, pp. 3179–96, Paris, 1922.

MONNERET DE VILLARD, U., *Aksum*, Rome, 1938.

MONTGOMERY, J. A., 'The Ethiopic text of the Acts of the Apostles' in *Harvard Theological Review*, xxvii, pp. 169 ff., Cambridge, Mass., 1934.

MONTI DELLA CORTE, A. A., *Lalibela*, Rome, 1940.

—— *I castelli di Gondar*, Rome, 1938.

MORDINI, A., 'Il Convento di Gunde Gundiè' in *RSE* 1953.

MORENO, M. M., 'Struttura e terminologia del Säwasew' in *RSE* viii, 1950.

MÜLLER, W. MAX, *Äthiopien*, Leipzig, 1904.

MUNZINGER, W., *Vocabulaire de la langue tigre* (Appendix to Dillmann's *Lexicon*), 1863.

MURAD KAMIL, Josippon's *History of the Jews*, New York–Berlin, 1937.

NAU, F. (ed.), 'Histoire de Akhoudemmeh', *Patrologia Orientalis*, iii, 1909.

NIELSEN, D., *Handbuch der alt-arabischen Altertumskunde*, Copenhagen, 1927.

NÖLDEKE, T., Review of Dillman's *Regierung*, insb. *Kirchenordnung des Zar'a-Jacob* (Berlin 1884) in *GGA* 1884.

—— *Kurzgefasste syrische Grammatik*², Leipzig, 1898.

—— *Neue Beiträge zur semitischen Sprachwissenschaft*, Strasbourg, 1910.

—— 'Semitic languages' in *Encyclopaedia Britannica*¹³.

—— *Geschichte des Qorāns* (reprint), Hildesheim, 1961.

OESTERLEY, W. O. E., *The Jewish background of the Christian Liturgy*, Oxford, 1925.

PAIS, PÊRO, *Historia de Etiopia*, 3 vols., Porto, 1945.

PALMER, F. R., *The morphology of the Tigre noun*, Oxford, 1962.

PANKHURST, R., *An introduction to the economic history of Ethiopia from early times to 1800*, 1961.

PARKYNS, MANSFIELD, *Life in Abyssinia*, London 1966 impression of 2nd ed. 1868 (1st ed. 1853).

Peake's commentary on the Bible (ed. by M. Black and H. H. Rowley), 1962.

PEARCE, NATHANIEL, *The life and adventures of Nathaniel Pearce*, written by himself, London, 1831.

PEREIRA, F. M. ESTEVES, *Patrologia Orientalis*, Ethiopic text edition of *Job* (1907); *Esther* (1913); *Amos* (1917); *Ezra-Nehemia* (1919).

PERHAM, M., *The Government of Ethiopia*, London, 1948.,

Periplus Maris Erythraei, see SCHOFF, W. H.

PERRUCHON, J., *Les Chroniques de Zar'a Ya'qob et de Ba'eda Maryam*, Paris, 1893.

—— 'Histoire des guerres d'Amda Syon' in *JA* 1889.

PETRUS AETHIOPS (FRATER), *Testamentum Novum cum Epistola Pauli ad Hebraeos*, Rome, 1548.

PLATT, THOMAS PELL (ed.), *Evangelia Sancta, sub auspiciis D. Asselini, rerum gallicarum apud Aegyptios procuratoris, in linguam amharicam, vertit Abu Rumi habessinus*, London, 1824.

—— *Testamentum Novum, Domini Nostri et Servatoris Jesu Christi, sub auspiciis D. Asselini . . . in linguam amharicam vertit Abu Rumi habessinus*, London, 1829.

—— *The Ethiopic Didascalia* (Eth. text, Engl. transl.), London, 1834.

—— *Biblia sacra amharice, sub auspiciis D. Asselini in linguam amharicam vertit Abu Rumi*, London, 1840.

PLAYNE, B., *St. George for Ethiopia*, London, 1954.

POLLERA, A., *Lo Stato etiopico e la sua Chiesa*, Rome–Milan, 1926.

—— *Le popolazioni indigene dell'Eritrea*, Bologna, 1935.

—— *L'Abissinia di ieri*, Rome, 1940.

POLOTSKY, H. J., 'Aramaic, Syriac and Ge'ez' in *Ethiopian Studies* (*JSS* ix. 1), 1964.

—— 'Semitics' in *The world history of the Jewish people*, vol. i (p. 107), London, 1964.

POTKEN, J., *Alphabetum seu potius syllabarium literarum Chaldaearum, Psalterium Chaldaeum*, Rome, 1513.

PRAETORIUS, F., *Fabula de regina Sabaea apud Aethiopes*, Halle, 1870.

—— *Grammatik der Tigrinasprache in Abessinien*, Halle, 1871.

—— *Die amharische Sprache*, Halle, 1879.

—— *Aethiopische Grammatik*, Leipzig, 1886.

—— 'Beiträge zur äthiopischen Grammatik und Etymologie' in *Beiträge zur Assyriologie*, i, 1890.

—— 'Äthiopische Bibelübersetzungen' in Herzog's *Realencyklopaedie*[3], iii, 1897.

—— *Über die Herkunft der hebräischen Accente*, Berlin, 1901.

PRITCHARD, J. B. (ed.), *Ancient Near Eastern texts relating to the O.T.*[2], Princeton University Press, 1955.

Psalms in Tigre (ed. and transl. by G. R. Sundström), Asmara, 1925.

RABIN, C., *Ancient West Arabian*, London, 1951.

RAHLFS, A., 'Nissel und Petraeus, ihre aethiopischen Textausgaben und Typen' in *Nachrichten von d. Königl. Gesellschaft der Wissenschaften*, Göttingen, 1917.

—— *Septuaginta Studien*, i–iii, 2nd ed., Göttingen, 1965.

—— 'Die äthiopische Bibelübersetzung' in *Septuaginta Studien* (pp. 659–681), Göttingen, 1965.

RATHJENS, C., *Die Juden in Abessinien*, Hamburg, 1921.

Reale Società Geografica Italiana, *L'Africa Orientale*, Bologna, 1936.

RECKENDORF, S., 'Über den Wert der alt-aethiopischen Pentateuch-übersetzung' in *ZAW* vii, Gießen, 1887.

RHODOKANAKIS, N., *Die äthiopischen Handschriften der K. K. Hofbibliothek zu Wien*, Vienna, 1906.

RICCI, L., *Maṣḥafa Berhan, see under* CONTI ROSSINI, C.

RINCK, F. T., *Macrizi Historia Regum Islamiticorum in Abyssinia* (Arabic text and Latin transl.), Leiden, 1790.

ROBERTSON SMITH, W., *The religion of the Semites*, London, 1907.

RODEN, K. G., *Le tribù dei Mensa* (Tigre text and Italian transl.), Asmara and Stockholm, 1913.

RODINSON, M., 'Sur éth. *tābōt*, ar. *tābūt* et les noms sémitiques de l'Arche' in *GLECS* ix, 1962.

—— 'Sur la question des "influences juives" en Éthiopie' in *Ethiopian Studies* (*JSS* ix. 1), 1964.

—— Review of E. Ullendorff's, *The Ethiopians* in *Bi Or* xxi. 3–4, 1964.

—— 'Ghidhā'' in *Encyclopaedia of Islam²*, vol. ii (pp. 1057–72).

RÖNSCH, H., *Das Buch der Jubiläen oder Die kleine Genesis* (lateinische Fragmente der Ambrosiana sowie eine von Dillmann aus 2 aeth. MSS gefertigten lat. Übertr.), Leipzig, 1874.

RÖNSCH, G., 'Die Königin von Saba als Königin Bilqis' in *Jahrbuch für Protestantische Theologie*, vi, 1880.

ROSENTHAL, F. (transl.), Ibn Khaldun, *Muqaddimah*, 3 vols., London, 1958.

ROTHMÜLLER, A. M., *The music of the Jews*, London, 1953.

ROUPP, N., 'Die älteste äthiopische Handschrift der vier Bücher der Könige' in *ZA* xvi, 1902.

ROWLEY, H. H., and GRANT, F. C., *Dictionary of the Bible²* (revised one-vol. ed. of Hastings's *Dict. of the Bible*), Edinburgh, 1963.

RUBENSON, S., 'The lion of the tribe of Judah, Christian symbol and/or Imperial title' in *JES* iii. 2, 1965.

RÜPPELL, E., *Reise in Abessinien*, 2 vols., Frankfort, 1838–40.

RUSSELL, BERTRAND, 'The Queen of Sheba's nightmare' in *Nightmares of eminent persons*, Penguin, 1962.

RYCKMANS, G., 'Inscriptions sud-arabes' (Xᵉ série) in *Le Muséon*, lxvi (3–4), 1953.

—— 'Inscriptions sud-arabes' (XIᵉ série) in *Le Muséon*, lxvii, 1954.

—— *Les Religions arabes préislamiques²* (*L'Histoire générale des religions*), 1960.

RYCKMANS, J., *L'Institution monarchique en Arabie méridionale*, Louvain, 1951.

—— 'Le christianisme en Arabie du Sud préislamique' in *L'Oriente cristiano nella storia della civiltà* (Accademia dei Lincei), Rome, 1964.

SABELLI, LUCA DEI, *Storia di Abissinia*, Rome, 1936–8.

SALT, H., *A voyage to Abyssinia*, London, 1814.

SALZBERGER, G., *Die Salomo-Sage in der semitischen Literatur*, Berlin, 1907.

SCHÄFERS, J., *Die äthiopische Übersetzung des Propheten Jeremias*, Freiburg, 1912.

SCHIRMANN, J., 'Hebrew Liturgical Poetry and Christian Hymnology' in *JQR*, October, 1953.

Schoff, W. H. (transl. and ed.), *The periplus of the Erythraean Sea*, New York, 1912.

Segal, M. Z., *Ben Sira* (in Hebrew), Jerusalem, 1953.

Shihāb ad-Dīn, *see* Basset, R.

Skinner, J., *Genesis*, 2nd ed., I.C.C., Edinburgh, 1930–51.

Smith, Sidney, 'Events in Arabia in the 6th cent. A.D.' in *BSOAS* xvi. 3, 1954.

Stern, H. A., *Wanderings among the Falashas in Abyssinia*, London, 1862.

Strelcyn, S., 'Quelques éléments du vocabulaire magique éthiopien' in *GLECS* v, 1949.

—— *Catalogue des manuscrits éthiopiens* (*Collection Griaule*), tome iv, Paris, 1954.

—— *Prières magiques éthiopiennes pour délier les charmes* (*Rocznik Orientalistyczny*, xviii), Warsaw, 1955.

—— 'Un traité éthiopien d'hygiène et de diététique' in *Africana*, i, 1964.

Swedish Evangelical Mission, *Evangelium enligt Markus på Tigre-Språket*, tryckt på Missionspressen i Monkullo, 1889.

Täsämma Habtä Mika'el, *Käsate Bərhan Täsämma: yä'aməraňňa mäzgäbä qalat*, Addis Ababa, 1958/9.

Tisserant, E., *Ascension d'Isaïe* (traduction de la version éthiopienne), Paris, 1909.

Trevaskis, G. K. N., *Eritrea. A colony in transition 1941–52*, Oxford, 1960.

Trimingham, J. S., *Islam in Ethiopia*, London, 1952.

Turaiev, Boris, 'Testi etiopici in manoscritti di Leningrado' in *RSE* vii. 1, 1948.

—— *Vitae Sanctorum Indigenarum, Acta S. Eustathii* (Latin transl.), C.S.C.O., Louvain, 1955.

Ullendorff, Edward, *Catalogue of Ethiopic MSS. in the Bodleian Library*, Oxford, 1951.

—— 'Ugaritic marginalia' in *Orientalia*, 1951.

—— 'The obelisk of Matara' in *JRAS* 1951.

—— 'Studies in the Ethiopic syllabary' in *Africa*, 1951.

—— Review of Leslau's *Falasha anthology* in *BSOAS* xv. 1, 1953.

—— 'James Bruce of Kinnaird' in *Scottish Historical Review*, October 1953.

—— 'The Ethiopic manuscripts in the Royal Library, Windsor Castle' in *RSE* xii, 1953.

—— *The Semitic languages of Ethiopia*, London, 1955.

—— 'The Semitic languages of Ethiopia and their contribution to general Semitic studies' in *Africa*, April 1955.

—— 'Candace (Acts VIII, 27) and The Queen of Sheba' in *New Testament Studies*, ii, September 1955.

—— 'Hebraic-Jewish elements in Abyssinian (Monophysite) Christianity' in *JSS*, July 1956.

—— 'The contribution of South Semitics to Hebrew lexicography' in *Vetus Testamentum*, April 1956.

—— 'The Biblical sources of the Ethiopian national saga' (in Hebrew) in *Sefer Ṭur-Sinai*, Jerusalem, 1960.

—— 'An Aramaic *Vorlage* of the Ethiopic text of Enoch?' in *Atti del Conv. Internaz. di Studi Etiopici*, Rome, 1960.

—— 'The "Death of Moses" in the literature of the Falashas' in *BSOAS*, October 1961.

—— 'The Queen of Sheba' in *Bulletin of the John Rylands Library*, March 1963.

—— *The Ethiopians*², Oxford University Press, 1965.

—— *An Amharic Chrestomathy*, Oxford University Press, 1965.

—— 'Bilḳīs' in *Encyclopaedia of Islam*, 2nd ed.

—— and WRIGHT, S., *Catalogue of Ethiopian manuscripts in the Cambridge University Library*, Cambridge, 1961.

URSIN, M., *Aethiopien. Impressionen aus einem altchristlichen Land*, Mannheim, 1958.

U.S. Army, *Area handbook for Ethiopia*, Washington, 1960.

VARENBERGH, J., 'Studien zur abessinischen Reichsordnung (Šerʿata Mangešt)' in *ZA*, vol. 30, 1915.

DE VAUX, R., *Ancient Israel, its life and institutions* (transl. by J. McHugh), London, 1961.

VERMES, G., 'The use of Bar Nash/Bar Nasha in Jewish Aramaic', a contribution to: Matthew Black, *An Aramaic approach to the Gospels and Acts* (new ed.); Clarendon Press, 1968.

VÖÖBUS, A., *Die Spuren eines älteren aethiopischen Evangelientextes im Lichte der literarischen Monumente*, Stockholm, 1951.

—— *Early versions of the New Testament*, Stockholm, 1954.

WALKER, C. H., *The Abyssinian at home*, London, 1933.

WATT, W. MONTGOMERY, *Muhammad at Medina*, Oxford, 1956.

WEIL, G., *Biblische Legenden der Muselmänner*, Frankfort, 1845.

WELLESZ, E., 'Studien zur aethiopischen Kirchenmusk' in *Oriens Christianus*, 1920.

—— *History of Byzantine music and hymnography*, Oxford, 1949.

—— (ed.), *Ancient and Oriental music*, London, 1957.

WELLHAUSEN, J., *Reste arabischen Heidentums*, 3rd ed., 1961.

WENDT, K., 'Die theologischen Auseinandersetzungen in der äthiopischen Kirche zur Zeit der Reformen des XV. Jahrhunderts' in *Atti del Conv. Internaz. di Studi Etiopici*, 1960.

—— *Das Maṣḥafa Milad (Liber Nativitatis) und Maṣḥafa Sellase (Liber Trinitatis) des Kaisers Zarʾa Yaʿqob; C.S.C.O.* (4 vols.); (1) Eth. text 221/41—transl. 222/42, 1962; (2) Eth. text 235/43—transl. 236/44, 1963.

WESTCOTT, B. F., and HORT, F. J. A., edition of the *Greek New Testament*, 1881.

WHISTON, W., Translation of *Flavius Josephus' Works* (Antiquities; Wars of the Jews; Against Apion; Dissertations), London, 1841.

WHITEWAY, R. S. (transl. and ed.), *The Portuguese expedition to Abyssinia 1541–1543* (as narrated by Castanhoso, with extracts from Bermudez and Correa), Hakluyt Society, London, 1902.

WISSMANN, H. VON, *Zur Geschichte und Landeskunde von Alt-Südarabien*, Vienna, 1964.

—— and HÖFNER, M., *Zur historischen Geographie des vorislamischen Südarabien*, Wiesbaden, 1953.

WORRELL, W. H., 'Studien zum abessinischen Zauberwesen' in *ZA* 1910.

WRIGHT, S., LEROY, J., and JÄGER, O., *Ethiopia. Illuminated manuscripts*, UNESCO, 1961.

WRIGHT, W., *Catalogue of Ethiopic MSS. in the British Museum*, London, 1877.

WURMBRAND, M., *The death of Aaron* (Eth. text ed., transl. into Hebrew, annotated, and introd.); publ. by the Circle of Friends of the Faitlovitch Library, Tel Aviv, 1961.

—— *The Falasha Arde'et* (transl., annotated, and introd.; in Hebrew), Tel Aviv, 1964.

YARON, R., *The law of the Elephantine documents* (in Hebrew), Jerusalem, 1961.

ZANUTTO, S., *Bibliografia etiopica: manoscritti etiopici*, Rome, 1932.

ZOTENBERG, H., *Catalogue des mss. Éthiopiens de la Bibliothèque nationale*, Paris, 1877.

INDEX

Aaron, 8, 26.
Aaronite, 24.
d'Abbadie, A., 35.
Abbay (Blue Nile), 2.
Abercrombie, L., 143.
'abiy sänbät, 109.
Abraha, 21.
Abraham, 3, 76.
Abraham, Testament of, 118.
Abraham, M., 13.
Abu Rumi (Abi Ruhh, Abu Ruhh, Abba Rukh Habessinus), 63–67, 70, 93.
Abu Ṣāliḥ, 26, 27, 83.
Abuna, 58.
Acts, 10, 50, 101.
Addis Ababa, 33, 67, 73, 100, 108, 112, 131.
'adīm, 126.
'dm, 126.
'adom, 126.
Adonay, 80, 81.
Adoniah, 13.
Adulis, 23.
Adwa (Adoa), 69, 70.
Aeglippus, 12, 13.
Aelius Gallus, 18.
Aescoly, A. Z., 26, 30, 102, 108, 115, 116, 118.
Africa, 1, 3, 4, 6, 7, 14, 63, 80, 90, 105, 117, 118, 127, 131, 134, 135, 141.
Agaw, 116, 118.
Aggadic, 19, 22.
Ahasuerus, 14.
Aḥmad Grañ, 35.
Akhudemmeh, 22.
Akkadian, 126–8.
Aksum, Aksumite, 1, 10, 18, 20, 21, 23, 24, 25, 35, 41, 46, 47, 50, 51, 54, 56, 58, 71, 74, 75, 83, 84, 87, 88, 94, 112, 117, 121, 131, 135, 141, 142.
Albright, W. F., 6, 133.
Alexander (the Great), 2, 10, 134, 142.
Alexandria (Creed, Church), 1, 37, 38, 48, 78, 101.
Alexandrinus (Codex), 38, 48.
Allah, 81, 136.
Alliance Israélite Universelle, 116.
Almemor, 86.
Alphabet of Ben Sira, 136, 139.
Alvares, F., 107, 134.
amäru, 127.
'Amda Ṣəyon, 28, 35, 114.
America, 105.
Amhara, 63, 70.
Amharic, 5, 44, 62–67, 69, 70, 74, 75, 82, 91–94, 99, 101, 103, 108, 109, 112, 132.
Amos, 8, 34, 128.
'mr, 127.

'anbäsa, 127.
Angels, Book of, 118.
Ankober, 102.
Antioch, 40, 46, 48.
Apocrypha, 12, 13, 33, 35, 55, 61, 75.
Apocryphal Acts of the Apostles, 12, 13, 134.
Apostles, 10, 12, 50, 101, 110, 111, 144.
'Aqabah, 17.
'Aqiba, Rabbi, 17.
'arä, 126.
Arabia, Arabian, 3, 4, 6, 8, 17–25, 41, 76, 101, 117, 121, 132, 135, 136.
Arabic, 8, 19, 26, 28, 32, 36–38, 42–44, 47–49, 51–53, 55, 57–59, 63–65, 75, 83, 86, 91, 93, 97, 104, 118–20, 123, 124, 126–9, 136–8, 141, 142.
Arabs, 17, 19, 75, 105, 134.
Aramaean, 39–41, 43, 45, 46.
Aramaic, 16, 19, 24, 34, 39–41, 43, 45–47, 51, 53, 61, 62, 75, 82, 108, 119–28.
'arami, 122.
'arammi, 122.
'araray, 97.
'arb, 123.
'rg, 129.
Ark of the Covenant, 25, 26, 74, 78, 82–85, 87, 89, 91, 92, 135, 141, 142.
'armäyä, 122.
Armenia, 66.
Armenian, 26.
Aron, 85.
aru, 126.
'aruḫtä, 123.
'arwe, 126.
'aryeh, 126, 127.
Asia, 1, 6, 41, 90.
'askema, 123.
al-Asmā' al-ḥusnā, 81.
Asmara, 34, 59, 60, 71, 72, 77, 93.
'asmat, 81.
'asot, 124.
Asselin de Cherville, 63–66.
'asūṭä, 124.
Aswan, 6, 12.
'asyūṭä, 124.
Atbara, 6.
'aṭharä, 123.
Australia, 105.
Awash, 2.
Azqir, Acts of, 19.

Baars, W., 34, 61.
Baba Batra, 135, 137.
Babylon, 7.
Bachmann, Johannes, 34.
bädr, 114.

BIBLICAL REFERENCES